Leisure Gu

KENT

Born in Nottingham, at the age of ten Pat Davis had his first love affair – with Kent cricket. He spent his schooldays in Lakeland. Wartime chance posted him to Walderslade, Chatham and Rochester, there he grew to love Kent itself. In between playing village cricket at Bourne Park, tennis for Canterbury, county badminton for Kent, and writing eight books on the latter sport including *The Encyclopaedia of Badminton* (also published by Robert Hale), Pat Davis explored and photographed the Garden of England.

Between books Pat Davis has written freelance countryside and cricket contributions for *Evergreen, This England, Country, The Cricketer* and *Kent Life* including series on Kentish vineyards and Kent villages. His latest book *A Picture of Kent* will be published in late 1989. Pat Davis lives in Canterbury with his wife and invaluable PA, Patricia.

Leisure Guides

KENT

Pat Davis

ROBERT HALE · LONDON

© *Pat Davis 1989*
First published in Great Britain 1989

Robert Hale Limited
Clerkenwell House
Clerkenwell Green
London EC1R 0HT

British Library Cataloguing-in-Publication Data

Davis, Pat
 Leisure Guides: Kent
 1. Kent. Visitors' guide
 I. Title
 914.22'304858

ISBN 0-7090-3566-7

Photoset in Palatino by
Derek Doyle & Associates, Mold, Clwyd.
Printed in Great Britain by
St Edmundsbury Press Ltd, Bury St Edmunds, Suffolk.
Bound by WBC Bookbinders Limited.

Contents

Maps	9
Introduction	29
Animals and Birds	32
Aquarium, Butterflies and Wildlife	32
Aviaries	33
Zoo Parks	34
Archaeological Sites	35
Pre-history	35
Roman	36
The Arts	39
Art Galleries	39
Brass-Rubbing Centres	40
Music	41
Theatres	42
Countryside	47
Country Parks	47
Nature Reserves	56
Picnic Sites	61
Tours – by car, by cycle	61
Walks – circular, long-distance, waterside	70
Eating and Drinking	90
Cafés and Tea-Rooms (Morning Coffee)	90
Inns	93
Restaurants	100

Farms — 104
- Farms and Farm Trails — 104
- Pick-Your-Own and Farm Shops — 107
- Vineyards — 109

Gardens — 111
- Gardens — 111
- Garden Centres — 116
- Town Parks — 118

Historical Buildings — 121
- Abbeys — 121
- Castles — 122
- Cathedrals — 125
- Churches — 125
- Forts — 132
- Historic Homes — 134
- Other Historical Buildings — 140

Museums — 144
- Agricultural — 144
- Army, Navy and Air Force — 145
- General Interest — 148
- Industrial — 152
- Local and Heritage — 154
- Transport — 160
- Windmills and Watermills — 163

Seaside Attractions — 167
- Amusement Parks and Arcades — 167
- Beaches and Coastal Towns — 168
- Lifeboats and Lighthouses — 177

Shopping Centres — 179
- Antiques — 179
- Arcades — 181
- Auctions — 183
- Crafts — 185
- Markets – General, WI — 189

Contents 7

Sport 196
  Angling 196
  Badminton 202
  Bowls (Indoor) 202
  Bowling (Ten Pin) 203
  Flying 204
  Golf 204
  Leisure and Sport Centres (Indoor) 211
  Leisure and Sport Centres (Outdoor) 216
  Riding 218
  Skating and Ski-ing 220
  Spectator Sports – Badminton, Cricket, Rugby, Soccer, Racing (cars, greyhounds, horses, point-to-point) 221
  Squash 226
  Swimming-pools 226
  Windsurfing 229

Towns and Villages 231
  Larger Towns 231
  Small Towns and Villages 237
  Town Trails 254

Unusual Excursions 257
  Aeroplanes 257
  Boats 257
  Pony and Trap 260
  Railways 261
  Tourist Information Centres 262

Appendix: Annual Events 265
Further Reading 277
Index 279

Maps

General map   10-11

Area maps
  1. Dartford – Maidstone   12-13
  2. Tonbridge – Hawkhurst   14-15
  3. Sheppey – Swale   16-17
  4. Hollingbourne – Ashford   18-19
  5. Benenden – Dungeness   20-1
  6. Canterbury – Ramsgate   22-3
  7. Deal – Hythe   24-5

Open Spaces map   26-8

Maps by EDANART. Crown copyright reserved.

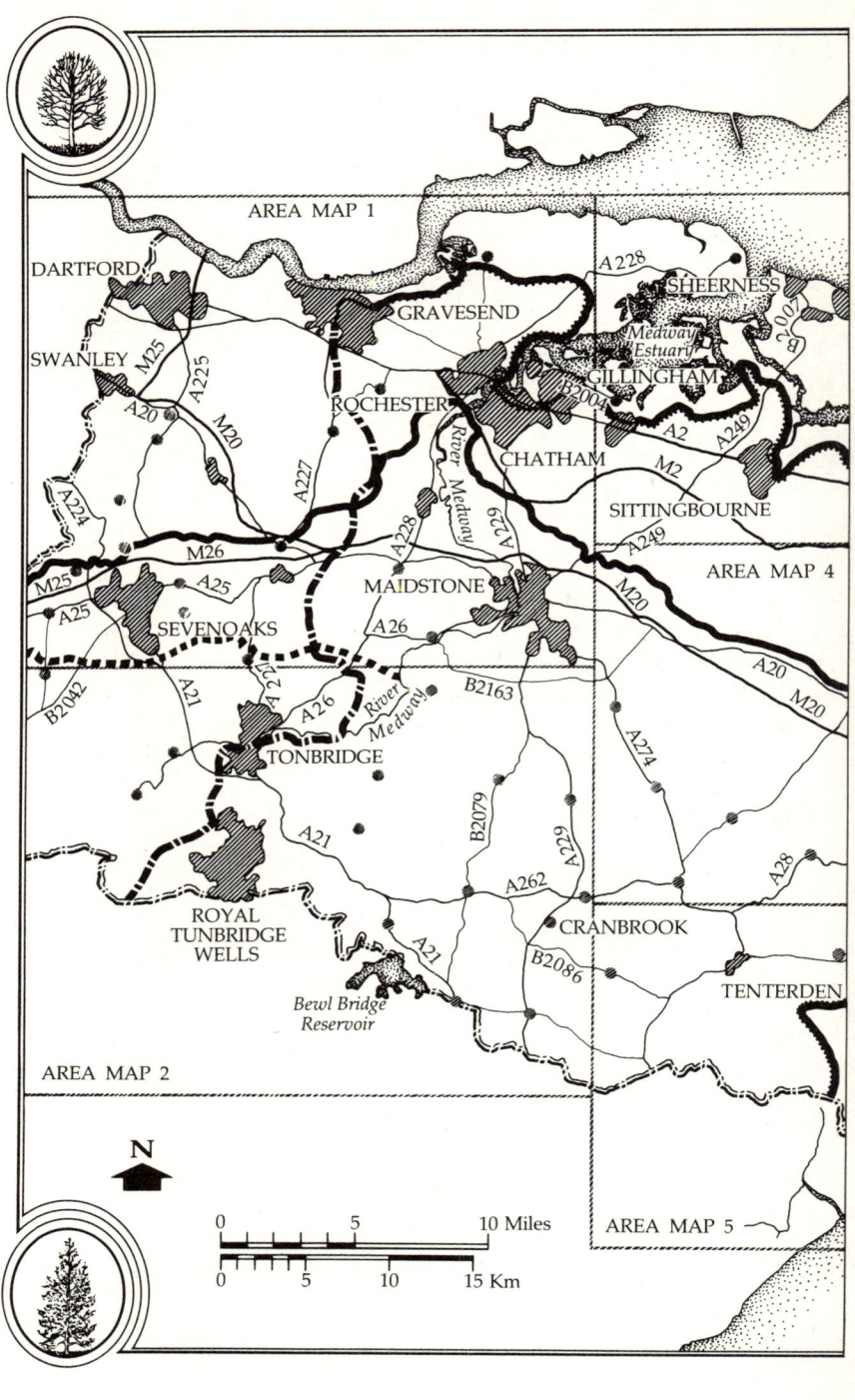

KENT
General Map

AREA MAP 3

AREA MAP 6

Isle of Sheppey
The Swale
WHITSTABLE
HERNE BAY
MARGATE
BROADSTAIRS
A299
A28
A253
A256
RAMSGATE
A2
A299
FAVERSHAM
A290
CANTERBURY
A28
River Stour
Pegwell Bay
A2
A257
SANDWICH
A251
A258
DEAL
A252
B2068
A28
A2
A258
B2068
A260
ASHFORD
DOVER
A20
M20
A261
FOLKESTONE
B2067
HYTHE
AREA MAP 7
B2070
A259

Key
- Main towns
- Major roads
- County Boundary

Long Distance Footpaths
- North Downs Way ✳
- Wealdway
- Saxon Shore
- Greensand Way

✳ The ancient Pilgrims Way and the modern North Downs Way follow much the same route except that the Pilgrims Way generally keeps to the lower slopes of the Downs and also had a short-cut across the Medway from Snodland to near Kits Coty House

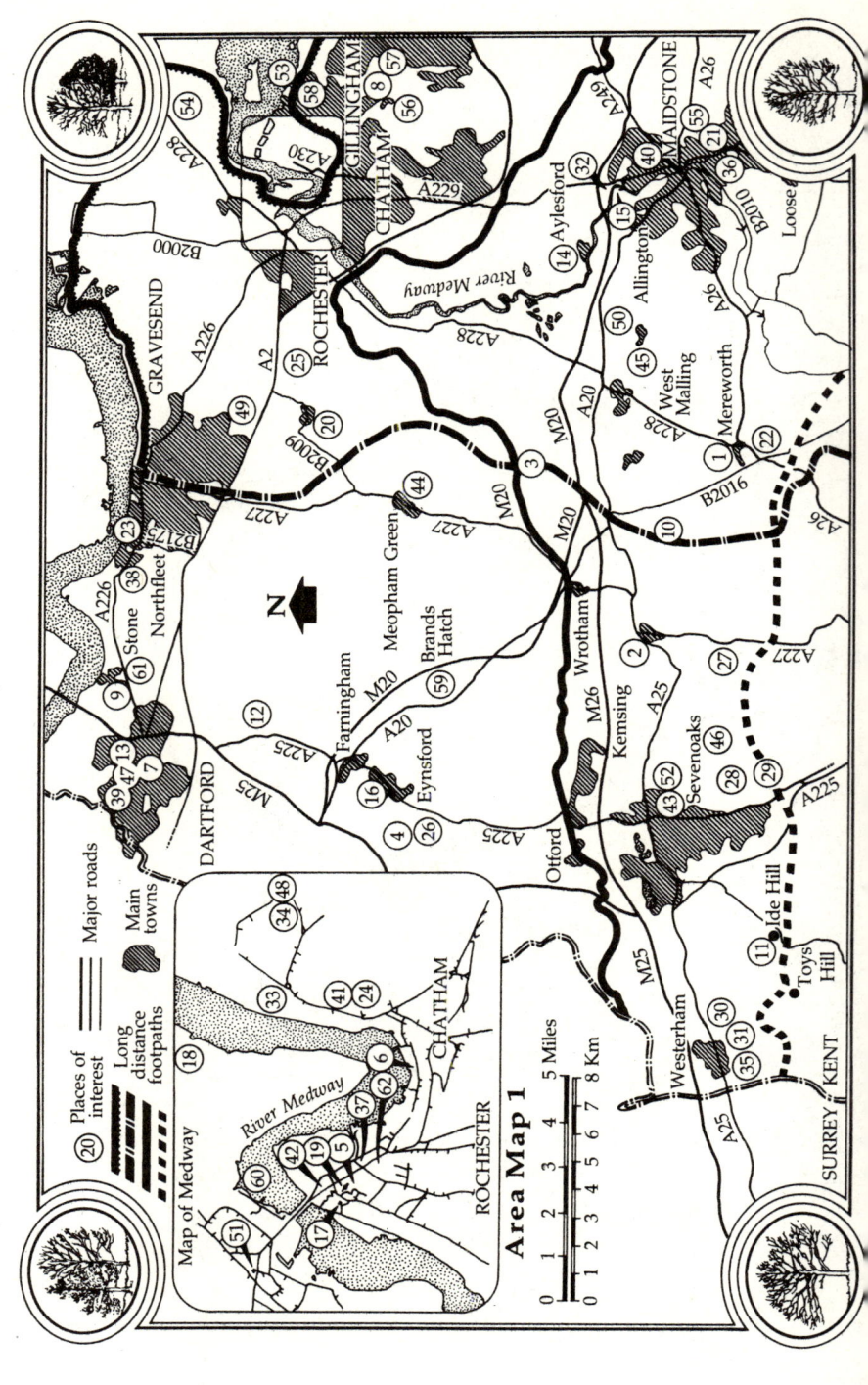

1. Dartford – Maidstone

Location	Page
1. Mereworth Parrot Park	33
2. Oldbury Fort	53
3. Coldrum Long Barrow	36
4. Lullingstone Villa	37
5. Rochester: Cathedral Brass Rubbing Centre	40
6. Chatham: Central Hall Theatre	43
7. Dartford: Orchard Theatre	43
8. Gillingham: Star Farm	105
9. Stone Lodge Farm Park	107
10. Great Comp Garden	112
11. Emmetts Garden	114
12. Sutton-at-Hone: St John's Jerusalem Garden	115
13. Dartford Central Park	119
14. Aylesford Friary	121
15. Allington Castle	134
16. Eynsford Castle	123
17. Rochester Castle	124
18. Upnor Castle	124
19. Rochester Cathedral	125
20. Cobham: St Mary Magdalene's Church	127
21. Maidstone: All Saints Church	130
22. Mereworth: St Lawrence's Church	131
23. Northfleet: St Botolph's Church	131
24. Chatham: Fort Amherst	132
25. Cobham Hall	136
26. Lullingstone Castle	136
27. Ightham Mote	137
28. Sevenoaks: Knole	139
29. Sevenoaks: Riverhill House	140
30. Westerham: Chartwell	140
31. Westerham: Squerryes Court	140

Location	Page
32. Sandling: Museum of Kent Rural Life	144
33. Chatham Historic Dockyard	146
34. Chatham: Royal Engineers' Museum	146
35. Westerham: Quebec House	148
36. Maidstone: Tyrwhitt Museum of Carriages	151
37. Rochester Dickens Centre	151
38. Northfleet: Blue Circle Heritage Centre	153
39. Dartford Borough Museum	155
40. Maidstone Museum	158
41. Medway Heritage Centre	155
42. Rochester: Guildhall Museum	159
43. Sevenoaks Museum	160
44. Meopham Windmill	165
45. West Malling: Mill Yard Craft Centre	189
46. Sevenoaks: Knole Park Golf Course	209
47. Dartford: Downs Sports Centre	212
48. Gillingham: Black Lion Sports Centre	213
49. Gravesend: Thong Lane Sports Centre	213
50. Maidstone: Larkfield Leisure Centre	214
51. Strood Sports Centre	215
52. Wildernesse Sports Centre	215
53. Gillingham: Strand Outdoor Leisure Park	217
54. Hoo: Deangate Ridge Sports Complex	217
55. Maidstone: Mote Park Outdoor Leisure Centre	227
56. Chatham: Alpine Ski Centre	220
57. Gillingham Ice Bowl	221
58. Gillingham Football Club	223
59. Fawkham: Brands Hatch Circuit	224
60. Strood: MV *Clyde* and *Kingswear Castle*	259
61. Stone Lodge Railway	261
62. Rochester: Kenneth Bills Motor Cycle Museum	163

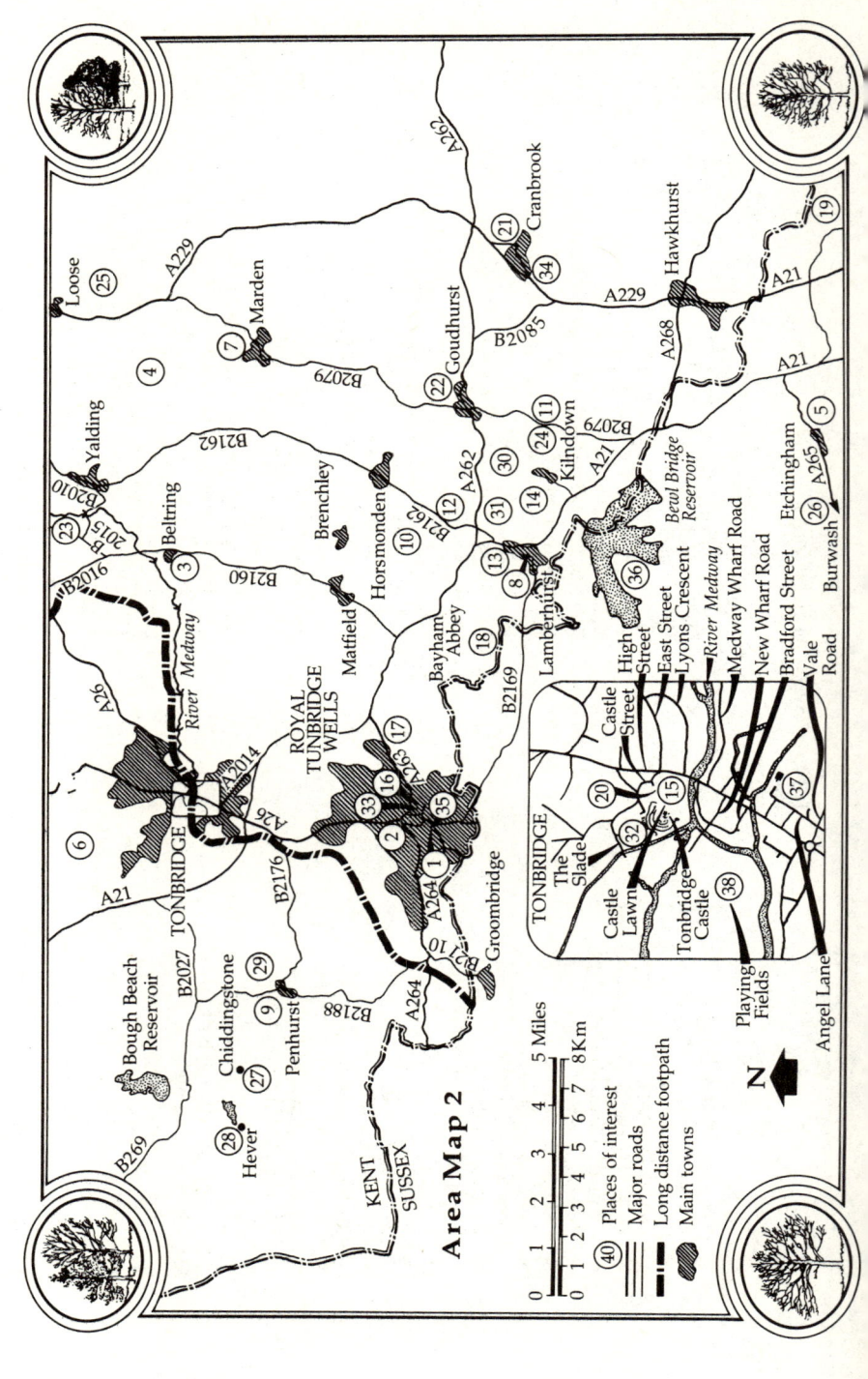

2. Tonbridge – Hawkhurst

Location	Page
1. Tunbridge Wells Brass Rubbing Centre	40
2. Tunbridge Wells: Trinity Arts Centre	46
3. Beltring: Whitbread's Hop Farm	104
4. Chainhurst: Reed Court Farm	105
5. Etchingham: Sussex Shire Horses	105
6. Hildenborough: Great Hollanden Farm	106
7. Marden: Goffs Oak Shire Horses	106
8. Lamberhurst Vineyard	109
9. Penshurst Vineyard	110
10. Brenchley: Marle Place	112
11. Bedgebury National Pinetum	113
12. Horsmonden: Sprivers	113
13. Lamberhurst: Owl House Gardens	114
14. Scotney Castle Gardens	114
15. Tonbridge Castle Grounds	120
16. Tunbridge Wells: Calverley Gardens	120
17. Tunbridge Wells: Dunorlan Park	120
18. Bayham Abbey	121
19. Bodiam Castle	122

Location	Page
20. Tonbridge Castle	124
21. Cranbrook: St Dunstan's Church	127
22. Goudhurst: St Mary's Church	128
23. Nettlestead: St Mary's Church	131
24. Kilndown: Christ Church	130
25. Boughton Monchelsea Place	135
26. Burwash: Bateman's	135
27. Chiddingstone Castle	135
28. Hever Castle	136
29. Penshurst Place	139
30. Goudhurst: Finchcocks	150
31. Lamberhurst: Mr Hever's Model Museum	151
32. Tonbridge: Milne Museum	153
33. Tunbridge Wells Museum	160
34. Cranbrook Union Mill	163
35. Tunbridge Wells: The Pantiles	183
36. Bewl Water Reservoir	217
37. Tonbridge: Angel Leisure Centre	216
38. Tonbridge Sports Ground	218

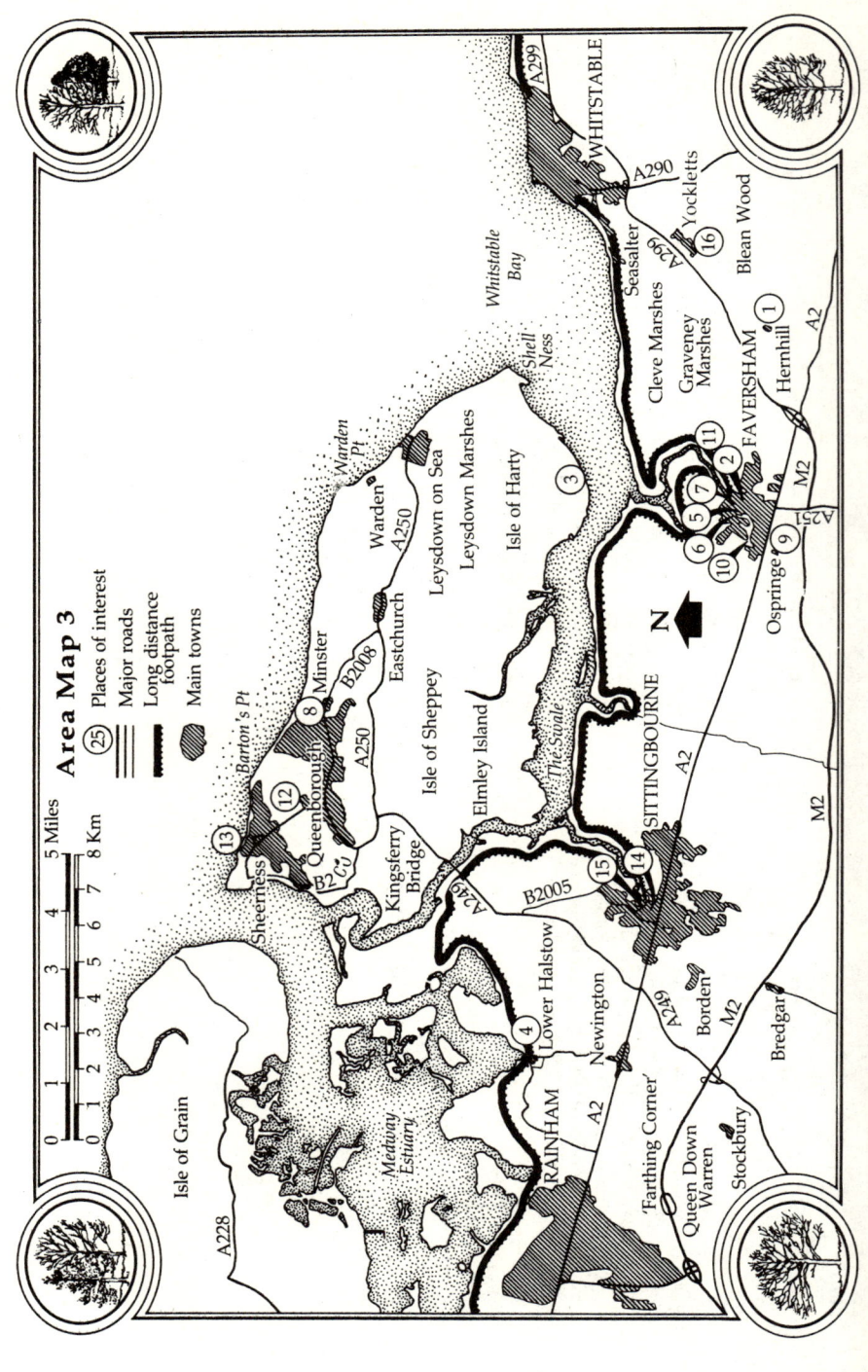

3. Sheppey – Swale

Location	Page
1. Hernhill: Mount Ephraim Gardens	113
2. Faversham: St Mary of Charity Church	128
3. Isle of Harty: St Thomas's Church	129
4. Lower Halstow: St Margaret's Church	130
5. Faversham: Abbey Street	141
6. Faversham: Chart Gunpowder Works	153
7. Faversham: Fleur de Lys Heritage Centre	157
8. Minster: Abbey Gate Museum	159
9. Ospringe: Maison Dieu Museum	159
10. Faversham: Shepherd Neame Brewery	187
11. Tonge: Old Mill Craft Centre	188
12. Sheerness Golf Club	209
13. Sheerness Sea Front Sports Centre	215
14. Sittingbourne & Kemsley Light Railway	261
15. Sittingbourne: Dolphin Yard Barge Museum	163
16. Yockletts Nature Reserve	56

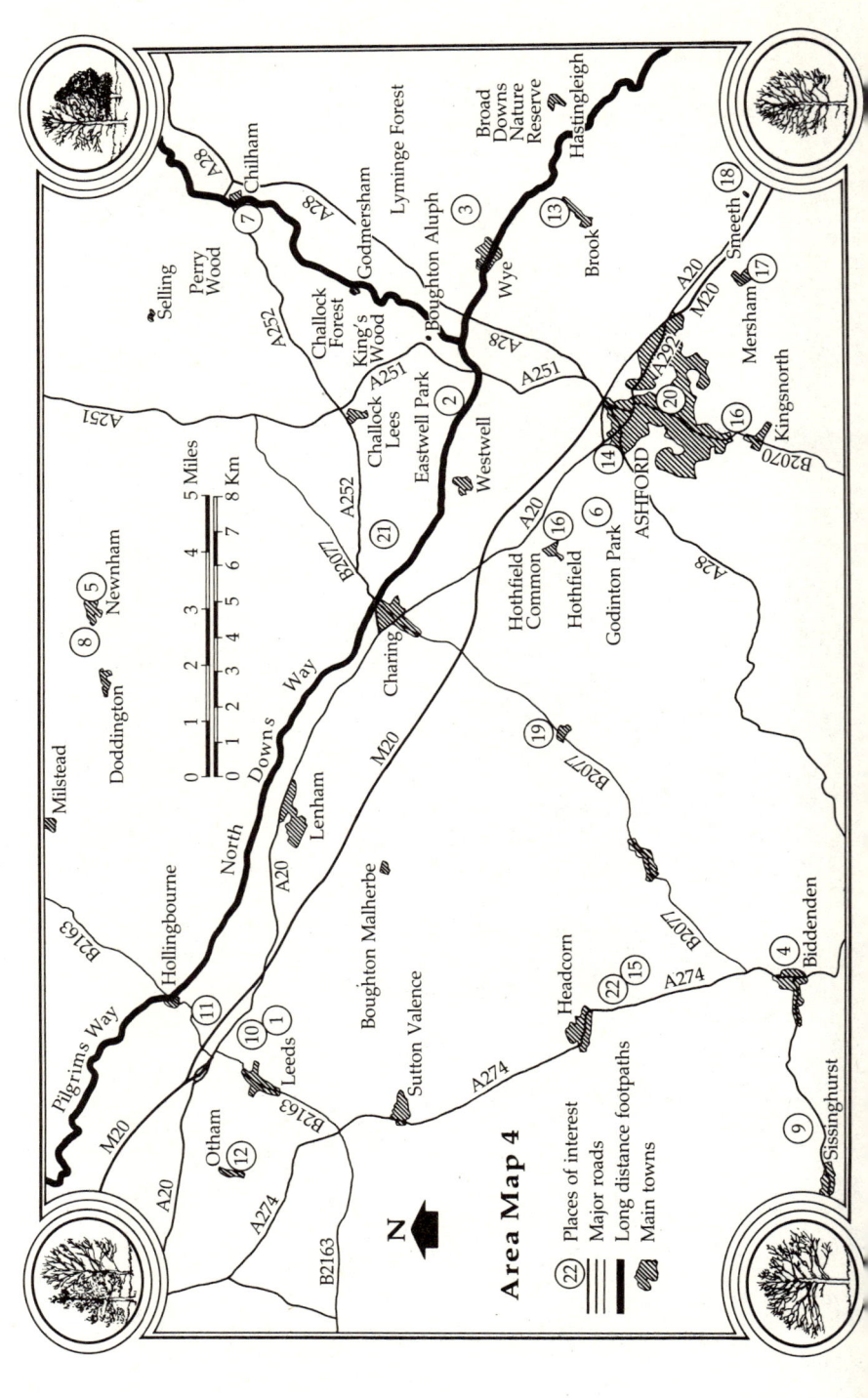

4. Hollingbourne – Ashford

Location	Page
1. Leeds Castle Aviaries	33
2. Eastwell Park	100
3. Wye College Farm	107
4. Biddenden Vineyard	109
5. Newnham: Syndale Valley Vineyard	110
6. Godinton Park	134
7. Chilham Castle and Gardens	112
8. Doddington Place Gardens	112
9. Sissinghurst Castle and Garden	115
10. Leeds Castle	137
11. Eythorne Manor	137
12. Otham: Stoneacre	142
13. Wye College Agricultural Museum	144
14. Ashford: Intelligence Corps Museum	145
15. Lashenden Air Warfare Museum	147
16. Kingsnorth Museum	150
17. Lower Mersham: Swanton Mill	164
18. Smeeth: Evegate Mill	165
19. Pluckley: Lambden Trout Fishery	199
20. Ashford: Stour Leisure Centre	212
21. Challock: Kent Gliding Club	257
22. Headcorn Aerodrome	257

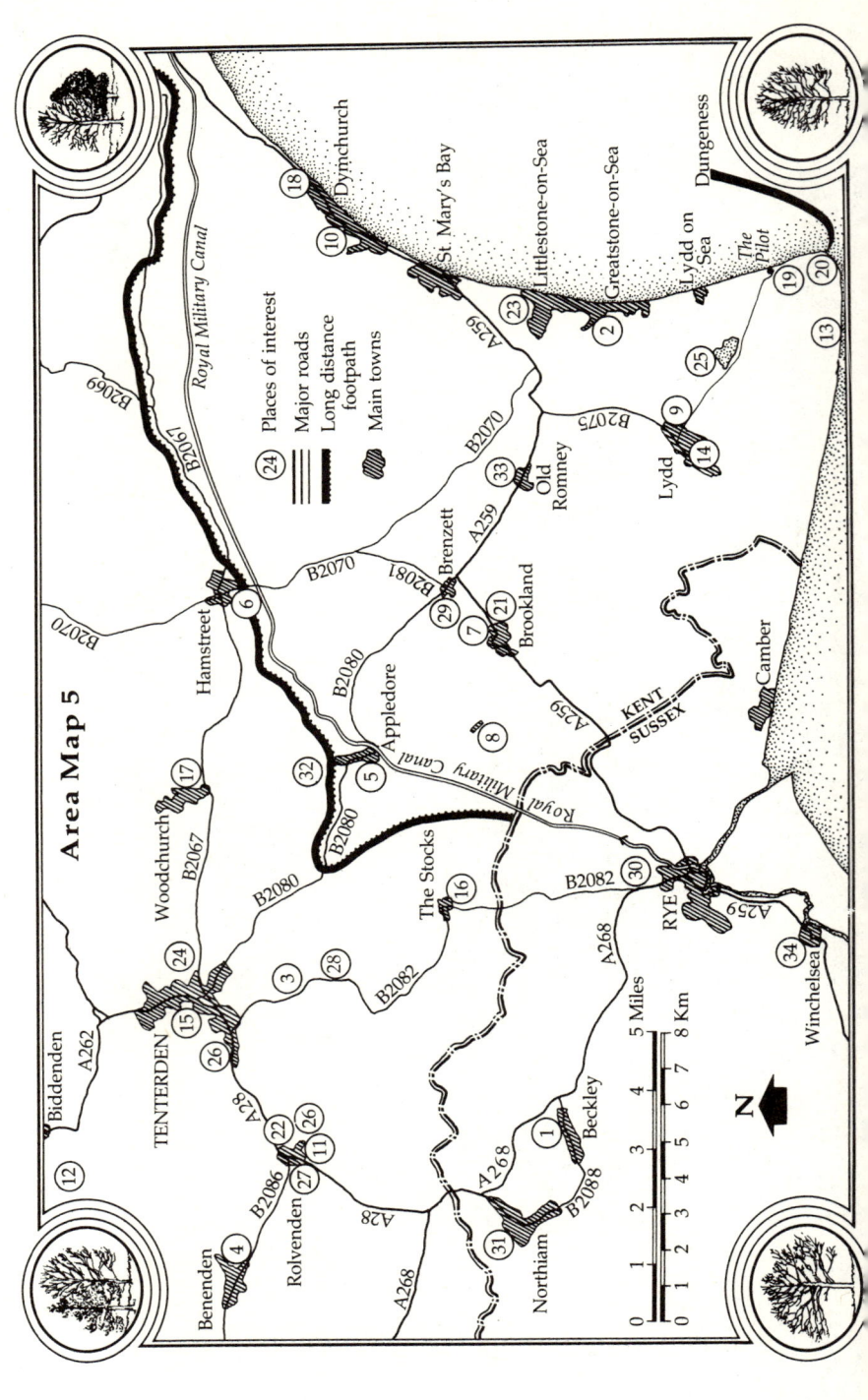

5. Benenden – Dungeness

Location	Page
1. Beckley Children's Farm	104
2. Greatstone: Dunrobin Shire Horse Stud	106
3. Tenterden Vineyard	110
4. Benenden Walled Garden	111
5. Appledore's Answer	116
6. Ham Street: Romney Marsh Garden Centre	117
7. Brookland: St Augustine's Church	126
8. Fairfield: St Thomas à Becket Church	128
9. Lydd: All Saints Church	130
10. Dymchurch: Martello Tower	133
11. Rolvenden: Great Maytham Hall	139
12. Biddenden: Bettenham Manor Baby Carriage Collection	148
13. Dungeness 'A' Power Station	152
14. Lydd Town Museum	158
15. Tenterden & District Museum	160
16. Wittersham: Stocks Mill	166
17. Woodchurch Windmill	166

Location	Page
18. Dymchurch Phoenix Amusements	167
19. Dungeness Lifeboat	177
20. Dungeness Lighthouse	177-8
21. Brookland: Phillipine Village Craft Centre	186
22. Rolvenden: Lake at Pooh Corner	199
23. Littlestone Golf Club	208
24. Tenterden Golf Club	210
25. Romney Marsh Windsurf Centre, Lydd	229
26. Kent and East Sussex Railway	262
27. Rolvenden Historic Vehicles Museum	163
28. Smallhythe Place Theatrical Museum	152
29. Brenzett Aeronautical Museum	145
30. Rye	250
31. Northiam: Great Dixter	138
32. Horne's Place Chapel	126
33. Old Romney	248
34. Winchelsea	253

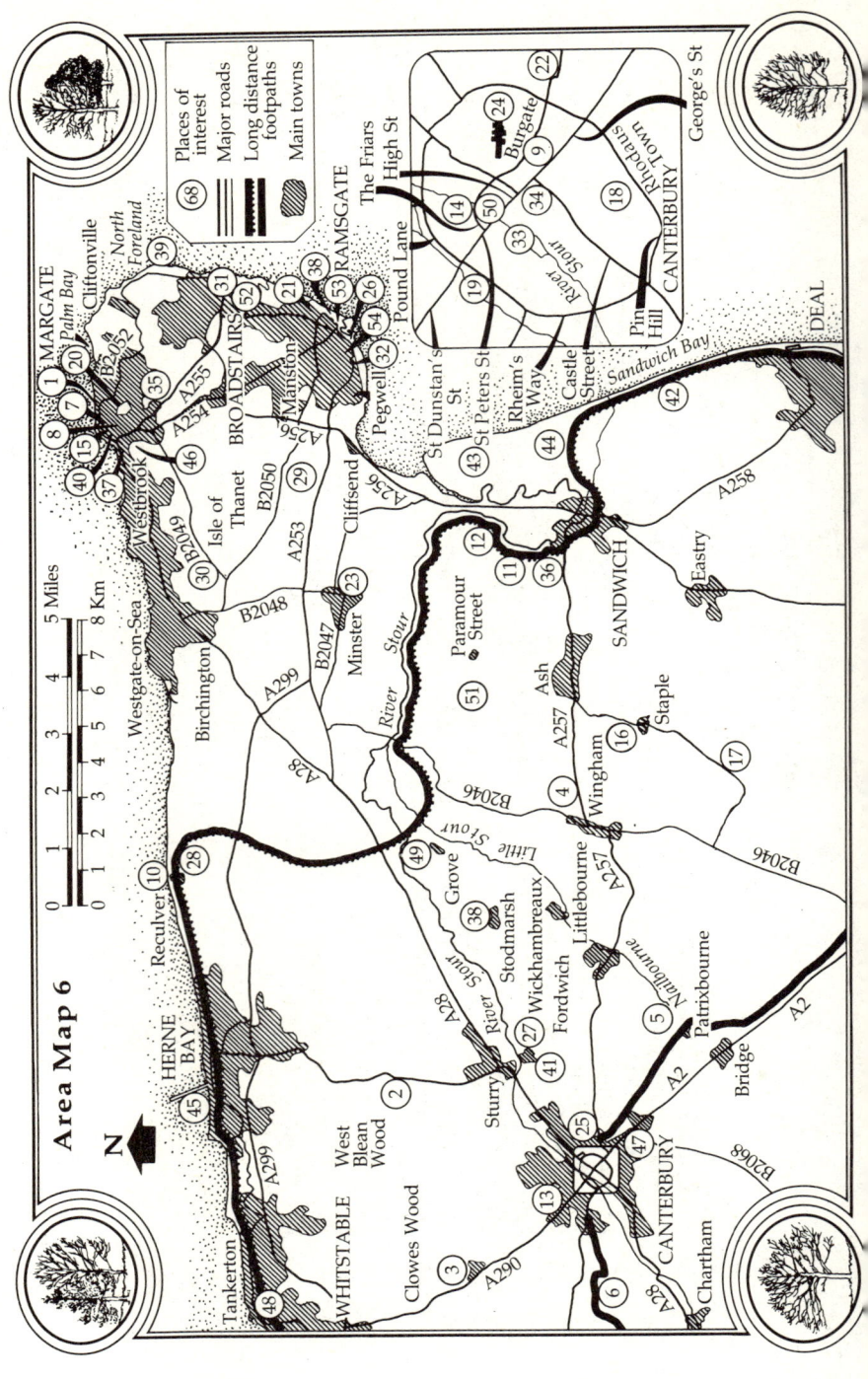

6. Canterbury – Ramsgate

Location	Page	Location	Page
1. Cliftonville: Aquarium	32	29. Manston Spitfire Memorial Pavilion	148
2. Herne Bay: Brambles English Wildlife	32	30. Birchington: Quex House and Powell-Cotton Museum	148
3. Blean Bird Park	33	31. Broadstairs: Bleak House	149
4. Wingham Bird Park	33	32. Ramsgate Model Village	151
5. Bekesbourne: Howletts Zoo Park	34	33. Canterbury Heritage Museum	154
6. Bigbury Fort	35	34. Canterbury Pilgrims Way Time-Walk	154
7. Margate Caves	36	35. Margate: Draper's Windmill	165
8. Margate: Shell Grotto	36	36. Sandwich: White Mill	165
9. Canterbury: Roman Pavement	36	37. Margate: Bembom Theme Park	167
10. Reculver Fort	38	38. Ramsgate: Pleasure Park	168
11. Richborough: Roman Amphitheatre	38	39. North Foreland Lighthouse	177
12. Richborough Fort	38	40. Margate Lifeboat	178
13. Canterbury: Gulbenkian Theatre	42	41. Canterbury Golf Club	205
14. Canterbury: Marlowe Theatre	43	42. Deal: Royal Cinque Ports Golf Club	206
15. Margate: Winter Gardens	45	43. Sandwich: Princes Golf Club	208
16. Staple Vineyard	110	44. Sandwich: Royal St George's Golf Club	209
17. Goodnestone Park Gardens	113	45. Herne Bay Pier Pavilion Sports Centre	214
18. Canterbury: Dane John Gardens	118	46. Margate: Hartsdown Sports Centre	214
19. Canterbury: West Gate Gardens	118	47. Canterbury: St Lawrence Cricket Ground	221
20. Margate: Dane Park	119	48. Whitstable Windsurfing	230
21. Ramsgate: King George VI Park	119	49. Grove Ferry River Trips	258
22. Canterbury: St Augustine's Abbey	121	50. Canterbury: Weavers Boat Trips	257
23. Minster Abbey	122	51. Padbrook Carriage Driving Centre	219
24. Canterbury Cathedral	125	52. Broadstairs: Crampton Tower	161
25. Canterbury: St Martin's Church	126	53. Ramsgate Maritime Museum	162
26. Ramsgate: St Augustine's Church	131	54. Ramsgate Motor Museum	162
27. Fordwich Town Hall	141		
28. Reculver Towers	142		

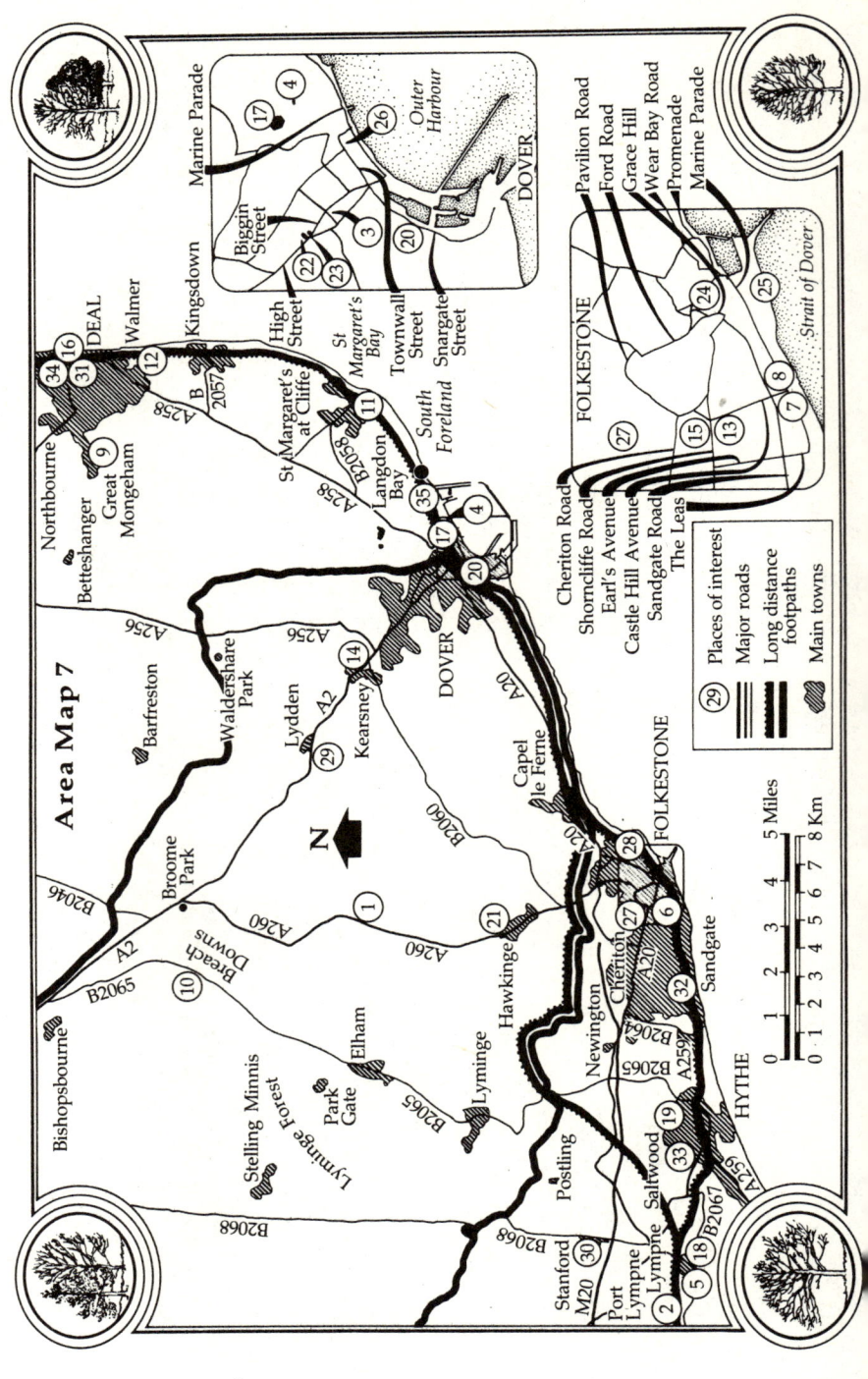

7. Deal – Hythe

Location	Page
1. Swingfield: Butterfly Centre	34
2. Port Lympne Zoo Park and Mansion	34
3. Dover: Painted House	37
4. Dover: Pharos	37
5. Stutfall Castle	37
6. Folkestone: Metropole Arts Centre	39
7. Folkestone: Leas Bandstand	41
8. Folkestone: Leas Cliff Hall	43
9. Great Mongeham: Solly's Farm Tour	106
10. Elham Valley Vineyards	109
11. St Margaret's Bay: Pines Garden	114
12. Walmer Castle and Garden	124
13. Folkestone: Kennedy's Garden Centre	117
14. Kearsney: Abbey Park	119
15. Folkestone: Kingsnorth Gardens	119
16. Deal Castle	123
17. Dover Castle	123
18. Lympne Castle	138

Location	Page
19. Hythe: St Leonard's Church	129
20. Dover Grand Shaft	133
21. Hawkinge: Battle of Britain Museum	147
22. Dover Maison Dieu	156
23. Dover Museum	156
24. Folkestone Museum	157
25. Folkestone Rotunda	167
26. Dover Sports Centre	212
27. Folkestone Sports Centre	213
28. Folkestone: East Cliff Outdoor Sports Centre	217
29. Lydden Motor Racing Circuit	224
30. Folkestone Race Course	225
31. Deal Swimming-Pool	227
32. Sandgate: Windsurfing	229
33. Romney, Hythe and Dymchurch Railway	261
34. Deal: Time-ball Tower	161
35. Port of Dover Tours	162

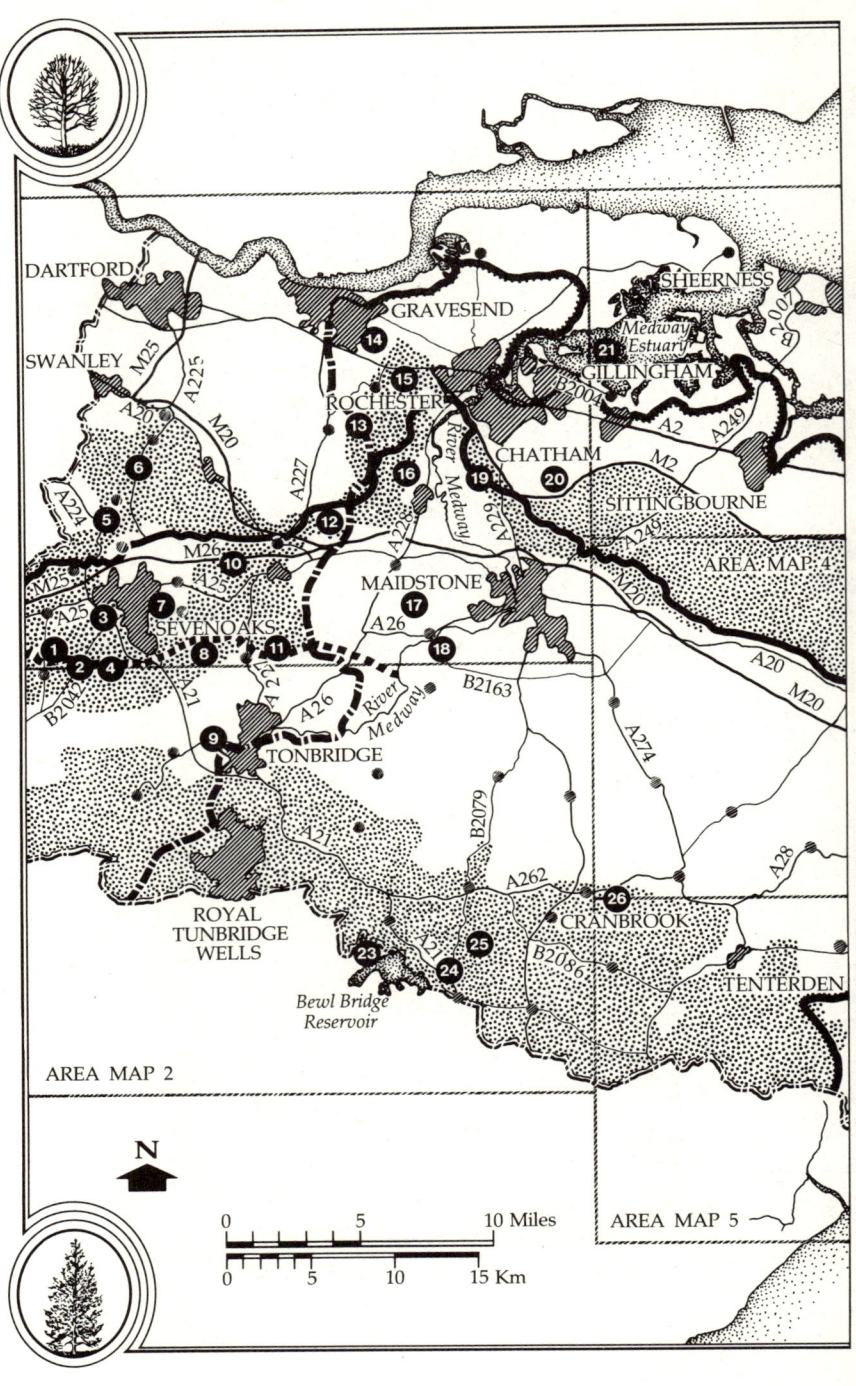

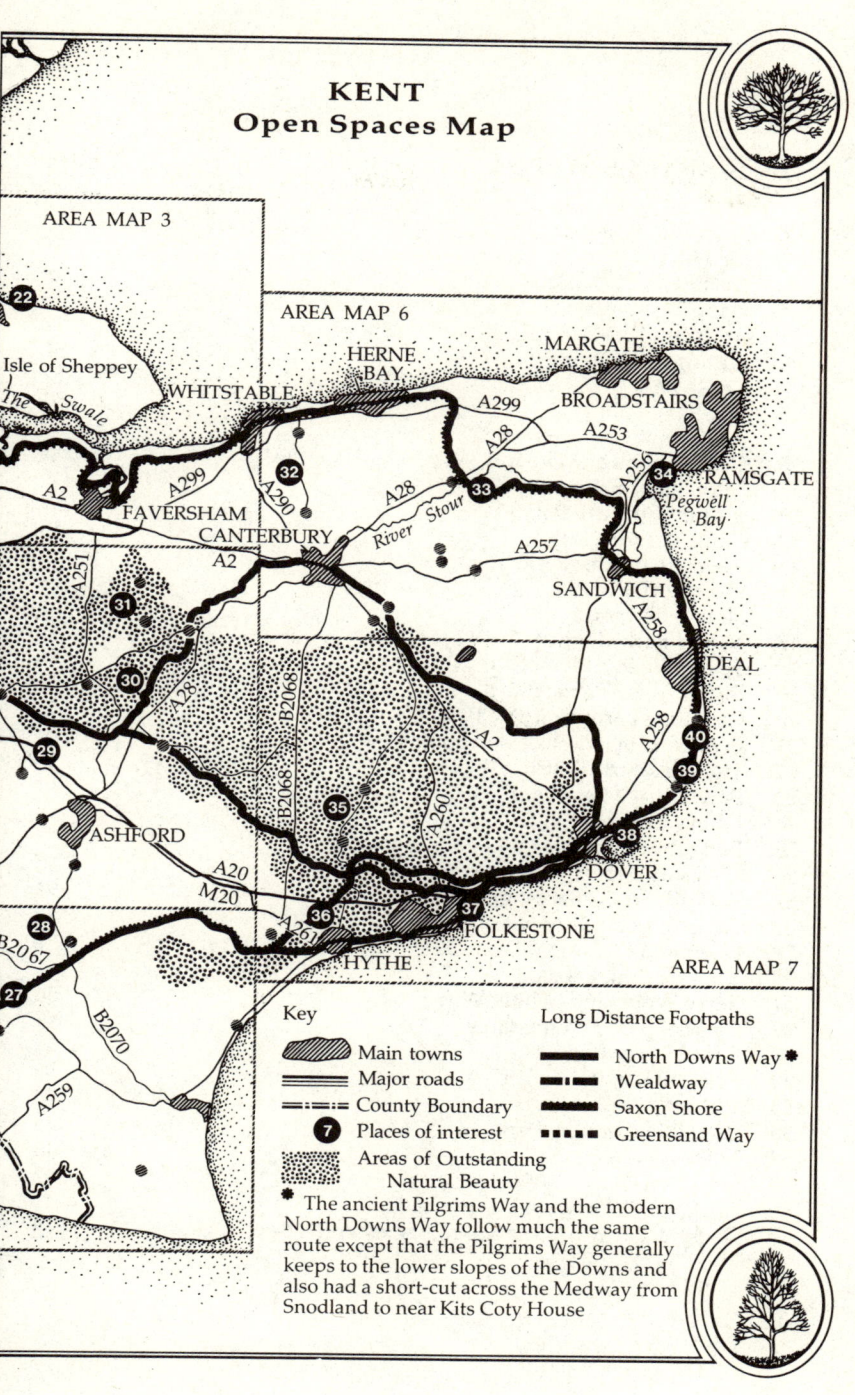

OPEN SPACES MAP   *Page*

1.	Toys Hill, Brasted	54
2.	Ide Hill	51
3.	Dryhill Picnic Park	49
4.	Hanging Bank and Brockhoult Mount	50
5.	Andrews Wood, Badgers Mount, Shoreham	47
6.	Lullingstone Park	52
7.	Knole Park	51
8.	One Tree Hill	53
9.	Barnetts Wood	47
10.	Oldbury Hill and Styants Wood	53
11.	Dene Park, Shipbourne	49
12.	Trosley Country Park	55
13.	Camer Country Park	48
14.	Shorne Country Park	54
15.	Shepherds Gate	54
16.	Holly Hill Wood	51
17.	Manor Park Country Park	52
18.	Teston Bridge Picnic Site	54
19.	Bluebell Hill Picnic Site	47
20.	Capstone Farm Country Park	48
21.	Eastcourt Meadows Country Park	49
22.	The Leas and Clifftop Minster	52
23.	Bewl Bridge Reservoir	217
24.	Pillory Corner	55
25.	Bedgebury Pinetum and Bedgebury Forest	113
26.	Hemsted Forest, Cranbrook	50
27.	Park Wood, Kenardington	53
28.	Faggs Wood, Orlestone	49
29.	Hothfield Common Picnic Site	51
30.	Kings Wood, Challock	51
31.	Perry Wood and Selling Wood	54
32.	Clowes Wood, Whitstable	49
33.	Grove Ferry Picnic Site	50
34.	Pegwell Bay Picnic Site	53
35.	West Wood, Lyminge	55
36.	Brockhill Country Park	48
37.	Folkestone Warren	49
38.	Langdon Cliffs	52
39.	Bockell Hill Viewing Point	48
40.	Bockhill Farm and the Leas, St Margaret's Bay	48

Introduction

With more and more people enjoying more and more leisure, it is hoped that this compact book will offer a wealth of ideas and a constant and ready answer to that perennial and daunting question 'Wherever can we go that's new?'

SCOPE

With fifteen main and some eighty sub-headings, it caters for all tastes and presents hundreds of attractions, ranging from abbeys to zoos, that may lead to new interests.

It covers the whole of Kent, from Chatham in the north down to Tenterden in the south and from Sevenoaks in the west across to Ramsgate in the east. Greater London is not covered but occasional forays have been made a short way into Sussex when the attraction is great enough to transcend county boundaries.

EASY REFERENCE

The book has been designed to be readable yet ideal for simple and quick reference. To that end sections and individual entries are in *alphabetical order*, the latter under the nearest town or village.

If you already know where you wish to go, simply use the index to find the page giving the necessary details. If you know roughly the kind of 'day out' you want, look at the Contents List and under 'Farms', 'Museums' etc you'll find a list of such places in alphabetical order; simply skim through the section until you find an entry whose details appeal to you.

If you are at a loss for a new outing, you could look down the Contents list until a main heading catches the imagination. Then glance through sub-headings and entries listed under them to find one that sounds interesting to you. If you want a second attraction for the afternoon or evening, look at the relevant map; the 'Town and Village' chapter also shows nearby places of interest. At the end of the book is a brief guide to annual events taking place in particular centres.

DETAILS

Each entry gives (a) the name of the *attraction*; (b) the exact *address* and, in case you wish to check some detail, the *phone number*; (c) except where details make too long or involved an entry, a necessarily brief guideline *location*, which can be supplemented by a larger map or town guide (more and more leisure attractions are being signposted); (d) *details* of the main attraction and its facilities; (e) *opening and closing times* etc; periods shown are inclusive; 'daily' means seven days a week but it should be borne in mind that a large majority of attractions will be closed on Christmas Day; (f) where *'free'* or *'small fee'* (i.e. generally under 60p) is *not* indicated, a charge is made; exact amounts have not been shown as they are constantly changing.

ABBREVIATIONS

For the sake of conciseness, these occur frequently. Although commonly accepted, they are listed below:

BD = Boxing Day
BHM = Bank Holiday Monday
D = A part, but possibly not all, of the site is suitable for the disabled. The absence of such a symbol does not *necessarily* mean it is entirely impracticable for disabled people.
EH = English Heritage
GF = Good Friday
KNCC = Kent Nature Conservancy Council
KTNC = Kent Trust for Nature Conservation
LA = Last admission (generally half or one hour before closing time)

NT   = National Trust
NYD = New Year's Day
RSPB = Royal Society for the Protection of Birds
XD   = Christmas Day

ENGLISH HERITAGE OR DEPARTMENT OF THE ENVIRONMENT
Opening and closing times are as follows:

	Mid-March–Mid-October	Mid October–Mid-March
Standard	Monday–Saturday 9.30–6.30 Sunday 2–6.30	9.30–4 2–4
Standard and summer Sunday mornings	As above, but also open from 9.30 on Sundays from 1 April to 30 September	
Summer season, standard	1 April to 30 September, Mon-Sat 9.30–6.30, Sunday 2-6.30	
Summer season, standard and Sunday mornings	1 April to 30 September, daily 9.30–6.30	

All sites are closed 24-6 December and 1 January; some close for one or 2 rest days each week in winter. A number may close for lunch 1-2.

Every care has been taken in compiling the following entries but it should be appreciated that changes do take place from time to time. Before setting out on a trip, it is always a good idea to telephone and check details.

The author would be pleased to receive notification of any such changes. They should be addressed to him c/o Robert Hale Ltd, Clerkenwell House, 45-47 Clerkenwell Green, London EC1R 0HT.

The author and publishers regret they cannot accept any liability whatsoever for errors or omissions.

Animals and Birds

AQUARIUM, BUTTERFLIES AND WILDLIFE

Cliftonville: The Aquarium
Palm Bay Avenue, Palm Bay, Cliftonville (0843 221951)
Displays of marine, tropical and cold water fish, reptiles and insects. Shop, cafeteria.
Daily: 9.30–5; from Whitsun, until 10

Herne Bay: Brambles English Wildlife and Rare Breeds
Wealden Forest Park, Herne (0227 712379)
Midway between Canterbury and Herne Bay on A291
20 acres of natural woodland in which live deer, owls and foxes. Rare-breed farm animals too. Enclosed garden with ponds containing fish and amphibians. 'Butterfly World': free-flying butterflies amid their natural surroundings, if sunny. Adventure and Under-5 playgrounds. Tea-room, gift shop, picnic area.
Mid-April–October: daily, 10–5

Swingfield: Butterfly Centre
Swingfield, near Folkestone (0303 83244)
On main A260 Canterbury–Folkestone road, 4 miles N of Folkestone
A butterfly safari park amidst bougainvillea, banana, hibiscus, passion-flower, jacaranda in bloom. Free-flying butterflies from all over the world may be observed and photographed. Garden centre, coffee bar. D
April–October: daily, 10–5

AVIARIES

Blean: Blean Bird Park
Honey Hill, Blean, near Canterbury (0227 471666)
On A290, 3 miles NW of Canterbury
Most all-embracing breeding collection of macaws in England; also cockatoos, pheasants and softbills. Pets corner, free-flying parrots, tropical house, woodland walk. Tea-room with lawn, restaurant. D
March–November: daily, 10–6

Leeds: Leeds Castle Aviaries
Leeds Castle, near Maidstone (0622 65400)
Junction of A20 and M20, 4 miles E of Maidstone
50 uniquely designed and constructed aviaries house over 100 species of birds from Australia, South America, Africa and Asia, under the care of David Frank, formerly with the San Diego Wild Animal Park. Comfortable for the birds – practical for the public. (See also Castles, p.122.)
April–October: daily, 11–5 (LA); November–March: Saturday and Sunday only, 12–4 (LA)

Mereworth: Parrot Park
Seven Mile Lane, Mereworth, near Maidstone (0622 812045)
On A226, 7 miles W of Maidstone
10-acre country garden, a lovely setting for over 40 species of parrots, rare, tame and talking! Also peacocks, doves, pheasants etc. Refreshments, shop, picnic area, pets corner.
Easter–October: daily, 10-5 LA

Wingham: Bird Park
Little Rusham Bird Farm, Wingham, near Canterbury (0227 720836)
Off A257, 1 mile E of Wingham
Small conservation area for breeding of endangered species: waterfowl, cockatoos, macaws, owls, lorrys, lorikeets.
Picnic area near lake, pets corner, aviary and cage shop. PYO strawberries, apples, vegetables. Garden centre, tea-room.

Daily (except XD): 10–6
Fee for bird park, though disabled are admitted free

ZOO PARKS

Bekesbourne: Howletts Zoo Park
Bekesbourne, near Canterbury (0227 721286)
Turn off A257 in Littlebourne, 3 miles E of Canterbury; or off A2, 2 miles S of Canterbury
55 acres of mature parkland are home for a large number of endangered species: largest collection of tigers and largest breeding colony of gorillas in the world; also chimps, cheetahs, elephants etc. Cafeteria, shop.   D
All year: daily (except XD) 10–5 (LA) or one hour before dusk in winter months

Lympne: Port Lympne Zoo Park
Lympne, near Hythe (0303 64646)
2 miles W of Hythe, off B2067; Exit 11 off M20
The mansion contains fine rooms superbly decorated, and animal paintings and sculptures. 15 acres of varied terraced gardens give sweeping marshland and Channel views. 270 acres of safari park are a spacious home for endangered species that range from tigers and elephants to leopards and chimps. Safari trailer available. Picnic area, cafeteria, shop.
All the year: daily (except XD), 10–5 (or dusk) (LA one hour before dusk in winter)

Archaeological Sites

The following museums (in the section p.154) have archaeological displays: Birchington (Powell Cotton), Canterbury (Royal), Dartford (Borough), Deal (Archaeological), Folkestone, Gravesend, Hythe (Local History), Ospringe (Maison Dieu), Sevenoaks and Tunbridge Wells.

PRE-HISTORY

Aylesford: Kits Coty and Little Kits Coty (EH)
Aylesford, near Maidstone
4 miles N of Maidstone just off A229 near junction with Burham road
Monolithic stones, part of prehistoric burial chambers, once covered by long earthen mounds. Downland setting with fine views. Little Kits Coty is ½ mile S of Kits Coty.
Any reasonable time   Free

Canterbury: Bigbury Fort
1¼ miles SW of Harbledown on Chartham Hatch road (rough going)
A Belgic hill-fort or tribal capital before Durovernum (Canterbury) was founded in the valley below. Here the Belgae probably made their last stand against the Romans. Chariot equipment and slave chains found.
Any reasonable time   Free

Ightham: Oldbury Fort (NT)
N side of A25 above Ightham, near lay-by (rough going)

The S half of an Iron Age fort built about 100 BC on a hill-top. On E side are rock shelters used by palaeolithic hunters.
Any reasonable time   Free

Margate: Margate Caves
Lower end Northdown Road, Margate (0843 220139)
3 minute walk from Winter Gardens and Lido
Hewn out of Thanet's chalk over 1,000 years ago, these cathedral-like caves are decorated with unusual wall-paintings. They have been used for religious ceremonies and as torture chambers and smugglers' hide-outs.
Easter–September: daily, including Sunday, 10–5
Small fee

Margate: Shell Grotto
Grotto Hill, Margate (0843 220008)
Off Northdown Road
An ancient and possibly unique shell temple whose origin is still a mystery. Millions of shells have been used to decorate 2,000 square feet of winding passages with mosaic designs. Gift shop.
April–mid-October: weekdays, 10–5; Saturday, 10–12; Sunday (during high season), 10–4

Trottiscliffe: Coldrum Long Barrow (NT)
Between Pilgrims Way and M20, 1 mile E of Trottiscliffe
Impressively sited, exposed stones of burial chamber of a megalithic long barrow. A fitting memorial to the Ightham grocer Benjamin Harrison who became an archaeologist of international repute.
Any reasonable time   Free

ROMAN

Canterbury: Roman Pavement
Butchery Lane, Canterbury (0227 52747)
Off The Parade, near the cathedral
Underground museum in remains of town-house with

Archaeological Sites

hypocaust and pavement. Also other Roman exhibits from Canterbury sites.
April–September: Monday–Saturday, 10–1. October–March: Monday–Saturday, 2–4
Small fee

Dover: Painted House
New Street, Dover (0304 203279)
Close to Market Square and Priory Station
Britain's Pompeii! Although buried by the Roman Army in AD 270, walls, floors, elaborate hypocaust, fort wall, bastion and best-preserved wall-paintings in Britain still survive. Displays show its history and that of medieval Dover.
April–October: daily (except non BH Mondays), 10–5
Small fee

Dover: Dover Pharos (EH)
Castle Hill, Dover
Within the castle walls, near St Mary-in-Castro
Hollow tower, square inside; octagonal outside, of rubble, tufa, ashlar tiles and pink mortar, with keyhole-shape windows to prevent undue draught to beacon-fire above. 62 feet of its original 80 feet still standing. (More than can be said of its devastated twin on Western Heights across the harbour.)
EH Standard and Sunday mornings

Lullingstone: Lullingstone Villa (EH)
Lullingstone, near Eynsford (0322 863467)
½ mile SE of Eynsford, off A225
Foundations of important country villa under nearly 400 years of Roman occupation showing 4 distinct periods of building. Contains the only Christian chapel found in a Roman house, full hypocaust and splendid mosaics. Also fascinating and very human relics. The whole is under cover. Picnics allowed   D – ground floor only
EH Standard and summer Sunday mornings

Lympne: Stutfall Castle (Port Lemanis)
Picturesque but hardly distinguishable remains of Port Lemanis which slid down the clay slopes below Lympne Castle.
Free

Reculver: Reculver Fort (Regulbium) (EH)
Off A299, at Roman Galley, 3 miles E of Herne Bay
Foundations of a 7½-acre fort built on a hillock then well above the sea, commanding entrance to the Wantsum Channel. Within them was built St Mary's Abbey.
EH Standard times, June–August

Richborough: Roman Amphitheatre (EH)
Richborough, near Sandwich
1½ miles N of Sandwich off A256; ¼ mile SW of Richborough Castle
Roman amphitheatre associated with the nearby 3rd century castle.
Any reasonable time   Free

Richborough: Richborough Fort (EH)
Richborough, near Sandwich (0304 612013)
Off A257, 1 mile N of Sandwich
Towering and massive walls and defensive earthworks of sea port where Romans landed in AD 43. Became main supply base for whole Roman invasion and chief in their line of Saxon shore forts. Site museum.   D
EH Standard time but museum closed on Friday

The Arts

ART GALLERIES

Most 'Historic Homes' have, as part of the décor, fine paintings; those listed below have particularly rich collections or galleries of their own.

See also, in the section 'Historic Homes', p.134: Hever Castle; Lympne (Port Lympne); Penshurst Place, Sevenoaks (Knole) and Westerham (Chartwell and Squerryes Court); in the chapter 'Museums', p.154: Canterbury (Beaney Museum and Art Gallery), Maidstone Museum and Art Gallery and Tunbridge Wells Museum and Art Gallery; and under 'Theatres', p.42, Tunbridge Wells (Trinity Arts Centre).

Canterbury: Graphics Gallery
University of Kent at Canterbury, Giles Lane (0227 66822)
Off Canterbury-Whitstable A290 road, 1 m N of town centre
Housed in the university's splendid library building, throughout the year it has various interesting and unusual exhibitions of cartoons, caricatures etc.
Weekdays: 9–7; Saturday: 9–1. Closed BHs. Times may alter during vacations   Free

Folkestone: Metropole Arts Centre
The Leas, Folkestone (0303 55070)
On the cliff-top promenade off Sandgate Road
A former luxury Edwardian hotel with a Channel view: talks and textiles; dance and drama; music and mime; painting and poetry.

Cafeteria, shop   D – every help given
All the year: Monday–Saturday, 10–5; Sunday, 2.30–5.
                                       Free, except for special exhibitions

BRASS-RUBBING CENTRES

Cobham: Church of St Mary Magdalene
Cobham, near Rochester (0474 814332)
In Cobham on B2009, Halfpence Lane
Finest collection of monumental brasses in the world, dating from the 13th century. A veritable dream for brass-rubbing enthusiasts! Limited materials available.
Phone for appointment. Daily, except Sunday, services permitting. 4-hourly sessions, 9–1, 2–6

Rochester: Rochester Cathedral Brass-Rubbing Centre
Cathedral crypt
An opportunity to make rubbings from replicas of medieval knights and ladies etc. Materials and tuition provided.
Last week of June to end of August: Monday–Saturday, 10.30–5.

Tunbridge Wells: Tunbridge Wells Brass-Rubbing Centre
Fonthill, The Common, Tunbridge Wells (0892 46832 during opening hours or 0892 27901)
Near The Pantiles
Brass-rubbing from replicas; tuition and material provided. Also exhibition of history of Tunbridge Wells.
7 days a week: April, May, June, September, October, 1.30–5.30; July, August, 10.30–5.30

The following are churches in various parts of the county which have a number of brasses, e.g. (7), that are generally available to *experienced* brass-rubbers when services are not being held. A modest fee is usually charged per session or per brass.

Naturally, an appointment should be made by phone or letter with the vicar and every care taken to ensure that the brass is not damaged in any way.

Biddenden, All Saints (9); Birchington, All Saints (6); Chartham, St Mary (5, including Sir Robert de Septvans, one of the finest brasses of its kind in England); Dartford, Holy Trinity (2); Faversham, St Mary of Charity (9); Goudhurst, St Mary (3); Great Chart, St Mary Virgin (7); Hever, St Peter (3, including Sir Thomas Bullen – Anne Boleyn's father); Hoo, St Werburgh (7); Lydd, All Saints (8); Newington Juxta Hythe, St Nicholas (7); Otterden, St Lawrence (5); Pluckley, St Nicholas (8); Rainham, St Margaret (4); Southfleet, St Nicholas (5); Ulcombe, All Saints (3); Westerham, St Mary Virgin (7); Woodchurch, All Saints (3, including Nichol de Gore); Wrotham, St George (8).

MUSIC

There are no halls *solely* dedicated to concerts. Most are held in theatres, town halls, churches etc. Even outdoor bandstands are often used only sporadically.

Series of concerts are often held at fairly regular intervals at Canterbury's Marlowe Theatre, Dartford's Orchard Theatre, Folkestone's Leas Cliff Hall and Tunbridge Wells Assembly Rooms.

See also Museums: Goudhurst, Finchcocks Living Museum of Music (p.150).

Folkestone: The Leas Bandstand
On Folkestone's cliff-top promenade, The Leas, off Sandgate Road, opposite Castle Hill Avenue
A wide variety of bands, jazz, military, accordion, pipes and drums; or Michelle, with her accordion in 'Sing-a-long', 'Songs from the Shows' or 'Musical World'; entertainment in sheltered enclosure.
Last week May–September: daily, 2.30; sometimes 7.45
Deck-chairs are free but collection for charity

Tunbridge Wells: Pantiles Bandstand
In The Pantiles itself
Town and military bands play here in the pleasantest of settings, with cafés near at hand.

June–August: Sunday only. Town bands: 3 p.m. Military bands: 2.30, 5.30. Children's entertainments also: Mid-July–August, 11, 3
Free

THEATRES

The theatres listed below offer a wide range of entertainment. Some will be by amateur companies, some by professional. The form of entertainment may range from one-night stands to week-long runs. Drama and variety, musicals and opera, ballet and concerts all have their place.

It is obviously not possible to give exact details of performances as, except at Canterbury's Marlowe Theatre and Dartford's The Orchard, they are not a *regular* 6-days-a-week feature. It is therefore advisable to see the local press announcements, obtain a 'List of Attractions' or phone the box-office number given for each theatre.

Broadstairs: Pavilion Theatre
The Promenade, near Harbour Street, Broadstairs (0843 64682)
A theatre close to the sea and set amidst lawns and flowers. Every night of the week in season, a different offering: children's party shows, dancing, music hall, orchestral nights.

Canterbury: Gulbenkian Theatre
University of Kent at Canterbury, Giles Lane, Canterbury (0227 69075)
Off A290 (Canterbury–Whitstable road), 1 mile N of Canterbury. Signposted
Centrally positioned on the university campus, the Gulbenkian is a striking, modern theatre 'in the round'. University, touring and local companies present a very wide variety of programmes. Also Cinema 3, lectures, concerts and recitals. Art exhibitions in the foyer. Bar; bar snacks on Thursdays.
Box office: 2–5.30. Closed during university vacations

The Arts

Canterbury: Marlowe Theatre
The Friars, Canterbury (0227 67246)
Off St Peter's Street, before Westgate Towers
Fine modern theatre upholds honour of Canterburian playwright Christopher Marlowe. Wide-ranging week runs and one-night acts by well-known companies and 'stars'. Grand opera, ballet and concerts, especially during the autumn Canterbury Festival. Bar, kiosk. D
All the year

Chatham: Central Hall Theatre
170 High Street, Chatham (0634 403868)
Originally a Methodist church, now offering a wide range of entertainments: orchestras, bands, drama, operas, fashion shows and individual acts. Bar. D
All the year. Box office: 10–5

Cliftonville: Tom Thumb Theatre
2a Eastern Esplanade, Cliftonville (0843 221791)
Miniscule theatre that produces occasional plays etc.

Dartford: Orchard Theatre
Home Gardens, Dartford (0322 34333)
Near railway station
Modern theatre-cum-concert-and-exhibition-hall with versatile auditoria and adaptable proscenium arch. Some week runs of plays, comedies, musicals etc and more one-night stands of music and humour etc. Stalls bar for coffee and snacks, morning, lunch-time and evening. Loop system for hard of hearing; wheel-chair facilities. D
Box office: Monday–Saturday, 9.30–5.30

Deal: Astor Theatre
Stanhope Road, Deal (0304 361161, ext 266)
Off High Street, behind the sea-front, near Royal Hotel
Small local hall, with stage facilities, used for occasional concerts, plays and other productions.

Folkestone: Leas Cliff Hall
The Leas, Folkestone (0303 53191)
Magnificently sited hall, built into the cliff face high above

the beach. Wide range of entertainment from disco to Olde Tyme dancing, big band to ballet, folk to Viennese nights, Chinese acrobats to all-in-wrestling – and a galaxy of one-night stars. Big-name concerts, too. Afternoon tea-dances on Wednesdays, June–August.
All the year

Gillingham: Oast House Theatre
Watling Street, Gillingham (0634 372121)
Off A2, 2 miles E of town centre
One-time oast-houses have been skilfully converted into a superb community theatre. Throughout the year sporadic programmes include drama, dance and pantomimes etc to suit all tastes and ages.

Gravesend: Woodville Halls
Civic Centre, Wrotham Road, Gravesend (0474 337460)
Offers wide variety of music and dance, drama and disco, exhibitions etc.
Box office: Monday–Saturday, 10.30–4.30

Herne Bay: King's Hall
The Downs, Herne Bay (0227 361911)
¾ mile E of the pier on the sea-front
Recently refurbished, it has 650 seats to choose from after a day on the beach. It has a 9-week summer season and at other times is used by local dramatic societies and for one-night shows and concerts.

Hever: Hever Castle
Hever, near Edenbridge (0732 866114)
From Edenbridge (B2026) follow clear signs
An open-air theatre in the perfect setting of an Italian garden created by an American multi-millionaire in the grounds where Henry VIII courted Anne Boleyn. A colonnaded loggia beside the lake makes an incomparable stage for music and drama under the auspices of Kent Repertory Company. The auditorium can be covered. Restaurant, bars, light meals and snacks, picnic area, festival dinners every Saturday.
Mid-June to first week in September: 8 p.m.

The Arts

Maidstone: Hazlitt Theatre
Earl Street, Maidstone (0622 58611)
Earl Street runs between Fairmeadow and Week Street in town centre
Amateur and professional productions are held in this intimate theatre during 40 weeks of the year.

Margate: Winter Gardens
Fort Crescent, Margate (0843 292795)
Along the sea-front just east of the harbour
Artistes have ranged from Sir Harry Lauder to Anna Pavlova. Today a wide variety of entertainment is provided, ranging from pantomime to one-night stands by equally famous stars, band concerts to musicals, and orchestras to drama.
Box office: Monday–Friday, 10-1, 2.15–5 (extended to 8 on show nights)

Ramsgate: Granville Theatre
Victoria Parade, Ramsgate (0843 591750)
In season entertainment is offered by Channel Theatre Co's plays, revues, or music hall. Occasional winter shows.

Southborough: Royal Victoria Hall
London Road, Southborough, Tunbridge Wells (0892 291761)
A small theatre used for a variety of entertainments and functions from locally produced music halls and shows to pantomime and smaller visiting professional dance and theatre companies.   Bar

Tonbridge: Medway Hall
The Angel Centre, Angel Lane, Tonbridge (0732 359966)
Off the High Street, just N of railway station and opposite the public library
A multi-purpose hall in a leisure centre with theatre lighting, sound system and stage facilities, capability of adding tiered theatre seats. It provides a variety of musical shows and plays, mainly produced by local entertainers.
Restaurant open Monday–Saturday, 10–4.30. Bar, vending machines

Tunbridge Wells: Assembly Hall
Crescent Road, Tunbridge Wells (0892 30613)
Next to town hall, just off Mount Pleasant Road (A26)
A variety of professional and amateur shows, including concerts by the excellent town orchestra, plays and dances. Entertainments for children also.
Most of the year

Tunbridge Wells: Trinity Arts Centre
Church Road, Tunbridge Wells (0892 44699)
Off Mount Pleasant Road, opposite town hall (A26)
A Decimus Burton church, Grade A listed, although Newman tersely dismissed it as 'cost £10,591 ... and looks worth every penny of it'. Now with raked auditorium, gallery, bar and buffet, seats 300 for regular lunchtime and evening performances and concerts several times a week. Also modern art exhibitions.   D
All year: Monday–Saturday, 10–2.30 (box office)

Whitstable: The Playhouse
104 High Street, Whitstable (0227 272042)
A 'little theatre' which features plays by local Lindley Players and visiting companies, as well as concerts, fashion shows, dance and choral groups etc. Bar.
Open at irregular intervals throughout the year
Box office: 10.30–12.30

Countryside

COUNTRY PARKS

Leaflets may be obtained from Kent County Council, Planning Department, Springfield, Maidstone.

All country parks are free except a few where a small parking fee is shown. Parking is generally available, and the parks are open throughout the day, 9 a.m. until dusk.

See also 'Gardens', Goudhurst (Bedgebury Pinetum), p.113, and 'Leisure Centres': Lamberhurst (Bewl Bridge Reservoir), p.217.

Andrews Wood, Badgers Mount, Shoreham
¼ mile E of A21 roundabout junction with A224
Nearly 200 acres of mixed woodland. 1 m walk. Picnic area.

Barnetts Wood
Adjoining A21, 4 miles S of Sevenoaks
8-acre picnic site of grassland set amid trees. D

Bluebell Hill Picnic Site
From A229 (Rochester–Maidstone road) at top of Bluebell Hill, just S of M2 Junction 3 interchange, turn into Common Road, opposite Upper Bell public house
From the car-park, one of SE England's finest views across the Medway valley to the hazy South Downs. 13 sunny acres of chalk downland pitted with intriguing, overgrown quarries. The North Downs Way skirts one edge

and leads (¾ mile) to neolithic Kits Coty and Lower Kits Coty.
Closed XD

Bockell Hill Viewing Point
From A258 (Dover–Deal road) take B2058 to St Margaret's at Cliffe. From B2058 turn left along Granville Road for ¾ mile. Viewing-point is on the left
11 acres of cliff-top with spectacular views of the sea. Nearby is the imposing Dover Patrol Memorial.

Brockhill Country Park
½ mile S of Sandling railway station on Sandling–Saltwood road. Shares joint entrance with secondary school. Signposted from Junction 11 off M20
Delightful 54-acre grassy valley with a lake of its own and woodland at its head. Sea views, trails, information area.   D
Closed XD   Small parking fee

Bockhill Farm and The Leas, St Margaret's Bay
Access is as for Bockell Hill viewing-point (above), which adjoins this site.
Bockhill Farm includes nearly a mile of cliff-top and other walks. The Leas is a 10-acre cliff-top area with good views to the east of St Margaret's Bay.

Camer Country Park
From A227 (Gravesend–Wrotham road) turn E onto B2009 just N of Meopham. Entrance 500 yards on right
Small, only 46 acres, but pleasant mature parkland for stroll or informal games.

Capstone Farm Country Park
2 miles S of Chatham on Capstone road
Countryside in the town? 280 acres of open countryside. Walking, picnicking, fishing, riding, archery and nature trails. Refreshment kiosk, Easter–October
Closed XD

Clowes Wood, Whitstable
On W side of Canterbury–Whitstable road (via Tyler Hill), 5 miles N of Canterbury, 2 miles S of Chestfield
580 acres of mixed woodland with broad rides. A 2-mile waymarked path gives unusual and splendid views of the Swale. Picnic site.

Dene Park, Shipbourne
From A227, at crossroads 1½ miles S of Shipbourne, take road signposted Plaxtol. Access ½ mile on left
A wealth of natural beauty! Over 200 acres of mixed hardwoods and conifers in Shipbourne Forest. 1½-mile walk along grassy rides offers interesting views. Picnic area, information point.

Dryhill Picnic Park
1½ miles W of Sevenoaks. Turn S from A25, ¼ mile W of junction with A21, at signpost
22 acres of grassland and young woodland. Former ragstone quarry shows strange rock formations. Picnic area and shelter. Leaflet at park or by post.   D
Closed XD   Small parking fee

Eastcourt Meadows Country Park
1 mile E of The Strand at Gillingham. Turn N off B2004 (Lower Rainham Road) just E of B2004/Lower Twydall Lane junction
60 acres of riverside walking and picnicking. Ideal haunt for bird-watchers and maritime enthusiasts.

Faggs Wood, Orlestone
4¼ miles S of Ashford. From B2070 (Ashford to Ham Street road) turn W at third crossroads south of Kingsnorth village. Take first road on left
350 acres of mixed woodland. 2½-mile waymarked forest walk yields sweeping views over the Weald towards 'Tenterden's steeple'.

Folkestone Warren
From roundabout junction of A20 and A260 continue E along A20 to next roundabout. There turn right and

continue to junction with Dover road. Carry straight on across into Wear Bay Road opposite. Grassy cliff-top car-park ½ mile on
From car-park (with splendid sea and shipping views) paths lead down into 350 acres of miniature jungle (rich in insects, flowers and fossils) formed when tens of thousands of tons of chalk collapsed as they slowly slid over wet gault clay. Bathing on beach. Bracing walk along massive sea-wall beneath towering white cliffs.
Small parking fee

Great Farthingloe, Dover (NT)
Access from Dover by car through Aycliffe along the Old Folkestone Road
A walk over 67 acres of farmland extending along magnificent cliffs midway between Capel-le-Ferne and Dover.

Grove Ferry Picnic Site
Turn S off A28 (Canterbury–Margate road) just E of Upstreet at signposts. Site is over railway and river and welcomely adjoining Grove Ferry Inn
A site with a difference. 11 acres of flat meadowland offering pleasant and easy riverside walking – or just a chair in the sun. Fishing (on a day ticket obtainable from local bailiff).
D
Closed XD

Hanging Bank and Brockhoult Mount
½ mile E of Ide Hill, along B2042, turn into minor road at Y-junction
Almost 100 acres of fine mixed woodland on crestline with views across Bough Beech Reservoir and Weald.

Hemsted Forest, Cranbrook
From A262 (Biddenden–Goudhurst road) at Sissinghurst turn S onto Benenden road. Turn E, 2 miles S of Sissinghurst. Access on left
One of the Weald's largest forests, 1,000 acres of it, offers a picnic area in an attractive larch wood.

High Rocks
High Rocks Lane, Tunbridge Wells (0892 26074)
From Mount Ephraim take Fir Tree and Hungershall Park Roads to Groombridge
In woodland setting, 50–70-feet-high rock outcrops, much admired by James II, with scenic paths between, spanned by high bridges. Restaurant/pub opposite.
All year: daily, sunrise to sunset.

Private property: Small fee

Holly Hill Wood
Turn W off A228 at Snodland crossroads. After 150 yards carry straight on for 1½ miles. At T-junction turn right up Birling Hill. At top of Downs, turn right up Holly Hill for 500 yards to car-park
A small wood with big views across the Medway valley from one of the highest points in Kent.

Hothfield Common Picnic Site
3 miles NW of Ashford signposted from A20. Take road S towards Hothfield. Picnic site is 150 yards on left just beyond car-park
Nearby Hothfield Common, 140 acres of heathland and woods, is a KTNC nature reserve. Waymarked nature trail.

Ide Hill
From A25 at Riverhead turn S on B2042 for 3 miles. Site is S of the village
32 acres of wooded hillside overlooking the Weald.

King's Wood, Challock
South on A251 (Faversham–Ashford road) from Challock crossroads for ¾ mile. Fork left (along minor road to Wye) for 500 yards
King's Wood by name – and by size, too. 1,400 acres of hardwood and conifer woodland with interspersed chestnut coppice. 2½-mile waymarked path, along which you may see deer.

Knole Park
Off main road at S end of Sevenoaks. No entry for cars

unless visiting Knole House
A historic deer park of 1,000 acres with avenues of majestic trees. Open by courtesy of Lord Sackville. Please do not trespass on golf course. No dogs because of grazing deer.

Langdon Cliffs
From Dover take A258 (Dover–Sandwich road) to top of Castle Hill Road. Pass the castle and take first road on right for 1 mile. Site is signposted on right at U-bend
Terraced car-park offers superb, sweeping Channel seascapes and fascinating bird's-eye view of the Eastern Docks 'ant-heap' immediately below. Equally splendid, the white cliff-top walk (with optional dizzy views to beach far below) to St Margaret's Bay. Chalkland flowers and butterflies.

Lighthouse Down (NT)
Accessible by footpath from St Margaret's Bay
10 acres of ground on the South Foreland near lighthouse giving short cliff-top walk.

Lullingstone Park
½ mile S of Eynsford. Turn W off A225 along Farningham–Sevenoaks road signposted 'Castle Farm'
A huge 300 acres of park and woodland. Also public golf course, restaurant and two car-parks.

Manor Park Country Park
Just S of West Malling on E side of A228
Only 52 acres of mature parkland but with a 3-acre lake. Four waymarked circular walks; informal games and picnicking; playlog for children near car-park. Information leaflet and walk guides at park or by post.   D
Closed XD   Small parking fee

Minster: The Leas and Cliff-Top
At Minster turn N off B2008 along the Broadway opposite Harps Inn. At sea-front turn right
Short walks or long. 4 grassy cliff-top acres that roll gently down to the beach. Walk can be continued E to Warden

Point. Shipping, beach and marshland views, walking and picnicking.

Oldbury Hill and Styants Wood (NT)
On N side of A25, 2 miles W of Borough Green
A fine combination: 150 acres of woodland, more than 600 feet above sea-level; the southern part of an Iron Age hill-fort of about 100 BC refortified by the Belgae, and Stone Age cave-dwellings. Downland views.

One Tree Hill (NT)
2 miles SE of Sevenoaks. From A25 at Seal, turn S and continue past Godden Green for 1 mile to crossroads. Woodlands ½ mile to S
Belies its name with beautiful crestline woodlands – and views of the Weald.

Park Wood
Woodland Trust, Dysart Road, Grantham (0476 74297)
1½ miles W of Chilham on A252
55 acres of coppiced woodland, the northernmost tip of extensive Challock Forest. Also fine beeches, unusual pollarded hornbeams, orchids, albino deer, goldcrest and nightingales etc. Leaflet from above.

Park Wood, Kenardington
4½ miles E of Tenterden. Turn S off B2067 (Hythe–Tenterden road) at Woodchurch onto Appledore road for 2 miles. Park Wood is the most southerly part of woodland on the left
40 acres of woodland offers oaks, woodland walks and panoramic views.

Pegwell Bay Picnic Site
Pegwell Bay, near Ramsgate (0622 671411 ext 3031)
Off A256 Sandwich Road
Coastal picnic site close to Viking ship *Hugin* and St Augustine's Ebbsfleet Monument, with short walk to River Stour through conservation area with much bird life.   Small car-park free

Perry Wood and Selling Wood
At Chilham, 2 miles NW of A252 (Canterbury–Charing road). Woods lie between Selling to N and Shottenden to S. Access via footpaths
150 acres of unspoilt woodland, once owned by Corpus Christi, Oxford. Dissected by footpaths and tracks. Rhododendrons. Two mesolithic sites (c. 1800 BC). 'Pulpit' at 504 feet gives splendid views. Picnic area. Trail for the disabled, including one for the blind.   D

Pillory Corner
Adjoining A21, ½ mile N of Flimwell on Hastings–London road
Tiny picnic area but worthwhile views southwards across the Weald.   D

Potters Hole
E of Platt, close to A25
Pleasant woodland which gives many opportunities for short walks. There are many varied tree species to be enjoyed, as the area was originally an ornamental woodland garden.

Shepherds Gate
Adjoining A2 at Cobham/Shorne interchange
3 acres of woodland and picnic site.

Shorne Wood Country Park
Brewers Lane, Shorne (0474 823800)
Off A2 on Shorne road, at Cobham/Shorne interchange
174 acres of woods and meadow, 5 miles of waymarked paths. Wild flower garden, horse-riding bridle route, fishing (day tickets), orienteering course.
                                        Small car-park fee

Teston Bridge Picnic Site
From A26, Maidstone–Tonbridge road, turn S on B2163. Entrance on right between level-crossing and river
24 acres of flat water-meadows by an interesting lock and medieval bridge. Walks along the Medway, fishing.
Closed XD   Small parking fee

Toys Hill, Brasted (NT)
2½ miles S of A25 at Brasted on Brasted–Toys Hill road

330 acres of delightful mixed woodlands on ridge of high land (800 feet) giving wide Wealden views.
Small parking fee

Trosley Country Park
2 miles NE of Wrotham, signposted from A227
160 acres of woods and downland with panoramic views over the Weald. Woodland strolls or more strenuous walks on the Downs. Springtime bluebells. Information centre. Walk and nature trail guides at park or by post. Three waymarked paths (3½–7 miles); 4,000-year-old barrow – Coldrum Stones.   D
Closed XD   Small parking fee

Tunbridge Wells, The Common
At S end of town, opposite the famous Pantiles shopping centre
250 acres of unspoilt woods and heathland criss-crossed with paths and within walking distance of the town centre. Ideal for picnicking, especially near Wellington Rocks, a safe scramble for even young children. Higher and Lower Cricket Grounds provide weekend cricket viewing.

West Wood, Lyminge
9 miles S of Canterbury. From B2068 (Canterbury–Hythe road) turn E at 6 Mile Garage along minor road for ½ mile
Extensive woodlands (440 acres) through which runs a majestic 2¼-mile waymarked path. Picnic area.

Woods Meadow
Adjacent to the A20 immediately N of the junction with the A228, West Malling road
An open space only 6 acres in extent but which provides quiet and pleasant walks and is a small refuge for a variety of flora and fauna. Maintained in conjunction with Kent Trust for Nature Conservation.

Wrotham Hill Viewpoint
On the A20, 1 mile NW of Wrotham
Only an acre in extent but with disproportionately enormous views. Picnic area.

Leisure Guide to Kent

NATURE RESERVES

These are extremely fragile. It is therefore more than ever essential that the Country Code be observed; that visitors park carefully to ensure there is no damage or obstruction; that information boards are carefully read; that only permitted paths are followed and closely kept to; and that any 'special areas' are respected. All are *free* except Dungeness, High Halstow and Sevenoaks, and all are open daily unless otherwise stated.

The survival of these reserves is in the hands (and under the feet) of each visitor.

Leaflets are available from:
The Kent Nature Conservancy Council, Zealds, Church Street, Wye TW25 5BW
The Kent Trust for Nature Conservation, PO Box 29, Maidstone ME14 1YH
The Royal Society for the Protection of Birds, 8 Church Street, Shoreham by Sea, West Sussex BN4 5DQ (0273 463642)

Bossingham: Yockletts Bank (KTNC)
Southbound, turn right off B2068 (Canterbury–Hythe road) along Waddenhall Lane, just after Bossingham turning, for 1½ miles
A narrow, 60-acre strip of coppiced woodland with stands of hornbeam and hazel and some open grassland. Spring wild flowers; woodland butterflies in early summer; orchids; tits, warblers, finches and even nightingales; badgers; golden oat and tor grass.

Canterbury: Church Wood, Blean (RSPB)
Rough Common, Canterbury
From A290, turn left ('Rough Common') 1½ miles N of Canterbury. 500 yards on, park in Ross Gardens
2,000 acres of deciduous woodland and some conifers harbour a wide range of birds from three species of woodpecker to blackcaps and redpolls. The yellow cow-wheat provides food for the endangered heath fritillary caterpillar. Public footpaths.   D
Free

Canterbury: Stodmarsh (KNCC)
Warden: Reedlings, Stodmarsh, near Canterbury (0227 277)
Turn off the A257 (Canterbury–Sandwich road) just beyond the golf course. Stodmarsh is some 3 miles NE. Parking (*not* in the village, please) is just off the drove road past the Red Lion
Subsidence due to underground colliery workings has created rough pasture, reed marsh and open water. Here many different wildfowl and marshland birds breed or overwinter; swans and wild geese occasionally make a winter visit. Wide range of aquatic plants.

Dungeness: Dungeness Bird Reserve (RSPB)
Off the Dungeness–Lydd road, 2 miles from Dungeness
A wide variety of birds may be seen at all times (270 species in recent years), more especially in the migration period, when this unusual 2,000-acre shingle habitat makes a very welcome landfall. A paradise for botanists and entomologists too. Reception centre, 'three 'hides', 1½-mile visitor route, leaflet. D
Daily (except Tuesday): 9–9

Elham: Park Gate Down (KTNC)
Off B2065, 1 mile N of Elham on minor road to Stelling Minnis. Or off B2068, some 8 miles S of Canterbury, between Stelling Minnis and Elham. (Please park well off the road.)
Wide range of downland flora and fauna. Rich in orchids, especially in spring, and chalk herbs (fairy flax wild thyme). Butterflies (common blue, brown argus and Essex skippers), lizards and adders, yellow-hammers and green woodpeckers, even kestrels and sparrow-hawks. Warden at peak times.

Faversham: Oare Marshes (KTNC)
From Oare (1 mile NW of Faversham) travel N along Church Road towards S bank of The Swale
170 acres of grazing marsh dissected by fresh and brackish water dykes and bounded by an earth sea-wall and some saltmarsh. Many birds: waders and wildfowl; kingfisher

and heron etc. Plants: frogbit, water parsnip, sea wormweed, golden samphire etc; reed bed.

Farningham: Farningham Woods
From Swanley roundabout, take A20 southbound to Farningham; then first left into Button Street for 1½ miles
175 acres of varied woodland rising to a height of 412 feet. Paths and rides from which may be seen, *inter alia*, heather and lily of the valley, yellow archangel, butchers' broom and orpine, Deptford pink and Solomon's seal; ringlet and gatekeeper butterflies; hawfinch, kestrel and tree-pipit.

Gillingham: Riverside Country Park and Berengrave Nature Reserve (KTNC)
Lower Rainham Road, Gillingham (0634 378898)
Off B2004 about 2 miles E of town centre
25 acres offer riverside walks with panoramic views over Kent marshes and estuary, picnic areas, nature reserve and self-guided trails, pond, reed bed and woodland.

Ham Street: Ham Street Woods (KNCC)
Off B2067, ¼ mile N of Ham Street
42 acres sloping from Weald to Romney Marsh, of coppice-with-standards (oaks) woodland. 90 species of birds have been recorded. Information centre at N end.

Hartlip: Queendown Warren (KTNC)
Near Hartlip, Sittingbourne
Signposted from Hartlip, Bredhurst, Stockbury and Yelsted
50 acres of grassland and coppiced woodland on North Downs. Rich orchid flora, butterflies, warblers etc.

High Halstow: Northward Hill Nature Reserve (RSPB)
High Halstow, near Rochester (0273 463642)
1 mile N of High Halstow reached from A228 (Rochester–Grain road)
Largest heronry in Britain, in oak woods: 220 pairs feed on the marshes below (February–July only); nightingales, turtle doves and woodland birds too. Butterflies and wild flowers. Paths – but no close viewing except on escorted

Countryside

visit (fee). Viewpoint under construction.   Free

Hothfield: Hothfield Common (KTNC)
South side of A20 at Hothfield
Open space with sandy common (heather, bracken, birches), bog (asphodel and orchid) and woodland (beech and Scots pines etc). Picnic site adjoining.

Leigh: Bough Beech Reservoir and Information Centre (KTNC)
Winkhurst Green, Ide Hill, near Sevenoaks
Off B2042 S of Winkhurst Green
Reservoir with angling and boat fishing (permit only). Nature reserve. Wide variety of birds, especially duck and geese. Information centre in old oast illustrates history of valley, oast-houses and waterworks. Nature trail.
April–October: Wednesday, Saturday, Sunday, 11–4.30

Leysdown: Shell Ness (KTNC)
Shell Ness, Isle of Sheppey
Most easterly tip of island. Access along public paths and sea-wall
Walks, naturist beach, bird-watching, nearby remote Isle of Harty and church. Information boards.

Leysdown: The Swale (KNCC)
East end of the Isle of Sheppey at Shell Ness: foot access only 70 acres of salt marsh, grazing marsh, fleet and mudflats under possible threat from agriculture and industry. A wide variety of birds in large numbers (ranging from Brent geese, waders and ducks to perching birds, raptors and gulls) may be viewed from a war-time block-house 'hide'.

Maidstone: Burham Downs (KTNC)
W of the A229 Maidstone–Chatham road. Adjoining the KCC picnic site on Common Road, Bluebell Hill
Downland, woodland, scrub and 2 disused quarries. Downland herbs (fairy flax, wild thyme, milkwort), butterflies (adonis blue, meadow and hedge brown), flowers (cowslips, autumn gentian and orchids), trees

(silver birch and hazel), birds (woodpeckers and yellowhammers). Picnic site.

Monkton: Monkton Nature Reserve (KTNC)
Hard by the roundabout at junction of B2047 and A253
A 15-acre chalk pit, unused for years, finds a new lease of life as a nature reserve with varied flora and fauna, including orchids. Marked nature trails. Excellent Museum. Pond. Warden.
Friday, Saturday and Sunday only

Sandwich: Sandwich Bay (KTNC)
S of Pegwell Bay on either side of the River Stour estuary. Access via Sandwich Bay Estate (£2 toll). Paths
Dune pasture, saltmarsh and tidal mudflats. Plants: sea holly, sea lavender, cord grass and wild asparagus. Birds: gulls and waders. Butterflies: clouded yellow and painted lady.

Seasalter: South Swale (KTNC)
Graveney, near Whitstable
Along coastal wall, from Sportsman Inn, 1 mile W of Seasalter
Beach foreshore and some grassland of major importance for overwintering wild-fowl and passage migrants: up to 1,000 Brent geese and many waders. Saltmarsh flora.
Best viewing time: one hour before high tide

Sevenoaks: Sevenoaks Wildfowl Reserve
(0732 456407)
On A25 between Riverhead and Sevenoaks Bat & Ball railway station. Entrance signposted
Old gravel pits restored by father and son doctors. 135 acres of lakes, islands, river, woodland and grassland provide a sanctuary for wildfowl and other birds. Hides, exhibition hall, nature trail (1 mile) with leaflet.   D
All the year: Wednesday, Saturday and Sunday, 10–5

Sheerness: Elmley Marshes Nature and Bird Reserve (RSPB)
Kingshill Farm, off Sheppey Way, near Sheerness, Isle of Sheppey (0795 665969)

Off A249, ¾ mile after Kingsferry Bridge (rough track)
Windswept RSPB saltmarsh reserve with hides from which thousands of white-fronted geese, waders and ducks may be seen in winter. Also hen harrier, avocet, water fowl etc; marsh frogs; aquatic plants. Visitor route, leaflet.
All year. Daily (except Tuesday): 9–9 (or sunset if earlier)

Wye: Wye and Crundale Downs (KNCC)
On the Wye–Hastingleigh minor road: 5 miles NE of Ashford
250 acres of chalk downland on the steep face of the North Downs escarpment. Magnificent views and the dramatic dry valley, the 'Devil's Kneading Trough'.
A wealth of wild flowers and grasses includes 17 species of orchids; butterflies include the black and red six-spot burnet; lizards and adders; cuckoos, meadow pipits, skylarks, kestrels and a wide variety of other birds.

PICNIC SITES

With due observation of the Country Code, it is possible to picnic in most country parks. Picnic sites or areas are *specifically* designated at the following:
Dryhill, Andrews Wood, Lullingstone Park, Barnetts, Dene Park, Shorne, Manor Park, Teston Bridge, Capstone, Eastcourt Meadows, Minster Leas, Bewl Reservoir, Hothfield Common, West Wood.

TOURS: BY CAR

Kent County Council have thought out 3 excellent country tours which encompass the loveliest countryside and the most interesting villages and attractions. A few of the latter may be viewed only externally or with permission. Detailed leaflets on each tour are available from Tourist Information Centres and, to make assurance doubly sure, they are signposted throughout by individual brown-and-white indicators pointing out the basic routes and detours from it to nearby features of interest. Each route has a different symbol (tree, white horse, oasts) on its finger-posts.

The route is signed in an anti-clockwise direction and may, of course, be joined, and left, at any point.

East Kent Country Tour
Symbol: A white tree
Some 50 miles in length, this tour explores the peaceful countryside of the North Downs, south of Canterbury, and its picturesque villages
Among other attractions the following make ideal journey breaks:

Chilham	Kent's prettiest village? Church, castle
Selling	Perry Wood; walks and picnics
Sheldwich	Church and village green, Lees Court
Challock	King's Wood, walks and deer
Eastwell Park	Lake, ruined church, splendidly housed hotel
Wye	River, bridge, mill, church, college, village
Wye Downs	Memorial cross, Crundale Nature Reserve
Stelling Minnis	Windmill
West Wood	Forest walk and picnic site
Elham	Church, village, Abbot's Fireside, vineyard
Broome Park	Golf course, country club, Jacobean mansion
Goodnestone Park	Garden
Wingham	Village, church, Rusham Bird Park, Staple Vineyard
Littlebourne	Howletts Zoo Park
Patrixbourne	Village, church
Chartham Downs	Views
Chilham	As above

Heart of Kent Country Tour
Symbol: Invicta White Horse
A 50-mile tour through the Garden of England, the

orchard and hop-field region of Kent. In the spring, a sea of white blossom; in the early autumn, the dark green bines and yellow-green hops are heavy on the hop fields' straining wires. And at all seasons it is rich in architectural and historic interest. Woodland and Medway Valley; leafy lanes and views of Kent's North Downs and Greensand Ridge add to the pleasure.

Teston	Medieval bridge, picnic site
Wateringbury	Pleasant village
Mereworth	Superb church, Palladian villa
West Malling	Country town rich in buildings including an abbey
Manor Country Park	Lake, picnic site, walks
Offham	Attractive village, unique quintain on green
Great Comp	Garden
Old Soar Manor	13th-century solar
Plaxtol	Delightful village, forge
Hadlow	Impressive church and folly
Beltring	Magnificent collection of oasts; museum, shire horses etc
Badsell	Farm trail
Matfield	Peaceful village
Brenchley	Church, splendid 'black-and-white' houses
Gate House	Farm trail
Horsmonden	See the 2-mile distant church at all costs
Harpers	Farm trail
Brattles Farm	Museum
Staplehurst	Half-timbered hall-houses
Iden Croft	Herb garden
Reed Court	Farm trail
Yalding	Medway, bridges, church, village
West Farleigh	Mansion, fine orchard and hop gardens; Medway Valley and High Weald view

High Weald Country Tour
Symbol: Twin oasts

A circular tour through the Wealden countryside, once impenetrably forested and later the medieval 'Black Country' of England. Today the rolling landscape still has extensive woodlands. Streams and sleepy rivers wind between Kent's famous hop gardens, orchards and pastures. It is a delightful countryside dotted with Kent's unique, white-coned oast-houses and picturesque villages, rich in tile and brick, dark timber and white weather-boarding. About 70 miles.

The tour passes the following attractions:

Tonbridge	School, river walks, castle
Bough Beech Reservoir	Nature study
Hever Castle	Church, inn, superb castle and gardens
Chiddingstone	Unique National Trust village, church and castle
Penshurst	Another magnificent castle and grounds, and a vineyard trail
High Rocks	An enchanting miniature Switzerland
Tunbridge Wells	Spa, The Pantiles, Church of St Charles the Martyr
Bayham Abbey	Premonstratensian abbey and lake
Lamberhurst	Owl House garden, vineyard, Scotney Castle
Bewl Water	Open-air leisure complex
Bedgebury Pinetum	Superb National Pinetum
Benenden	Village, walled herb garden
Rolvenden	Village, C.M. Booth Motor Museum, Kent & East Sussex Railway, church, windmill
Tenterden	Charming town, Kent & East Sussex Railway workshops
Smallhythe	Ellen Terry Theatrical Museum (NT), Spots Farm Vineyard
Biddenden	Beautiful village, vineyard
Sissinghurst	Castle and garden

Countryside

Cranbrook	Church, Union Windmill
Goudhurst	Village, pinetum, church, Finchcocks Keyboard Museum, Mr Heaver's Model Museum

TOURS: BY CYCLE

Kent County Council have also published a free booklet of circular cycle tours of 15–50 miles. They embrace Kent's distinctive countryside of Romney Marsh, Weald, North Downs and north coast as well as its historic towns and villages.

Wherever possible, routes have been chosen on quiet roads where refreshment facilities are available and to which access is comparatively easy.

All tours are 'circular' and may therefore be started and finished at any point. The towns mentioned under the heading are the 2 farthest apart. Mileage shown, in miles and kilometres, is that of the whole tour.

Nearly all the places mentioned are on the route or need only a slight detour, and have been described in appropriate chapters.

The following are arranged in topographical order rather than alphabetical, so that tours may be inter-linked if desired.

Romney Marsh
Rye-Lympne (46 miles; 74 kilometres)

Rye	Historic town
Appledore	Bulb fields (Appledore's Answer)
Lympne	Wildlife park, mansion and garden, castle and church
Dymchurch	Martello tower, beach, pleasure park
St Mary-in-Marsh	Church
New Romney	Church
Dungeness	Atomic power station; Romney, Hythe & Dymchurch narrow-gauge railway terminus; lighthouses
Lydd	Church and museum
Brookland	Church, Philippine Village
Rye	See above

High Weald (East)
Rye–Cranbrook (30½ miles; 49.5 kilometres)

Rye	Historic town
Wittersham	Stocks windmill
Smallhythe	Ellen Terry Theatrical Museum (NT): Spots Vineyard
Tenterden	Historic town; Kent & East Sussex Railway
Biddenden	Beautiful village, vineyard
Sissinghurst	Famous gardens and castle (NT)
Cranbrook	Church, Union Windmill
Hawkhurst	Bedgebury Pinetum
Bodiam	Castle
Northiam	Gardens, museum
Rye	As above

High Weald (West)
Tunbridge Wells–Hawkhurst (11 miles; 17 kilometres)

Tunbridge Wells	Historic town, The Pantiles
Bewl Water	Open-air leisure complex
Scotney Castle	Garden
Flimwell	Bedgebury Pinetum
Hawkhurst	2 churches, one by Gilbert Scott; a huge green, Dunk's School and almshouses
Cranbrook	Church, Union Windmill
Goudhurst	Charming village, church, Finchcocks' Keyboard Museum
Horsmonden	Sprivers Garden, church, furnace pond
Brenchley	Splendid 'black-and-white' houses, church
Matfield	Delightful village with green, pond and manor
Tunbridge Wells	As above

Tunbridge Wells and North Downs
Groombridge–Teston (49 miles; 79 kilometres)

Tunbridge Wells	Historic town; The Pantiles
High Rocks	Picturesque rock outcrops make a miniature Switzerland

Groombridge	Beautiful village, church, mansion
Penshurst	Splendid mansion and gardens
Hever	Castle and superb gardens
Chiddingstone	National Trust Tudor village, castle
Bough Beech Reservoir	Picnic area and wildlife
Ide Hill	Viewpoint
Emmetts	National Trust garden
Sevenoaks	Knole House (National Trust)
Otford and Kemsing	Picturesque villages
Ightham Mote and Old Soar Manor	National Trust historic buildings
Gover Hill	Viewpoint
Teston	Medieval bridge and riverside picnic area
Yalding	Medieval bridges and charming village
Beltring	Huge oast-house complex, museum, shire horses etc
Matfield	Picturesque village
Tunbridge Wells	See above

Maidstone Circular
Hollingbourne–Teston (20 miles; 32 kilometres)

Maidstone	Kent County Cricket Mote Park Ground, historic town, museum and art gallery, Tyrwhitt-Drake Carriage Museum
Hollingbourne	Culpepper Chapel, charming village
Leeds	Magnificent castle
Sutton Valence	Village and views
Boughton Monchelsea	Stately home, church
Teston	Medieval bridge and riverside picnic area
Maidstone	As above

Medway and Dickens Trail
Maidstone–Cliffe (40 miles; 64 kilometres)

Maidstone	See above

Allington	Castle
Aylesford	Medieval bridge, friary, church, Museum of Rural Life
Rochester	Castle, cathedral, Dickens Centre, Guildhall Museum
Wainscott	Upnor Tudor Fort
Cooling and Cliffe	Castle, Dickens' churches
Higham	Dickens' house
Cobham	Stately home, church with world-famous brasses, almshouses, Owletts House, Leather Bottle Inn
Sole Street	Country park
Meopham	Windmill
Wrotham Heath	Great Comp Garden
West Malling	Manor Park Country Park, attractive small town
Maidstone	As above

Medway and North Downs
Maidstone–Sheerness–Faversham **(44 miles; 70 kilometres)**

Maidstone	As above
Aylesford	As above
Rochester	As above
Chatham	Historic dockyard, Heritage Centre, Fort Amherst
Gillingham	Ice Bowl, Royal Engineers' Museum, Black Lions Sports Centre, riverside country park
Sheerness	Leisure centre, swimming-pool
Milton Regis	Ancient court-house, museum
Sittingbourne	Sittingbourne & Kemsley Light Railway, Dolphin Barge Museum
Faversham	Historic town, 400 listed houses, Gunpowder Mill, Heritage Centre, guild-hall, church
Doddington	Doddington Place Gardens (Danger! Steep hill)
Boxley	Abbey
Maidstone	As above

Swale, North Kent Coast and Canterbury
Herne Bay–Chilham (37 miles; 60 kilometres)

Faversham	Historic town, 400 listed houses, gunpowder mill, Heritage Centre, guildhall, church
Whitstable	Small docks
Herne Bay	Pier pavilion; sea-front
Reculver	Church towers
Canterbury	Cathedral, St Augustine's Abbey, St Martin's Church, Heritage Centre, Pilgrims Way etc
Chilham	Very picturesque village, castle gardens
Faversham	As above

Canterbury to the Coast I
Canterbury–Ramsgate–Dover (44 miles; 70 kilometres)

Dover	Castle and Pharos, Roman house, docks, Blériot memorial
Bekesbourne	Howletts Zoo Park
Canterbury	As above
Richborough	Roman fort and amphitheatre
Sandwich	Historic town
Ramsgate	Marina and docks, model village, motor and maritime museums, amusement park
Deal	Castle, Time Ball Tower, pier
St Margaret's Bay	Pines Garden, Dover Patrol Memorial, picturesque bay
Dover	As above

Canterbury to the Coast II
Canterbury–Lympne–Folkestone (38 miles; 61 kilometres)

Canterbury	As above
Stelling Minnis	Windmill
Lyminge Forest	Picnic area, walks
Lympne	Port Lympne Zoo Park, mansion and garden, Lympne Castle, church
Hythe	Interesting old town, church, Romney, Hythe & Dymchurch Railway, Royal Military Canal

Folkestone	The Leas, fishing harbour, East Cliff Sands and Leisure Complex, sports centre, Leas Cliff Hall, open-air swimming-pool, beaches and White Cliffs
Elham	Abbot's Fireside, church
Bekesbourne	Howlett's Zoo Park
Canterbury	As above

WALKS: CIRCULAR

Despite modern developments, Kent still has many enjoyable short walks to offer. They are not easy to find unaided and finger-posts merely marked 'Footpath' do little to help.*

Kent County Council Planning Office have done a splendid job in printing over 200 brochures of interesting and attractive walks which are listed below. Some are obtainable separately, others in packs of five or six covering a limited area.

All are very modestly priced and add considerably to the enjoyment of a successful circular walk. They are available as shown from the appropriate Tourist Information Centre. (See p.262.)

* indicates that a path is waymarked. With very few exceptions (shown in leaflet), the walker has right of way.

The following may all be obtained from Canterbury TIC. Additionally, *Five Walks near Canterbury* (Forest of Blean) and *Six Walks along the Stour* are also available from Herne Bay and Whitstable; *Five Walks near Canterbury* (east of the city) and *Five Walks near Canterbury* (the city environs from Herne Bay.

Town	Miles	Scenic interest
Canterbury		
Circular Walks in East Kent		
1. Wye and Crundale	8	Downland
2. Lyminge and Newington	8	Downs

Countryside

3. Alkham and Newington   8   Downs and nature reserves

Five Walks near Canterbury
(Forest of Blean)
1. Broad Oak Valley   5   Woodland
2. East Blean Wood   4   Woodland
3. Stephenson's Railway   3   Woodland
4. The Radfall   5   Woodland
5. Bigbury Camp   4   Woodland

Five Walks near Canterbury
(east of the city)
1. The Orchard of England   6½   Orchards
2. Between Great and Little Stour   5   Orchards
3. By Fire and Water   6   Downland
4. Markets, Fairs and Wayfarers   5   Villages
5. Wantsum Marshes   6   Views of Wantsum Marshes

Five Walks near Canterbury
(south of the city)
1. 4-mile walk from Garlinge Green   4   Woodland
2. Knights and Smugglers   4   Woodland and orchards
3. The Manor of Swarling   5   Woodland and orchards
4. The Lands of Odo   5   Downland
5. Two Little Churches   5   Extensive views

Five Walks near Canterbury
(around Bridge and Bishopsbourne)
1. The Big House   5   Orchards and downland
2. Rendezvous on Barham Downs   6   Orchards and Downs
3. Off Watling Street   4   Parkland
4. Two Literary Giants   4-5   Downland and parkland

5. Downland, Farmland and Forest	4	Downland, farm and forest

Five Walks near Canterbury (the city environs)

1. The Port of Canterbury	4	
2. Salt Road, Turnpike and Railway	4	Woodland view of city
3. Town and Country Passages	5	Old railway, town
4. Highways Old and New	5-6	Orchards and downland
5. A Wood Given for Ever	4	Orchards and downland

Chartham Walks

1. A Walk by the River	3	River
2. Woods and Orchards	3	Woodland and orchards
3. Chartham Hatch	1½	Woodland and orchards
4. Through Hop Gardens to River and Lake	4½	Hop gardens and lake

Six Walks in Harbledown

1. Harbledown – Bigbury – Chartham Hatch – North Downs Way	4	Orchards and woodland
2. Harbledown – Golden Hill – Gorse Farm – Hospital Farm	4	Orchards and woodland
3. Rough Common – Jubilee Field, Faulkners Lane	3	Orchards and woodland
4. Stock Wood – Vernon Holme – Poldhurst Farm – Homestall Wood	4	Woodland and orchard
5. Harbledown – Rough Common – Church Wood	3	Woodland
6. Upper Harbledown – Denstead Farm – Poldhurst Farm	3	Orchards

Countryside

Six Walks along the Stour
1. Canterbury to Fordwich	7	River
2. Fordwich to Grove Ferry	11	River
3. Grove Ferry to Plucks Gutter	6	River
4. Plucks Gutter to Minster	8½	
5. Minster to Hoverport	4	Historic sites
6. Stourmouth to Richborough	11	Roman remains and orchards

Heritage Walking Trails
(East Kent: Book 1)
1. Town and University	5	Views of city
2. Radfall and Broad Oak Valley	5¾	Woodland
3. Landscapes and Lakes	6½	River and lakes
4. Blean Forest Churches	5¼	Woodland
5. Stephenson's Railway and Clowes Wood	4	Forest and old railway
6. 'Bright Island' from Saxon Shore Way	5	Spacious landscape
7. Escape with the Napoleonic Prisoners of War	8	Woodland and farm
8. Chestfield	6	Woodland
9. Herne Village	6	Village, woodland and windmill
10. Seasalter	5	
11. Maritime Whitstable	3¾	Town and harbour
12. Ancient Reculver	2-6	Coast and historic houses

Heritage Walking Trails
(East Kent: Book 2)
1. Canterbury	5¼	Town walk
2. Street End	6¾	Woodland and Downs
3. Valley of the Nail Bourne	6	Woodland and Downs
4. Stelling Minnis	7	Woodland and Downs
5. Denton and Downs	5¾	
6. Elham	5¾	Downland
7. Ridgeway	6¼	Downland
8. Battle of Britain	8⅓	Downland

9. Folkestone Warren	5½	Cliffs
10. Romney Marsh and Saxon Shore Cliffs	5¾	
11. England repels 'Old Boney'	6	Cinque Port
12. Victorian Folkestone	3¾	Victorian port and resort
Nature Trail and Tour of the Central Campus of the University of Kent*	2½	Woodland

The following may be obtained from the Cranbrook Tourist Information Centre:

Cranbrook
1. Angley Woods	2½	Woodland
2. Angley Woods	4	Woodland
3. Goudhurst	9	Wood and pastoral
4. Buckhurst Farm	3	Views of windmill
5. Sissinghurst Castle	6	Orchard, wood and fields
6. Paley Farm	6	

The following may all be obtained from Folkestone Tourist Information Centre. No. 1 is also available from Dover, and No. 2 from Deal.

Heritage Coast
1. Folkestone Warren	2¼	Access to unique coast
2. St Margaret's Down	5½	Cliffs and downland
3. South Foreland	5¼	View of French coast when clear

The following may all be obtained from Sevenoaks Tourist Information Centre:

Kemsing
A selection of walks in and around Kemsing to:
1. Otford – Shoreham – Upper Austin Lodge	8½	Valley and downland

Countryside

2. Seal – Greatness – Otford 5½
3. North Downs – Holmes- 5   North Downs
dale Valley
4. Heaverham and Noah's 3½ North Downs and
Ark   woodland
5. Knatts Valley – Romney 12 North Downs and
Street – Shoreham   woodland
6. Heaverham – Oldbury 6½ Woodland and orchard
Hill – Styants Bottom
7. Otford – Shoreham – 8½
Row Dow
8. Otford – Chipstead – 12½ North Downs, wood-
Dryhill Picnic Site – Whitley land, Sevenoaks
Forest – Sevenoaks
9. Cutman's Ash 2½
10. Seal – Godden Green – 6   Woodland
Seal Chart

The following may all be obtained from Swale Council Offices and/or Sittingbourne Tourist Information Centre:

Newington
Five Walks near Newington
1. The Valley of Watercress 4   Halstow Creek, water-
                                 cress and woodland
2. To Shoregate Creek 6   Medway estuary, little
                           harbours, creeks and
                           orchards
3. Monkey Island 4   Orchards
4. Around Standard Hill 5   Orchards
5. Almost to Stockbury 4   Orchards

The following may all be obtained from Maidstone Tourist Information Centre:

Maidstone
A Circular Walk
(Part I)
1. Detling Church to 8   Downland
Bearsted Church

2. Bearsted Church to Langley Green	7	
3. Langley Heath to Loose	11	Greensand Ridge

(Part II)
1. Sandling to Detling	8	
2. Loose to East Barming	8	Orchards
3. East Barming to Sandling	8	
4. Another Leeds Delight	5½	Castle and woodland

Local Walks
(Set I)
1. Yalding Down	4½	Orchards and Downs
2. Wateringbury	4½	Orchards
3. Reason Hill	5	Views of the Weald and orchards
4. Yalding	3	Orchards and River Beult
5. Nettlestead	6	Woodland and River Medway

More Local Walks
(Set II)
1. Benover	4½	Orchards
2. Hunton	5	Orchards and downland
3. West Farleigh	4½	River Medway and orchards
4. A Beultside Walk	7	River Beult
5. St Michael's Walk	6	Downs and woodland

Five Walks near Maidstone
(Set III)
1. A Walk in Barming Woods	5	
2. A Walk to Leeds Castle	5	Views of Leeds Castle, woodland
3. A Walk from Loose	5	Loose Village, Greensand Ridge and views over the Weald
4. A Hilltop Walk	6	Views of Weald and Medway Valley

5. The Loose Valley   4½   The Loose Valley

Five Walks near Tonbridge
1. Tudeley Walk   4½   Orchards and woodland
2. A West Peckham Walk   4½   Orchards and woodland
3. A Walk in Mereworth Wood 4½   Forestry
4. East Peckham   4½   Medway meadows
5. A Walk from Paddock Wood 7   The Weald, woodland and orchard

Five Walks round Staplehurst
1. Jubilee Walk (1)   4   Low Weald
2. Jubilee Walk (2)   3   Low Weald
3. Circular Walk via Cross at Hand   6½   Low Weald
4. Circular Walk via Chapmans Farm   4½   Low Weald
5. Linton to Staplehurst   7   Greensand Ridge and Beult Valley

Five More Walks around Staplehurst
1. Circular Walk   4   Low Weald
2. Circular Walk via Chickenden Lane and Little Craddock 4   Low Weald
3. Circular Walk to Headcorn   8   Low Weald
4. A Walk to Marden and back   7   Low Weald
5. Circular Walk to Frittenden   5½   Low Weald

The following may all be obtained from Manor Park Country Park Tourist Information Centre:

Manor Park Country Park
Waymarked Walks from Manor Park Country Park
1. The Quintain Walk*   4½   Fields and woods
2. Woods Meadow Walk*   3   Fields and woods
3. St Leonards Walk*   4   Fields, woods and meadows
4. Millstream Walk*   3¼   Watermills, oasts, orchards

The following may all be obtained from Swale Council Offices and/or Sittingbourne Tourist Information Centre:

Rainham
Five Walks near Rainham
1. The Roman Potteries (from Upchurch)   3   Estuary and orchards
2. Out to Hartlip   4
3. Over Hartlip Hill   5   Orchards
4. The Candle Snuffer Spire (not a circular walk)   4   Orchards
5. Queendown Warren   4-6 Orchards

The following may all be obtained from Hythe or New Romney Tourist Information Centres:

Romney Marsh
1. Circular Walk from New Romney to Midley and Old Romney   6½-7   Marsh and wildlife
2. Rural Walk from Lydd   3½   Marsh and sea wall

The following may all be obtained from Sevenoaks Tourist Information Centre:

Sevenoaks
Country Walks around Sevenoaks (Vol. I)
1. The Vine to Godden Green and Bowpits   4   Knole Park
2. Godden Green to Ightham Mote   5¼   Downland, woods and Ightham Mote

3. Godden Green to Nether Fawke, Bitchet Green and Stone Street — 4 — Woodland
4. Knole Park to Great Budds and Wilmot Cottage — 4½
5. Sevenoaks PO to Hubbards Hill and back by Knole Park — 6
6. Sevenoaks PO to Whitley Forest — 4½ — Woodland
7. Dibden Lane to Whitley Forest — 3½ — Woodland
8. Shrubs Corner to Sundridge Hospital — 4¾ — Woodland
9. Britannia Lane to Dryhill — 4½ — Woodland
10. Greatness Lane to the Downs via Kemsing and back through Otford — 6 — Downland
11. Otford Station to East Down — 4 — Downland

(*Vol. II*)
12. Shoreham to Upper Austin Lodge — 4¾ — Downland
13. Kemsing to Heaverham, Cobhams Ash and Woodlands — 4¾ — Downland
14. St Laurence Church to Oldbury Hill — 3½ — Iron Age fort
15. Shoreham to Lullingstone Park, the Terrace and Filston Mill — 6 — Darent Valley
16. Brasted to French Street and Emmetts Mill — 5¾ — Woodland, Emmetts Garden
17. Leigh to Powder Mills and the Medway — 4½ — Riverside (Medway)
18. Penshurst to Hoath Corner and Hill Hoath — 5¾ — Riverside and woodland
19. Chevening Church to North Downs Drive — 4¼ — North Downs and Chevening House

20. Knockholt Church to Horns Green and Bambers Farm return by North Downs Way	5	North Downs and Pilgrims Way
21. Leigh to Penshurst	5¼	River, park, woodland
Leigh to Penshurst (by Price's Farm)	6	River, park, woodland
Ensfield Bridge to Penshurst and back	4¼	River and park
22. Westerham to Chartwell, Mariners Hill, Crockham Hill Common and Squerryes Park	5¼	Downs, woodland, Chartwell, Squerryes Park

The following may be obtained from Tenterden Tourist Information Centre:

Tenterden

1. Chennel Park	3	Town, countryside
2. Belgar Hopes Grove, Six Fields	2	Town, orchards
3. Shoreham Lane	3	Town, Weald
4. The Bottoms	3	Primroses and bluebells in season
5. West View, Rolvenden Lane	4	Steam railway
6. Sandy Lane Forstal	3½	Woodland, orchard
7. Readers Bridge	4	Weald
8. Mill Ponds	3	Tenterden and Weald
Walks in the Weald	1	Tenterden and Weald
Four miles from Tenterden	4	

The following may all be obtained from Broadstairs, Margate or Ramsgate Tourist Information Centres:

Thanet Nature Trails
The Naturalist in Thanet

1. Minster Marshes	3	Minster Abbey and marshes
2. Botany Bay	1	Clifftop walk

Countryside

3. Pegwell Bay	2	Cliffs and Saxon landing-site
4. Sea Wall Walk	3¼	Minnis Bay and Reculver
5. Westbrook to Minnis Bay	4	Cliffs and bays

(Nos. 2, 3, 4 and 5 are not circular walks)

Trosley Country Park
Waymarked Walks

1. The Harvel Hike*	7	Views across the Weald and North Downs
2. The Trosley Ramble*	3½	Views across the Weald and North Downs
3. The Coldrum Trail*	6	Coldrum Stones

The following may be obtained from the Tunbridge Wells Tourist Information Centre:

Tunbridge Wells
Walking in the Borough
(Book I)

1. Ashurst	2	
2. Groombridge	5	Park, woodland
3. Pembury	3½	
4. Langton Green	3½	Park, woodland
5. Speldhurst	4	Woodland, park
6. Southborough and Bidborough	2½	Woodland

(Book II)

1. Brenchley	4	Orchard
2. Horsmonden	4½	Orchards and furnace ponds
3. Lamberhurst	5	Parkland, orchard and garden
4. Matfield	4	Orchards, woods, ponds
5. Paddock Wood	3½	Orchards

(Book III)

1. Benenden	4½	Weald

2. Cranbrook   5½   Weald
3. Frittenden   3
4. Goudhurst (a)   3¾
4. Goudhurst (b)   5¾
5. Hawkhurst   4¼   Weald
6. Sandhurst   5   Weald

Tunbridge Wells Town Area
(Book IV)
1. Pantiles – Happy Valley – 4   Weald
Rusthall – Toad Rock
2. Calverley Grounds – High 5½   Weald
Wood – Dunorlan
3. Pantiles – Hawkenbury   3½   Town
4. Town Hall – Speldhurst – 5   Woods
Rusthall
5. Pantiles – High Rocks – 5½   High rocks
Rusthall

The following may be obtained from Canterbury Tourist Information Centre (Nos. 2-4 and 6 only) and Tenterden Tourist Information Centre (all 7 walks):

Walks in the Weald
1. A 10-Mile Walk from   10   Sissinghurst Castle,
Cranbrook   woodlands
2. Bewl Bridge   5   Reservoir, water birds and
Reservoir   woodland
3. Four Miles from   4   Weald and town
Tenterden
4. From Goudhurst   8   Orchards and hopfields
through the Teise
Valley
5. Hawkhurst to   7   Woods and pasture
Benenden
6. The Railway Walk   6½   Steam railway, marsh, woodland and lake
7. The Beult Meadows   4¾

The following may be obtained from Dover and Deal Tourist Information Centres:

Walmer Castle, Kingsdown and Ringwould
6   Castle and coast

WALKS: LONG-DISTANCE

Kent is rich in walks, both in towns and in the countryside.

Most major towns now have a Town Trail (q.v.) – and the local Tourist Information Centre has a leaflet describing it. Leaflets are also available for individual and varied country walks.

Kent is also extremely fortunate in having 5 major long-distance walks: (i) The Greensand Way, (ii) The North Downs Way (iii) The Pilgrims Way, (iv) The Saxon Way and (v) The Wealdway. Brief details of all 5 are given in this section, and suitable books are recommended at the back of this book.

Guided walks in the country as well as the town are also available. An excellent list covering the whole of Kent and the whole of the summer is available from: Landscape Branch, Property Services Department, Kent County Council, Springfield, Maidstone ME14 2LT. It also includes delightful 'Special Events' held in country parks, ranging from a Teddy-Bears' Picnic to Teston Tots Day for the children and Bird-Watch Days and a Bat-Spottery Special for adults.

Few may have the time or energy to cover the whole distance but it is, of course, possible to join and leave the Way at any convenient place or to walk one of the sections listed below just to get the 'feel' of the whole walk. Each walk has its own signposts with its own symbol. Being country walks, they tend to avoid towns and crowded areas. Below, however, are listed the main natural features and villages directly on the route or comparatively nearby.

Greensand Way
Most recent of the long-distance footpaths and as yet unfinished. It enters Kent on the wooded ridge above Chartwell and runs as far as Yalding. In due course it will join the Saxon Shore Way near Hythe on the Channel.

It passes or is near to: Westerham; Squerryes Court; Chartwell (NT); Emmetts Garden (NT); Crockham Hill, Toys Hill and Ide Hill (viewpoints); Sevenoaks Weald (church); Knole (NT); Shipbourne; Hadlow (folly and church); Nettlestead (church and mansion); Yalding.

North Downs Way

DUNTON GREEN – TROTTISCLIFFE (8 MILES)

Otford; Wrotham; Pilgrims Way; Trosley Country Park; Trottiscliffe.

TROTTISCLIFFE – WOULDHAM (8 MILES)

Holly Hill, Upper Bush, Medway Bridge (Rochester); Wouldham.

WOULDHAM – HOLLINGBOURNE (14 MILES)

Bluebell Hill; Kits Coty; Aylesford; White Horse Stone; Boxley; Detling; Hollingbourne.

HOLLINGBOURNE – BOUGHTON LEES (9 MILES)

Pilgrims Way, Lenham 'Cross', Charing; Dunn Street; Eastwell Park; Boughton Lees.

BOUGHTON LEES – ETCHINGHILL (13½ MILES)

Wye; Wye Crown; Crundale Nature Reserve; Brabourne Downs; Stowting; Etchinghill.

ETCHINGHILL – DOVER (12 MILES)

Cheriton Hill; Castle Hill above Folkestone, and then along the cliff top to Dover.

BOUGHTON LEES – CANTERBURY (13¼ MILES)

Pilgrims Way; Boughton Aluph; Soakham Downs; King's Wood; Godmersham Park; Mountain Street; Chilham; Old Wives Lees; Chartham Hatch; Harbledown; Canterbury.

CANTERBURY – SHEPHERDSWELL (10 MILES)

Patrixbourne; Howletts Zoo; Barham Downs; Womensworld; Shepherdswell.

SHEPHERDSWELL – DOVER (7½ MILES)
Waldershare Park; Ashley; Connaught Park; Dover.

Pilgrim's Way
Medieval pilgrims undoubtedly travelled along it from Winchester to Canterbury, but it was neolithic man, travelling from Stonehenge to Dover, who, some 1,500 years earlier, had pioneered it. And it was only about 1880 that it was christened 'Pilgrims Way' and given the distinction of an Old English typeface on our maps by some romantically minded Ordnance Survey cartographer.

Today much of it is merged with the North Downs Way or under tarmac. For all that, it can still be followed along country lanes, across fields and round woods. Often skilfully contoured along the North Downs lower slopes, it offers worthwhile walking, fine views, interesting diversions – and even a hint of romance. No need today to put peas in one's shoes – as extra penance.

The Way passes through or near the following places: Westerham; Chevening; Otford; Kemsing; Trosley Country Park; Paddlesworth; Snodland; Burnham Old Church; Kits Coty; Boxley Abbey; Detling; Thurnham; Hollingbourne; Harrietsham; Charing; Westwell; Eastwell Park; Chilham; Old Wives Lees; Harbledown; Canterbury.

Saxon Shore Way
The Way, 140 miles long, is named after the forts built by the Romans in their ever-growing need of defence against rapacious Saxon pirates (c. AD 285). It is a far more diverse walk than the North Downs Way, more variable too in mood, and far richer in history. In content it varies from bleak marshland and muddy creeks, and from industrialization and over-population by the Thames Estuary to dunes and cliffs and to the quiet beaches and bustling seaside resorts of the Channel coast.

Walks can, of course, be tailored to individual tastes, but the following will appeal to strong walkers.

GRAVESEND – STROOD (19 MILES)
Thames-side; Milton Chantry; Shoremead Fort; Cliffe

Fort; Cliffe (Early English church views); Cooling Castle (massive 14th-century castle) and Dickens' *Great Expectations* church; Northward Hill (RSPB bird sanctuary and heronry); Medway riverside; Hoo St Werburgh (vast power station and church); Upnor (picture-book castle); Frindsbury (church on quarry edge, fine Medway views); Strood (Knights Templar manor).

STROOD – KINGSFERRY (18 MILES)

Rochester (castle, cathedral and much else); Chatham (historic dockyard, Heritage Centre, Great Lines); Gillingham (RE's Museum and Strand Riverside Leisure Complex); Riverside Country Park; marshland and creek; Lower Halstow (church); Chetney Lazaret; Swaleside; Kingsferry Bridge.

KINGSFERRY BRIDGE – FAVERSHAM (20 MILES)

Rhidham Dock; Milton Creek; Milton Regis (court house and church); Sittingbourne (Dolphin Barge Museum); sea wall; Oare; Faversham Creek; Faversham (houses, church, guildhall).

FAVERSHAM – HERNE BAY (14 MILES)

Swale Nature Reserve; Seasalter (golf course); Whitstable (Harbour); Tankerton; Swalecliffe; Herne Bay (pier pavilion).

HERNE BAY – SANDWICH (18 MILES)

Cliffs; Bishopstone Glen; Reculver (church; Roman fort); Marshside; Upstreet; Grove Ferry (picnic site, angling); Great Stour; Stourmouth; Plucks Gutter; Richborough (Roman fort); Sandwich (historic town, golf courses, nature reserve).

SANDWICH – DOVER (15 MILES)

Golf course; Sandown Castle; Deal (pier, castle); Walmer (castle); Kingsdown (cliffs; golf course); St Margaret's Bay (Pines Garden, Dover Patrol Memorial); South Foreland (windmill and lighthouse); Langdon Bay; Dover (harbour, castle).

Countryside

DOVER – HYTHE (13 MILES)

Western Heights; Shakespeare Cliff; Abbots Cliff; Folkestone East Cliff (open-air leisure complex); Folkestone (The Leas, harbour, rotunda); Sandgate (castle); Seabrook; Hythe (Romney, Hythe & Dymchurch Railway).

HYTHE – HAM STREET (12 MILES)

Lympne (castle, church, views, zoo park, mansion and garden); Royal Military Canal; Court at Street; Aldington (church, views); Bilsington Priory; Ham Street Woods; Ham Street.

HAM STREET – RYE (12 MILES)

Warehorne (Early English church); Royal Military Canal; Appledore (church, bulbfields); Stone (15th-century church and hall-house); River Rother; Rye Harbour; Rye.

Wealdway

A recently created path that runs through Kent from Gravesend in the north to Tunbridge Wells in the south. It then continues across the county border into Sussex to make its way to Eastbourne for a grand finale on Beachy Head.

It is a way that, largely shunning centres of population, makes the most of comparatively unknown but lovely countryside.

Places of interest *en route* or nearby are:

GRAVESEND – WROTHAM HEATH (11½ MILES)

Gravesend (Pocahontas statue, Milton Chantry, New Tavern Fort, Gordon Memorial Gardens and promenade with fine views of Thames); Nash Street; Sole Street (Tudor yeoman's half-timbered house); Camer Country Park; Luddesdown (picturesque village and church); Cobham (church with world-famous brasses, Priests' College, Elizabethan Hall, Leather Bottle Inn (Dickensiana), Owletts (NT); Trosley Country Park; Coldrum Stones; Coldrum Long Barrow; Wrotham Heath.

WROTHAM HEATH – TONBRIDGE (14 MILES)

Platt (Great Comp Garden); Mereworth Woods; Gover

Hill (NT viewpoint); West Peckham (village and church); Hadlow (church, 170-foot folly); Barnes Street; north bank of River Medway (East Lock, Porter's Lock, Hartlake Bridge, Eldridge Lock); Tonbridge (castle, public school, Port Reeve's House, Chequers Inn).

TONBRIDGE – FORDCOMBE (9½ MILES)

Hayesden Water (water sports); Bidborough (church, houses and gardens, panorama); Speldhurst (picturesque village, church with much stained glass, one of Kent's oldest inns); Tunbridge Wells (Church of King Charles the Martyr, The Pantiles); Bullingstone (cottages and manor); Penshurst (village, church, historic home); Avery's Wood; Fordcombe (pretty hillside hamlet).

FORDCOMBE – ASHDOWN FOREST (10 MILES)

Stone Cross; River Grom (tiny Medway tributary, Kent and Sussex border); Ashdown Forest.

And in Sussex:

ASHDOWN FOREST – BLACKBOYS (8½ MILES)
BLACKBOYS – HELLINGLY (9½ MILES)
HELLINGLY – WILMINGTON (8 MILES)
WILMINGTON – EASTBOURNE (7 MILES)

WALKS: WATERSIDE
(Other than those mentioned in Circular Walks)

Darent Valley Path

A delightful river and lakeside path following the Darent from Dartford's public library and Central Park to South Derenth. Mainly on footpaths, it passes Brooklands Lake, gunpowder mills, Darenth church, watercress beds and St John's Jerusalem Commandery (NT).

Can be traversed in 4-5 leisurely hours and, if wished, continued to Farningham still further up the delightful and interesting Darent Valley.

Medway Towpath

May not count as a long-distance footpath but ranks high

as a one-day marathon (18 miles) or a series of Sunday afternoon strolls.

It runs beside the best of the Medway from the outskirts of Maidstone (Maidstone bridges, Tovil) to those of Tonbridge (Cannon Bridge). Easy on the feet and the eye; attractive, unspoilt countryside, locks, bridges and pleasure craft. Picnic site at Teston Bridge.

Royal Military Canal
(i) Canal-side path from Hythe to below Court-at-Street
(ii) From Warehorne to Appledore on National Trust land

EATING AND DRINKING

All establishments are listed in alphabetical order of their town or village. Some tea-rooms (T) serve lunches (L) as well as cream teas and/or morning coffees. A growing number of inns (R) have a separate restaurant as well as serving lunch-time bar snacks.

The following are obviously only a few of a rapidly growing number. Choice has been based on proximity to other attractions; service and cuisine; historical associations and ambience; setting; and general character.

Opening and closing times may, of course, be varied to suit proprietors' particular needs. Christmas Day opening is often dependent on circumstances and demand.

CAFÉS AND TEA-ROOMS (MORNING COFFEE)

Biddenden: Claris's
3 High Street, Biddenden (0580 291025)
15th-century tea-rooms and craft shop. Claims its homemade cakes are 'irresistible' and coffee 'delightful'. Real Jersey cream too. Featured in *The Budget Good Food Guide, 1987*.
All the year. 6 days a week (except Mondays and Bank Holidays): 10.30–5.30

Burmarsh: Lathe Barn
Donkey Street, Burmarsh, near Dymchurch (0303 873618)
Off A259, 3 miles W of Hythe
After exploring Dr Syn country, you too could graze here

Eating and Drinking

in idyllic rural surroundings – on traditional teas: boiled egg and scone, cream tea and cakes. Children, not surprisingly, most welcome.
May–September: Tuesday–Sunday, 3–6

Chiddingstone: The Village Tea-Shop (L)
Chiddingstone, near Edenbridge (0892 870326)
Off B2027 at Bough Beech, 3 miles W of Leigh
Trim tea-shop and restaurant in the Old Coach House of Burghersh Court. Whole oak-smoked trout for lunch; Guernsey cream, jam and scones for tea. All from the hand of Ena Aitchison who won the Egon Ronay Award for Good Food and Value in 3 consecutive years. Ideal centre for 'castle fanatics': Hever, Penshurst, Chiddingstone, all nearby.
Daily (except Mondays) during the season: March–November 11–5.30

Fordwich: George & Dragon (L/R)
Fordwich, near Canterbury (0227 710661)
½ mile off A28 (Canterbury–Margate road) at Sturry
A picturesque little hotel in a still more picturesque village, with a big garden stretching down to a tree-lined River Stour. Beefeater waitresses!
All the year except XD: 12–2.15 but 12–10.30 on Sundays. Evenings 6–10.15 (10.30 on Fridays and Saturdays)

Goudhurst: Weekes of Goudhurst (L)
High Street, Goudhurst (0580 211380)
You can smell the fresh-baked bread! 16th-century tea-rooms hard by the village pond – and ducks.
Daily except XD: 8–5 but 9.30–5.30 Saturdays

Hythe: Kipps Tea-Rooms (L/R)
152 High Street, Hythe (0303 69669)
Opposite GPO
Here H.G. Wells set up Kipps in his longed-for bookshop, in Hythe's second oldest building – 12th century.
Daily: 10–6 but 12–6 on Sundays

Matfield: Cherry Trees Tea Gallery
The Green, Matfield, near Tunbridge Wells (0892 722187)
Old-world tea-rooms – and garden – picturesquely situated opposite the village green and pond. 'Everything homemade!' Décor of interesting old-time advertisements – and pianola. Small antiques for sale.
Summer: daily (except Wednesday), 9–1 and 2–5.30
Winter: daily (except Wednesday, Saturday and XD), 9–1 and 2–5.30

Penshurst: Fir Tree House
Penshurst, near Tonbridge (0892 870382)
Garden in summer; log fires in winter; magnificent guardian firs all the year. The cakes are pretty good too.
All the year (except November and December, and Mondays), 3–6; weekends only, January to Easter, 2.30–5.30

Rochester: Mr Tope's Gatehouse (L/R)
60 High Street, Rochester (0634 45270)
Next to Rochester Cathedral
Dickensian building in the very shadow of the cathedral
Daily: 10 a.m.–11 p.m.

Saltwood: Fountain Tea-Rooms (L)
The Green, Saltwood, near Hythe (0303 67158)
Main road junction in Saltwood
Ideally sited. Practically on the village green – with a pleasant stroll nearby past church and castle.
All the year (except XD); Tuesday–Saturday, 10.30–5.30; Sunday noon–5.30

Tunbridge Wells: Binns Corner House (L)
The Pantiles, Tunbridge Wells (0892 27690)
On the elegant Pantiles you can hear the bands in summer.
Daily: 9–5.30. XD: Lunch only

Wateringbury: The Riverside Restaurant (L/R)
Bow Bridge, Wateringbury, Maidstone (0622 812120)
Adjoining the River Medway

After a walk on the towpath or a row on the Medway itself, you can sit and watch the watery world go by.
Every day during the boating season (April–October), 10 a.m.–11 p.m. Also varied winter hours, including XD

Westerham: Pitts Cottage (L/R)
Westerham (0959 62125)
On the A25, Limpsfield Road, ½ mile W of Westerham
A 13th-century house, once the country home of William Pitt, at 24 Britain's youngest Premier. Original oak beams – and some rabbitskin windows.
Daily (except Sunday evening and XD) 10–12 (coffee); 12–2 (lunch); 7–9.30 (dinner)

INNS

At the time of writing, customary opening hours are as follows:
Weekdays: 10.30–2.30, 6–11. Sundays: 12–2, 7–10.30
By publication date, however, new legislation may permit the sale of alcoholic drinks 10 a.m.–11 p.m. Even then, landlords and breweries may still use their own discretion as to exactly what hours they keep, and whether or not they open on Christmas Day.

No alcoholic drinks may be served to those under 18, who, strictly speaking, should not be in the drinking-area. Many establishments now provide garden and/or indoor facilities to overcome this difficulty. These are often indicated outside the building by a green/brown symbol of parents and pram.

Inns, other than those listed in this section, with gardens (G) and/or playrooms, or play areas (P) are;: *Ashford*, Singleton (G/P); *Bapchild*, Fox & Goose (P); *Biddenden*, Chequers (P); *Bredhurst*, Bell (G/P); *East Farleigh*, Horseshoes (G); *Edenbridge*, Star (P); *Faversham*, Royal William (G); *Gillingham*, Black Lion (G/P); *Hadlow*, Harrow (P); *Herne Bay*, Hampton (P/G); *Lamberhurst*, Swan (G); *Maidstone*, Rising Sun (G/pets); *Minster*, Saddler (P/G); *New Romney*, Warren (G/goat); *Otford*, Bull (G/P); *Sevenoaks*, George & Dragon (G); *Woodchurch* (G/P); *Yalding*, Woolpack (G/P).

Addington Green: The Angel Inn
Addington Green, West Malling (0732 842117)
Off A20, 2 miles W of Leybourne
Lives up to its 14th-century tradition with inglenook and oak beams. Strong cricket flavour; 'kind and manly' Alfred Mynn played near here often. Homemade speciality dishes.
Ideal 'watering-hole' after Downland walks.

Aldington: Walnut Tree (R)
Aldington, near Ashford (0233 72298)
Off B2067, or A20, 4 miles W of Hythe
Fine springboard for Romney Marsh and smugglers – who were guided here by a lantern in its window. Pub snacks; mussels in garlic butter? Or restaurant: venison Stroganoff? Pub games. Garden.

Bredgar: The Sun
The Street, Bredgar, near Sittingbourne (0627 84221)
On B2163, 3 miles S of Sittingbourne
A converted 16th-century coaching inn with oak beams and log fire. Spacious garden. Varied selection of hot food and snacks. A 'family pub'.
Strategically placed for 'The Blossom Trail'.

Deal: Clarendon Hotel (R)
Beach Street, Deal (0304 374748)
Beside the promenade
Georgian, with sea views out to the Goodwin Sands. Fish couldn't be fresher: Dover sole *bonne femme*; or, for landlubbers, carbonnade of beef made with butter. Live music in summer.

Dungeness: The Pilot
Dungeness, New Romney (0679 20314)
1 mile N of lighthouse
Right on the coast, the pub's interior is designed to look like the inside of a ship. But no ship's biscuit here: The Pilot is noted for its food. Play facilities for children.
Time for a drink before catching the Romney, Hythe & Dymchurch train.

Eating and Drinking

Eynsford: The Malt Shovel (R)
Station Road, Eynsford, near Dartford (0322 862164)
This Jacobean inn has its own restaurant ('lobsters from the tank'), a garden leading to the River Darent – and a resident ghost!
Handy for Lullingstone Roman villa and castle.

Farningham: The Pied Bull
High Street, Farningham, near Dartford (0322 862125)
On A225, 4 miles S of Dartford
A traditional coaching inn that leads as a folk-music venue. Garden, pub games. Extensive menu and bar snacks.   D

Faversham: Chimney Boy (R)
Preston Street, Faversham (0795 532007)
Shopping centre
Don't be put off by the sad connotations of its name or feel guilty if you skip the excellent pub snacks and plump for scampi Port au Prince, chicken Kiev, or beef Stroganoff ...
Pub games, children's room.

Fordwich: Fordwich Arms (R)
Fordwich, near Sturry (0227 710444)
Off A28, 3 miles NE of Canterbury
A modern pub opposite one of the smallest and oldest town halls (and lock-ups) in the country. Alongside the pretty River Stour. Find peace and tranquillity here after the bustle of Canterbury. Meals and snacks.

Folkestone: Earl Grey
35 Old High Street, Folkestone (0303 56127)
Follow in smugglers' footsteps up Folkestone's quaint cobbled High Street from the harbour. Despite its name, tea is not the tipple here. Seafood and other honest-to-God snacks. Pub games, garden.

Golden Green: The Buck's Head
Golden Green, Sevenoaks (0732 61330)
On minor road skirting E boundary of Knole
A real country pub gleaming with copper and brass – next

to the village pond. Garden. Varied menu. Caters for all age-groups.

Goudhurst: The Star & Eagle (R)
High Street, Goudhurst (0580 211512)
14th-century and a smugglers' pub too – with tunnels connecting it to the church on the hilltop above. Magnificent Wealden views. Restaurant and large garden. Nearby Bedgebury Pinetum's glades can sharpen both appetite and thirst.

Groombridge: The Crown Inn (R)
Groombridge, near Tunbridge Wells (0892 76742)
Off B2110, 4 miles SW of Tunbridge Wells
A 16th-century Free House superbly sited above the charming village green, with a fascinating church and a stately home as nearby aperitifs. Patio, garden.

Gravesend: Three Daws
High Street, Gravesend
On the river-front near the Tilbury Ferry
Once the second home of river pilots and, at 500+ years, one of Kent's oldest pubs. Underground tunnels used by smugglers and desperate men fleeing the press gangs.

Halstow: The Three Tuns
Halstow, Sittingbourne (0795 842840)
Off A2, 2 miles W of Sittingbourne
500-year-old pub with, inside, oak beams and horse-brasses and, outside, garden, stream and ducks. Cooked meat and bar snacks at all times. Ideal refuge from a bleak nor'easter.

Herne: Fox & Hounds (R)
Herne, near Herne Bay (0227 374849)
On A291, midway between Canterbury and Herne Bay
5 successive Egon Ronay appearances equate with braised venison spliced with port and brandy; steak, kidney and oyster pie; Scotch salmon poached with hollandaise sauce. Hot and cold buffet.

Eating and Drinking

Ightham: George & Dragon
The Square, Ightham (0732 882440)
Just off A25, ½ mile W of Borough Green
Cosily set amid other half-timbered buildings, it is just as cosy inside, and as full of history as it is of oak beams.

Lamberhurst: The Chequers
Lamberhurst (0892 890260)
On A21, 5 miles E of Tunbridge Wells
A 15th-century inn and former coaching house ideally placed for visitors to Bewl Reservoir, Lamberhurst Vineyards and Owl House Gardens. Warranted a mention by Chaucer in *The Canterbury Tales* and one here for its excellent food, games room and views – over the nearby golf course.

Lenham: Dog & Bear (R)
Lenham, near Maidstone (0622 858219)
Just off the A20, 4 miles W of Charing
Nearly 400 years old and set in the delightful square of a delightful village. Good enough for Queen Anne (whose arms it proudly bears). Bar meals, restaurant and gamut of whiskies.

Maidstone: The British Queen (R)
Square Hill, Maidstone (0622 671118)
Off Lower Stone Street and Mote Road
A town tavern, once a drovers' inn, that has a maritime décor – and wishing-well. Restaurant; bar food at lunchtimes.

Marshside: Gate Inn
Marshside, near Herne Bay
1½ miles S of A299, turning right at the Roman Galley
Desolate outside, where Wantsum once made Thanet a *real* island; snug enough inside. Real ale, Egon Ronay recommended snacks; pub games, garden and children's room, no videos or fruit-machines; popular with 'mummers, bell-ringers, bird-watchers and assorted eccentrics'.

Sarre: Crown Inn (or Cherry Brandy House)
Sarre, near Margate (0843 47208)
At junction of A253 and A28, halfway between Canterbury and Margate
15th-century pub where Dickens wrote part of *Pickwick Papers* and where cherry brandy, made to a 17th-century Huguenot recipe, *must* be sold. Has known more famous stage, screen and Variety stars (listed on its walls) than a Palladium Royal Command Performance! Try the Blacksmith's Lunch. Garden.

Selling: White Lion (R)
Selling, near Faversham (0227 752211)
Off A2 and A251, 3 miles SE of Faversham
A 400-year-old coaching inn in orchard country; highwaymen have been its customers! Was it 'its legendary beef pudding' that was responsible for an Egon Ronay recommendation? *Good Beer Guide* citation also. Snacks.

Singleton: Singleton Barn (R)
Tythe Barn Lane, Singleton, near Ashford (0233 29379)
At the Great Chart bypass second roundabout, turn left for Singleton
Eat and drink in the second biggest barn in Kent, beautifully timbered, 17th-century, with moated Old Manor next door and with gallery restaurant, carvery and bar. Cold buffet, too. Garden, children's room.

Southfleet: The Ship Inn
Southfleet, Gravesend (0474 833238)
Off B262, 2 miles SW of Gravesend
Has just celebrated its 600th anniversary! Full of Olde Worlde charm. Garden – and good views of church and village. Steaks a speciality.

Staplehurst: King's Head
High Street, Staplehurst (0580 891231)
On the A229, 8 miles S of Maidstone
In its 300+ years life-span it has seen much excitement. Never more so than in 1865 when the London–Dover boat-train was de-railed, and Charles Dickens, though

severely shocked, risked his life to save others. Seafood specialities, children's room, garden and – a breath of France – *pétanque*.

Strood: The Crispin & Crispianus (R)
8 London Road, Strood, Rochester (0634 719912)
A 13th-century inn mentioned in Dickens' 'The Commercial Traveller' and furnished to match its association with Kent's greatest author, who often drank here. Separate restaurant. Rochester too is steeped in Dickens.

Sutton Valence: Swan Inn
Sutton Valence (0622 843212)
6 miles SE of Maidstone on A274
Long, and of gleaming white weather-board, it is as eye-catching as the splendid Wealden views from its terrace. Food too – but only at lunchtime.

Ulcombe: The Pepper Box (R)
Fairbourne Heath, near Ulcombe (0622 842558)
Off A20, near Harrietsham; follow signs for Fairbourne Heath
Perched on the Greensand hills, it has fine Wealden views. Log fires, garlands of dried hops, and shining horse-brasses add to the rural atmosphere. Fish, fresh from Dungeness, is a feature, as are Kent Korker sausages with free-range eggs. Also bar meals and sandwiches. Recommended by *Best of British Pubs*.

Wingham: The Red Lion Inn
Wingham, near Canterbury (0227 720217)
On corner of A257 and B2046, almost opposite the church near village centre
Spit-roast joints are at their best when cooked over an apple-log fire in a 700-year-old inn. Dover Sole and Kentish duckling also keep the county flag flying. Lunch and supper (except Sunday and Monday).

Woodchurch: The Stonebridge Inn
Woodchurch, near Ashford (0233 86289)
On B2062, 5 miles S of Ashford

Action as well as ale here: live entertainment, children's adventure playground, garden ... Bring your caravan too (CCC site). Meals evening and lunchtime, of course.

Wrotham: Rose & Crown (R)
High Street, Wrotham (0732 882409)
Good enough for the Hartley Morris Dancers – even though it claims *'substantial* bar meals'. Or round off a day's hard sightseeing with whitebait or veal *à la crême*.

Wye: The Tickled Trout (R)
Wye, near Ashford (0233 812227)
Next to Wye's charming bridge and with spacious gardens right down to the Great Stour. Ideal for a summer drink. Completes Stour Valley charm.

RESTAURANTS

Kent is rich in a wide variety of excellent restaurants far too numerous to mention. The following are just a few of those a little out of the ordinary in one way or another.
Christmas Day opening is often dependent on circumstances and demand and should be checked.

Boughton Aluph: Eastwell Manor
Eastwell Park, Boughton Aluph, near Ashford (0233 35751)
Off the A251, 2 miles N of Ashford
A historic house, sumptuously furnished, set in 62 acres of garden and rolling parkland – with lake. In the low-ceilinged, candelabra-lit, log-fire-warmed dining room, unobtrusive service will set before you *table d'Hôte, à la carte* or gourmet dinner. For the less demanding, an excellent two-course lunch *and* coffee for under £10. Egon Ronay recommended.
Daily: 12.30–2 L; 7.30–9.30 D (9 on Sunday)

Canterbury: Waterfields Restaurant
5 Best Lane, Canterbury (0227 450276)
Off High Street opposite GPO
This secluded riverside restaurant, formerly a forge, can

be an appetizing and imaginative jumping-off point for an evening at the nearby Marlowe Theatre. As an 'extra' you can land there from *The Weavers* tour-boat. Wines show 'breadth of price and pedigree'.
Monday–Saturday: set lunch noon–2; à la carte 7–10.30

Edenbridge: Honours Mill
87 High Street, Edenbridge (0732 866757)
Derelict mill reclaimed by two talented chefs. Unusual starters pave the way for chicken with pistachio mousse or noisettes of lamb. Rounded off with splendid sweets or an impressive cheese-board.
Daily (except Monday): 12.15–2, 7.15–10; closed Saturday lunch, Sunday dinner

Folkestone: La Tavernetta
Leaside Court, Clifton Gardens, Folkestone (0303 54955)
Off the cliff-top Leas, near the William Harvey statue
Sunny situation: equally sunny Italian welcome. Traditional favourites and 'seasonal specials', such as fresh salmon.
Monday–Saturday:12–2.30, 6.15–10.30

Hadlow: La Crémaillère (L/R)
The Square, Hadlow (0732 851489)
Hadlow is 5 miles NE of Tonbridge on the A26
Classic French provincial cuisine – the vegetables are even served in copper saucepans. In winter, dine by a huge open fire; in summer, in a vine-shaded conservatory. *Good Food Guide*.
Monday–Saturday (except Saturday lunch): 12.30–1.30, 8–9

Higham: The Knowle
School Lane, Higham, near Gravesend (047 4822262)
Off A226, 4 miles SE of Gravesend
Victorian Gothic house but there's nothing heavy about Peach Knowle as a starter, duck in Grand Marnier or a spectacular Kiwi fruit Pavlova.
Tuesday–Friday and Sunday: noon–1.30 p.m. Tuesday–Saturday: 7–10.30

Maidstone: Mr Jones's Pie Shop
90 Week Street, Maidstone (0622 672089)
Maidstone's main N–S shopping street
Dark panelling, candlelight and 1940 memorabilia create just the right atmosphere for, *inter alia*, a splendid variety of homemade pies.
Daily (except Sunday): 11–2.30, 6–11 (Saturday: 11–11)

Sevenoaks: Royal Oak (L/R)
Upper High Street, Sevenoaks (0732 451109)
Almost next door to ducal Knole (NT). 3- or 5-course meals: scallops in chive sauce, roast duckling with orange and red currants; strong on fish but not so good on sweets; 'service, young and personable'. *Good Food Guide*.
Daily (except Saturday lunch and Sunday dinner): 12.30–2, and 7.30–9.30

Shorne: The Inn on The Lake
Shorne, near Gravesend (047-482 3333)
On the M2, 4 miles N of Rochester
Formerly 'Laughing Water' but still with peaceful lake, water gusher, rhododendrons and a basically French cuisine. A caviare starter can lead to Tournedos Barca d'Ora and climax with a Pêche Flambée.
Daily: 12.30–2, 7.30–10

Sissinghurst; Rankins
The Street, Sissinghurst (0580 713964)
Hastings fish and local vegetables make a splendid get-together. The menu is short, so care and imagination produce delicious and unusual dishes.
Lunch: Sundays only, 12.30–1.45; dinner, Wednesday, Thursday, Friday and Saturday only, 7.30–9

Tenterden: Boswell's Coffee House
Sayers Lane, Tenterden (0580 5318)
Off High Street above arcade of shops
Morning coffee and afternoon tea; lunchtime Sussex 'Smokies', European sausages or Piazza Pasta (as eaten by Boswell in Milan in 1765). In the evening, French formality.

Daily (except Sunday, and Monday dinner): 9.30–5.30, 7.30– midnight

Tunbridge Wells: Downstairs at Thackeray's
85 London Road, Tunbridge Wells (0892 37559)
Near junction with Mount Ephraim
Thackeray lived – and, doubtless, lunched – here. Upstairs is classy; downstairs, less formal. In both, excellent cuisine is based on Kentish produce: Biddenden butter, Iden Croft herbs, Appledore quails, Matfield vegetables. *Good Food Guide* recommended. Tuesday–Saturday: 12.30–2.30, 7–10

Whitstable: Pearson's Crab and Oyster House
Sea Wall, Whitstable (0227 272005)
Off Sea Street
King prawns or hot mussels in wine and onion sauce, or Seafood Platter: with the added tang of a sea view.
Daily (except XD): lunch, 12–2; dinner, 6–10

Yalding: Cobblestones
Yalding (0622 814326)
6 miles SW of Maidstone
If you like variety, Cobblestones will serve you well. Homemade dishes, 7-course gourmet menu, Old English supper and wide-ranging *à la carte*.
Lunch, Tuesday–Friday and Sunday, 12–2; dinner, Tuesday–Saturday, 7–10

FARMS

FARMS AND FARM TRAILS

Beckley: Children's Farm
Great Knelle Farm, Beckley, near Rye, Sussex (079-726 250)
Off A268, at Four Oaks, on B2165
A wealth of attractions on a 600-acre working farm: rare breeds, aviary, butterflies, small domestic wild animals, farm animals, dairy, hop-picking, tractor train, adventure playground, craft shop, farm shop, nature trail, coarse fishing, cream teas.
May–October: Wednesday–Sunday, 10–5.30

Beltring: Whitbread's Hop Farm
Beltring (0622 872068)
On B2015 2 miles N of Paddock Wood
Largest collection of white-coned oasts in the world, on 1,000-acre farm. Comprehensive museums on hop-farming, rural crafts and agricultural machinery. Majestic Whitbread Shire horses, pets and play area, owls, nature trails. Craft centre, light refreshments, souvenir shop. A splendid full day out! D
Easter–late October: Tuesday–Sunday and BHM, 10–5.30
(LA 5)

Brenchley: Gate House Farm
Brenchley, near Tonbridge (0892 723723)
Brenchley, 1 mile off B2160, 2 miles S of Paddock Wood
80-acre working fruit farm trail (½ hour). Soft fruit, orchard, vineyard, lake and conservation area.
April–October: daily, 10–6　　　　　　　　　　　　Free

Farms

Chainhurst: Reed Court Farm
Chainhurst, near Marden (0627 2314)
2 miles N of Marden on by-roads to Yalding
Kentish Weald mixed farm of 400 acres producing fruit, hops, corn, beef, sheep, pigs and even cricket-bat willows. 2 separate farm trails: each takes 1½ hours. Comprehensive leaflet available. Stout footwear needed in rainy weather.
April–October: daily, during daylight hours   Free

Cliffsend: Lavender Farm
Cliffsend, off Sandwich Road, near Ramsgate
Visit a lavender farm opposite the monument commemorating the landing of St Augustine in AD 597. Farm shop. Easter–December: daily, 10–sunset.   Free

Etchingham: Sussex Shire Horses
The Stables, Haremere Hall, Etchingham, Sussex (0580-81 501)
On A265 2 miles W of Hurst Green on A21
Descriptive talk and working demonstrations of those 'gentle giants' Shires, Suffolk Punches, Ardennes etc. Cart rides, adventure playground, farm nature trail. Picnic areas, refreshments, souvenir shop.
Easter–October: Tuesday–Sunday and BHM 10.30–5.30. Demonstrations (under cover if wet) 11 and 3

Gillingham: Star Farm
Darland Avenue, Gillingham (0634 577547)
Off A2, near Will Adams Memorial
Small urban farm with a wide range of animals that delight young children especially. Occasional craft demonstrations and special events. Shop, picnic area.
Daily: 10–4   Small fee

Goudhurst: Harper's Farm Trail
Goudhurst (0580 211853)
Follow signs from B2079, Goudhurst–Marden road
A pleasant trail round a traditional Kentish hop and fruit farm, woodland and riverside rich in natural flora and fauna. Produce available in the season.
Daily: May–August, in daylight hours   Free

Greatstone: Dunrobin Shire Horse Stud
Dunes Road, Greatstone, near New Romney
Turn off the coast road at the Jolly Fisherman
Stallions, mares and often foals are to be seen. Collection of harness and farm machinery. Pedigree flock of Suffolk sheep, goats, pigs, donkeys and aviary. Donkey or pony rides for children. Picnic area, tea-room, gift shop.
Easter–September: daily, except Monday, 11–6

Great Mongeham: Solley's Farm Tour
Great Mongeham, Deal (0304 367437)
Off A258 just N of Deal
1½-hour tour on a tractor-drawn trailer of a working arable and dairy farm covering 900 acres.
School holidays: parties (prior booking), Monday–Friday; Individuals, Wednesday only, 2 p.m. prompt

Hernhill: Mount Ephraim Gardens
Hernhill, Faversham (0227 751496)
Off A299 or A2, 3 miles E of Faversham
Orchard walk through commercial fruit farm. Refreshments. See also Gardens, p.113
May–mid-September: Sundays and BHs

Hildenborough: Great Hollanden Farm
Mill Lane, Hildenborough, near Tonbridge (0732 832276)
Off B245
Survival centre for more than 50 different rare breeds of farm animals, including Eriskay pony, Bagot goats and Vietnamese pot-bellied pigs. PYO, shop, snacks, pets corner.
May–mid-October: daily, 10.30–5.30

Marden: Goffs Oak Shire Horses
Mount Pleasant Farm, Maidstone Road, Marden (0622 831182)
In Milebush Lane off B2079, 1 mile N of Marden
Shire horses at work; mares and foals; other farm animals. Picnic area, light refreshments.
Sunday: 2–5.30 from last Sunday in May to last Sunday in September

Matfield: Badsell Park Farm
Crittenden Road, Matfield, near Tonbridge (0892 832549)
On B2105; AA signs
Pet area, animal farm, nature trails, bird and insect displays, PYO. Farm shop, snack bar.
May–November: 9–6

Stone: Stone Lodge Farm Park
London Road, Stone (0322 343456)
Just off A226, E of Dartford
A working farm in an urbanized area. All farm animals and some farm processes (milking, ploughing, haymaking, shearing and spinning) can be seen. Rare Breeds Survival Centre. Pets corner, old-time farming implements, video films, souvenir shop, tea-room, outdoor and indoor picnic areas. The highlight? A wagon ride behind mighty Shires and Clydesdales.
April–September: daily (except Saturday) 10–5 Small fee
D

Wye: Wye College Farm
Wye, near Ashford (0233 812367)
E of Wye on Eastingleigh road
2½-mile farm trail (2½ hours), self-guided with leaflet, situated in lovely downland country. Passes fields and crops, a wood and nature reserve rich in orchids (19 varieties) and butterflies. Dairy unit can be visited if prior notice given. Picnic tables. See also Museums, p.144
All year, daily Free

PICK-YOUR-OWN AND FARM SHOPS

It is advisable to phone before you make your visit to ascertain: availability, price, opening hours and exact location.
   Out of courtesy, please keep to the PYO Code: no smoking, no dogs, careful picking.

Dp = Dairy produce; Eg – Eggs; Fr – Fruit trees; FS = Farm shop, Sf = Soft fruit; Tf = Top fruit; Ve = Vegetables

Ashford: Lenacre Hall Farm
Sandyhurst Lane, Ashford (0233 23618)
PYO/Sf

Borough Green: Crowhurst Farm
Crowhurst Lane, Borough Green, Sevenoaks (0732 882905)
PYO/Sf/Ve/Tf

Farnborough: Viners Farm
High Street, Farnborough, Orpington (0689 50680)
FS/Fr/Ve/Eg. PYO/Sf/Ve/Tf

Higham: Mockbeggar Farm
Cliffe Road, Higham, Rochester PYO: 0634 727136. FS: 0634 725664
FS/Fr/Ve/Dp/Eg. PYO/Sf/Tf

Luddenham: Four Oaks PYO
Luddenham, near Faversham (Evenings: 0795 536087)
FS/Fr/Ve. PYO/Sf/Ve/Tf

Matfield: Badsell Park Farm
Crittenden Road, Matfield, near Tonbridge (0892 832549)
FS/Fr/Ve/Eg. PYO/Sf/Tf

Orpington: Hewitts Farm
Chelsfield, Orpington (0950 34271)
2½ miles S of Orpington on A224 Orpington by-pass. 900 yards from junction 4 on M25 PYO farm. Wide variety of crops and leisure activities: combat zone 'Paintball' Games, Sunday market, dog show, marching bands, train, ARGOCAT, refreshments, rides, fruit festivals; world's biggest bowl of strawberries! Detailed brochure available. D

Pembury: Pippins Fruit Farm
Maidstone Road, Pembury, near Tunbridge Wells (0892 824569)
FS/Fr. PYO/Sf/Tf

Rainham: Mierscourt Farm Shop
Mierscourt Road, Rainham (0634 370283)
FS/Fr/Ve/Dp/Eg

Sutton-By-Dover: Sutton Court Farm
Sutton Court, Sutton-by-Dover CT15 5DF (0304 375033)
PYO/Sf

VINEYARDS

All have a shop selling their own wines and, often, other produce. The vineyard itself may be toured with a guide, generally by appointment (fee), or self-guided with an explanatory leaflet (free or nominal fee). Tasting is generally at a very nominal charge or sometimes free.
Only the large vineyards have their own winery.

Ash: St Nicholas Vineyard
Moat Farm, Moat Lane, Ash, near Canterbury (0304 812670)
Signposted off A257 in Ash
Vineyard and winery tours. Picnic area, teas on lawn by arrangement. Self-guided tours.
All year: daily, 9–6. Guided tours (groups by appointment): 11.30, 2 and 3.30

Barham: Elham Valley Vineyards
Breach, Barham, near Canterbury (0227 831266)
3 miles N of Elham on B2065
Vineyard and winery in the lovely Elham Valley.
June–September: closed Monday. Shop: May–Christmas, 10–6   Free

Biddenden Vineyard
Little Whatmans, Biddenden (0580 291726)
1½ miles W of Biddenden on Benenden road
Kent's oldest established vineyard (18 acres) offers a free self-guided tour. Shop.
All year: January–March and November–December: Monday–Friday, 9–5; Saturday, 11–2. April–October: Monday–Friday, 9–5; Saturday, 11–5; Sunday, 12–5   Free

Lamberhurst: Lamberhurst Vineyards
Ridge Farm, Lamberhurst, near Tunbridge Wells (0892 890844)

Signposted off A21 in village
Largest vineyard and winery in UK (50 acres). Self-guided trail and tasting: all the year. Refreshments.
All year: daily: January–April and November–December: Monday–Saturday, 9–1, 2–6; Sunday, 10–1, 2–5. May–October: Monday–Saturday, 9–6; Sunday, 10–5. Guided tours (2 hours): 1 May–31 October, by appointment only

Newnham: Syndale Valley Vineyards
Lady's Wood, Newnham, near Sittingbourne (0795 89693)
Turn off A2 at Ospringe
Wine-tasting and shop. 9 acres of vineyards and orchards. Woodland and nature walk. Guided tour (by arrangement) or self-guided.
Daily: 1 May–24 December, 10–5 Small fee

Penshurst: Penshurst Vineyards
Grove Road, Penshurst (0892 870255)
Self- or guided-tour (1½–2 hours) through vineyard and modern winery producing 60,000 bottles annually. Wallabies, black swans and rare sheep are unusual extras. D
1 April–24 December: daily, 10–6
Fee for guided tour only

Staple: Staple Vineyard
Church Farm, Staple, near Canterbury (0304 812571)
Off A257, 1½ miles SE of Wingham
Guided tour (appointment only) or self-guided tour. Herb garden, shop, picnic area, May–September: Monday–Saturday, 11–5; Sunday, 12–4 Fee for tour only

Tenterden: Tenterden Vineyards
Spots Farm, Smallhythe, Tenterden (0580 63033)
On B2082, 2 miles S of Tenterden
Vineyard, winery and extensive herb garden. Lake. Conducted (by appointment) and self-guided tours.
May–October: daily, 10–6

Gardens

GARDENS

This section lists very well known gardens, and others which are open on a fairly regular basis.

Many other, smaller gardens are also occasionally open to the public. As their times of opening are few and variable from one year to the next, they have not been included. Full details can be obtained, from the National Gardens Scheme pamphlet published each year. It is available at most public libraries for a nominal price.

See also, in the section 'Historic Homes', p.134: Ashford (Godinton Park), Birchington (Quex House), Boughton Monchelsea (Boughton Monchelsea Place), Cobham (Owletts), Hever Castle, Ightham Mote, Lympne (Port Lympne), Northiam (Great Dixter), Penshurst Place, Sevenoaks (Knole and Riverhill House) and Westerham (Chartwell and Squerryes Court).

Benenden: Benenden Walled Garden
Benenden, near Cranbrook (0580 240749)
In grounds of Benenden School, on Benenden–Sissinghurst road, 1 mile from Benenden crossroads
18th-century walled garden with culinary, medicinal, aromatic and decorative plants; ladies' garden and gourmets' vegetable garden, greenhouses and vinery. Butterflies and birds encouraged. D
Last week in March to last week in April; last week in May; mid-July–mid-September: 10–6   Fee (under-16s free)

Borough Green: Great Comp Garden
Comp Lane, Borough Green (0732 882669)
7-acre garden 'for all seasons', with trees and shrubs, terraces, walls, 'ruins' and 17th-century house as background. Nursery. Bi-annual musical festivals.
April–October: daily, 11–6

Brenchley: Marle Place Garden and Nursery
Brenchley (0892 722 304)
Off B2162, 1 mile SW of Horsmonden, turn E on Marle Place Road
A 10-acre Wealden plantsman's garden with trees and shrubs, Victorian gazebo, Edwardian rockery, walled garden and ornamental ponds.
Also a nursery specializing in culinary, medicinal and aromatic herbs. Home-made products sold.
Garden: April–September: Wednesdays, 10.30–5. Nursery: April–September: Monday–Saturday, 10.30–5   Free

Chilham: Chilham Castle Gardens
Chilham, near Canterbury (0227 730319)
6 miles SW of Canterbury on A252
Terraced flower borders fall away to lawn and fine topiary work. Walk round lake with its own water-garden. Park landscaped by 'Capability' Brown. Children's 'Petland'. Quiet garden in woodland setting, and rose garden. Flying display by birds of prey daily, except Monday and Friday. Exciting jousting on Sunday in season. Grand Tournament of Knights on BH Sundays and Mondays. Gift shop, restaurant, teas.
Early April–mid-October: daily, 11–5

Doddington: Doddington Place Gardens
Doddington, near Sittingbourne
Turn S off A2 at Teynham, 4 miles on
In downland countryside, 10 acres of landscaped gardens with extensive lawns, avenues and clipped yew hedges. Woodland garden with magnificent rhododendrons and azaleas. Rock and sunken gardens. Teas (May–June only).   D
May–September: Sunday and BHM, 2–6

Goodnestone: Goodnestone Park Gardens
Goodnestone, near Wingham
S of B2046 road from A2 to Wingham. Ignore 'No Through Road' sign
7–8 acres: trees, roses, walled and woodland gardens, views. Associations with Jane Austen. Plants. Picnic area, teas. D
Mid-April–early July and late August–September: Monday–Thursday, 11–5, and occasional Sundays, 2–6

Goudhurst: Bedgebury National Pinetum
Near Goudhurst (0580 211392)
Turn off A262 at Goudhurst, onto B2079 for 2½ miles
Kew comes to Kent – to avoid the smog! Forestry Commission's 150 undulating acres, including lake and streams, are an idyllic home for the scientific study, and public enjoyment, of every possible species of conifer. Ideal for sauntering, picnicking and arboreal amazement. Visitor centre, waymarked paths, booklet, mobile summer tea van.
   Adjoining 2,500 acres of Bedgebury Forest with public access to its rides and forest trail.
All year: daily, 10–dusk
            Fee, modestly incommensurate with beauty

Hernhill: Mount Ephraim Gardens
Hernhill, near Faversham (0227 751496)
3 miles E of Faversham, off either A2 or A299
7-acre garden, with spring flowers, rhododendrons, herbaceous border, roses and terraces descending to small lake. Also Japanese rock-garden with pools, topiary, woodland, interesting orchard walk, new vineyard, crafts centre. Cafeteria in Edwardian kitchen.
May–mid-September: Sunday and BHM only, 2–6

Horsmonden: Sprivers (NT)
Horsmonden (0892 723553)
2 miles N of Lamberhurst, just off B2162
Garden, with mid-18th-century house, rich in flowering and foliage shrubs, spring and summer bedding, herbaceous borders, old walls etc. No WC.

Garden only: May to last week in September, Wednesday only, 2–5.30 (LA 5)

Ide Hill: Emmetts Garden (NT)
Ide Hill, near Sevenoaks (0732 75429)
1½ miles S of A25 on Sundridge to Ide Hill road
Peaceful 5-acre hillside garden, one of the highest in Kent, noted for its rare trees and shrubs. Lovely spring and autumn colours. Terraced garden recently restored. Tea bar. Near NT viewpoints of Ide Hill and Toys Hill.
D: golf-buggy available
April–October: Tuesday–Friday, including GF and Sunday and BHM, 2–6 (LA 5)

Lamberhurst: Owl House Gardens
Lamberhurst (0892 890230)
Off A21, 1 mile N of Lamberhurst
13 acres of romantic walks and gardens (water gardens, azaleas, spring flowers, roses, rhododendrons etc) round quaint 16th-century smugglers' cottage (not open).
All year: daily, 11–6 except XD, BD and NYD
Fee goes to the Arthritics Centre

Lamberhurst: Scotney Castle Garden (NT)
Lamberhurst, near Tunbridge Wells (0890 890651)
On A21, 1½ miles S of Lamberhurst
One of England's most romantic gardens, landscaped around ruins of 14th-century moated castle. Open-air Shakespeare by moat in early September.
April–mid-November: Wednesday–Friday, 11–6 or sunset; Saturday, Sunday and BHM, 2–6 or sunset. Closed GF

St Margaret's Bay: Pines Garden
South Sands House, St Margaret's Bay, near Dover, (0304 853229)
Off Beach Road, 5 minutes from sea-front
Unusual 6-acre garden: lake and waterfall, Oscar Nemon's statue of Sir Winston Churchill, a Romany caravan, wishing-well, trees and shrubs, bog-garden, figure-heads. Walks to White Cliffs above. Plants. D
All year: daily, 10–6 (approx.) Small fee

Gardens

Sissinghurst: Sissinghurst Castle Garden (NT)
Sissinghurst, near Cranbrook (0580 712850)
On A262, 1 mile E of Sissinghurst
Unique 'gardens within a garden' created by writer Vita Sackville-West and diplomat husband Sir John Nicholson. Also the former's study in the fine Elizabethan tower, and the Long Library. Interesting historical display. NT shop, restaurant.
April–Mid-October: Tuesday–Friday, 10–6.30; Saturday, Sunday and GF, 10–6.30 (LA 6) Closed all Mondays including BH

Staplehurst: Iden Croft Herb Garden
Frittenden Road, Staplehurst (0580 891432)
Signposted from A229, S of Staplehurst
Acres of herb gardens – aromatic, culinary and medicinal – for beginner or expert. National Origanum Collection. Shop, light refreshments.
All the year: April–October, Monday–Saturday, 9–5; Sunday, 11–5. Winter: Monday–Saturday, 9–4; Sunday, closed

Sutton-at-Hone: St John's Jerusalem Garden (NT)
Sutton-at-Hone, Dartford (0892 890681)
3 miles S of Dartford on E side of A225
Former handsome Commandery of the Knights Hospitallers set in large (46-acre) beautifully treed garden, moated by the River Darent   D – garden only
Chapel and garden only: April–October, Wednesday only, 2–6 (LA 5.30)   Small fee

Walmer: Walmer Castle Garden (EH)
On the sea-front, 1 mile S of Walmer Green (0304 364288)
Attractive garden in the moat of a sturdy 'Tudor Rose' castle. Created by Lady Hester Stanhope and the Duke of Wellington; enjoyed today by the Lord Warden of the Cinque Ports: the Queen Mother. Wide sea views. (See also Castles, p.122).   D – gardens only
EH Standard but closed Monday except BHs and when the Lord Warden is in residence

GARDEN CENTRES

Appledore: Appledore's Answer
Appledore, Romney Marsh (023-383-285)
On B2080, near the Royal Military Canal
320 beds of bulbs including 145,000 tulips make a heartening spring sight. Shop, largest in SE, sells over 350 different varieties. Landscaped show area. Tea-room. D
Late March–mid-May (depending on weather): daily, 10–6 including BHs

Ash: Five Acres Nurseries Garden
Saunders Lane, Ash, near Sandwich (0304 812475)
E side of Ash just off A257
A large collection of aromatic, medicinal and culinary herbs and alpine plants displayed in gardens – with Richborough Castle only just down the road. Plants for sale. D
All year: daily, Monday–Saturday, 10–5, Sunday, 2–5   Free

Challock: Kent Country Nurseries
Goodpark Ltd, Challock, near Ashford (0233 74256)
On A252 Canterbury–Charing road, 3 miles E of Charing, opposite Challock Lees
One of Kent's biggest nurseries where, in the open and under glass, there is an all-embracing selection of plants, shrubs, trees etc, including a number of exotic and intriguingly unusual ones.
All the year: daily, except XD, BD and NYD. Spring and summer: weekdays, 9–6; Sunday, 10–6. Winter: weekdays, 9–5; Sunday, 10–5   Free

Faversham: McKenade Garden Centre
London Road, Faversham (0795 531213)
On the A2 at Faversham
House and herbaceous plants; summer bedding and shrubs; trees.
7 days a week: 8–6   Free

Faversham: Notcutts Garden Centre
Newnham Court Farm, Bearsted Road, Weavering, near Faversham (0622 36472)

Gardens

Just off M20 at Junction 7
Farm shop, pets centre, craft and wool shop, PYO, butterfly pavilions, coffee corner, farm freezer shop, florist shop.
All the year: daily – weekdays, 9–5.45; Sunday, 10–5.30
Free

Folkestone: Kennedy's Garden Centre
Ingles Meadow, Jointon Road, Folkestone (0303 58100)
Off Cheriton Road, opposite Kingsnorth Gardens
'Everything you need', in large, centrally situated 'garden'. Café. An admirable foil for Kingsnorth Gardens nearby.
7 days a week
Free

Greatstone: Greatstone Nursery
8 Coast Drive, Greatstone (0679 64380)
near Jolly Fisherman
A plantsman's paradise! Huge variety of plants, shrubs etc, includes 400 varieties of fuchsia and 300 of clematis.
Daily: 9–dusk
Free

Ham Street: Romney Marsh Garden Centre
Ham Street, near Ashford (0233 732613)
5 miles S of Ashford on B2070
8-acre garden centre. Herb house, pet shop, children's farm, machinery centre, fuchsia collections, aquatic section with thousands of fish, hot-houses, adventure playground.
All year: daily, including BHs, 10–6
Free

Hawkhurst: Springfield Garden Centre and Nursery
Cranbrook Road, Hawkhurst (05805 3108)
Wide selection of plants and shrubs, conifers and sundries.
7 days a week 9–5
Free

Strood: Pocock Garden Centre
Dillywood Lane, Higham, Strood, Rochester (0634 719889)
Off Gravesend road, first right after fire station. Next to Stone Horse pub

Plants, shrubs, trees and conifers, miniatures and dwarfs. Pet centre, water gardens, tropical and marine fish.
7 days a week 9–5　　　　　　　　　　　　　　　　Free

TOWN PARKS

Broadstairs: Pierremont Park
On the corner of Pierremont Avenue and High Street
A spacious park with children's play area and the mansion where Queen Victoria spent her childhood holidays; a charming garden with fountain.　　　　　　　　　　Free

Broadstairs: Victoria Garden
On Victoria Parade, off High Street
Fine floral displays and seascape views from above Viking Bay. Walks, rockery, clock-tower and occasional concerts from bandstand.　　　　　　　　　　　　　　　　Free

Canterbury: Dane John Gardens
Adjoining the bus station
The city wall runs above them; a splendid lime avenue, through them. Among lawns and flower-beds stand a delicate Christopher Marlowe statuette, a rugged Boer War memorial with inscriptions by Eric Gill, and the unusual 60-foot-high Dane John itself, a sepulchral and then defensive mound, path-ringed.　　　　　　　Free

Canterbury: Westgate Gardens
At the end of St Peter's Street
Rose garden, lawns and brilliant spring bulb and summer bedding displays, running beside the willow-shaded River Stour with majestic Westgate Towers as handsome back-drop.　　　　　　　　　　　　　　　　　　Free

Dover: Connaught Park
On Connaught Road off Castle Hill
Fine views and fine displays on an airy site above the town　　　　　　　　　　　　　　　　　　　　　　Free

Gardens

Dover: Kearsney Abbey
Just off the A2 at Kearsney at entrance to delightful Alkham Valley
Spacious park with sizeable lake. Café.   Free

Dartford: Central Park
Off Market Street and next to the library
27 acres include prize-winning floral displays and large play area for children with most modern equipment and an adventure playground complete with Viking ship.
   Free

Folkestone: Kingsnorth Gardens
Shorncliffe Road, Folkestone
Lawns, big rose-garden, maples, herbaceous borders, goldfish and water-lily pool, spring bulbs. Shelter.   Free

Gravesend: Gordon Promenade and Gardens
Alongside the Thames, E of the piers
Promenade with fine Thames shipping views and pleasant gardens surrounding Gordon's statue.   Free

Hythe: Royal Military Canal
Pleasant shady lawns and paths, and gardens, by and close to the serenity of the canal.   Free

Margate: Dane Park
From the harbour, follow King Street into Dane Road
Splendid bedding displays and fountain. Cricket and bowls to watch.   Free

Margate: Northdown Park
From Northdown Road (B2052), turn right up Queen Elizabeth Avenue, or from Palm Bay Avenue up Princess Margaret Avenue
Spacious, with lawns, trees and flowers; it also has charming Memorial Garden, with loggia and pool.   Free

Ramsgate: King George VI Park
On Ramsgate East Cliff
A pleasant park pleasantly sited, with the additional interest of the recently refurbished (£15,000) 18th-century

Italianate greenhouse originally built by Sir Moses Montefiore. Cliff walks via Dumpton Gap to Broadstairs.   Free

Rochester: Eastgate House
Off the High Street
From the hanging baskets of the shopping precinct it is only a step to a small but charming formal garden, with fish-pond and arboured seats, in the shadow of Charles Dickens' famous chalet and flamboyant Eastgate House.
Free

Rochester: Esplanade
Next to Rochester Bridge
Spacious lawns and flower-beds beside the Medway itself. And above it, within the castle walls, still more lawns.
Free

Tonbridge: Castle Grounds
Off High Street, Tonbridge
Lawns, gardens, terraces, nature trail, lily pond, river walks, children's playground nearby, wildlife and waterbirds. See also Castles, p.124.   Free

Tunbridge Wells: Calverley Gardens
Near town centre, off Mount Pleasant Road, near Central Station
Lawns, gardens, including a sunken rose-garden, paddling-pool, putting, tennis, bowls, summer café.   D
Free

Tunbridge Wells: Dunorlan Park
Off A264, Pembury Road, 1¼ miles E of town centre
50 acres of lawns and trees sweep down to a large lake, ideal for boating, angling – and ducks. Once the garden of a wealthy Tasmanian businessman, friend of Salvationist William Booth. Fine for picnics and games. Café.   Free

Tunbridge Wells: The Common
Near The Pantiles
250 breezy, unspoilt acres of gorse, bracken, grass and trees with a variety of strange sandstone rock outcrops.
Free

HISTORIC BUILDINGS

ABBEYS

Aylesford: Aylesford Friary
The Friary, Aylesford, Maidstone (0622 77272)
Signposted from Sandling roundabout on A229 or from Ditton on A20
13th-century friary on bank of Medway imaginatively restored by Carmelite friars after World War II. Original cloisters. Impressive Shrine of Our Lady with contemporary sculpture and ceramics. Shop, café.
All year: daily: 9–dusk   Donation

Canterbury: St Augustine's Abbey (EH)
Longport, Canterbury (0227 65029)
¼ mile immediately E of cathedral
Ruins of the once important Benedictine St Augustine's Abbey church and monastic buildings, built over the centuries on the site of that founded in AD 598 by St Augustine himself. Burial place of 7 kings, 3 queens, 11 archbishops – and, once, St Augustine. Within the abbey are also the ruins of the 7th-century Saxon church of St Pancras, with fine Roman brick. Small site exhibition.   D
EH Standard times

Lamberhurst: Bayham Abbey (EH)
Lamberhurst (0892 890381)
1¾ miles W of Lamberhurst, off B2169
Picturesque riverside 13th-century ruins of Premonstratensian monks – a stone's throw into Sussex!
Standard EH opening times

Margate: Salmestone Grange
Nash Road, Margate (0843 21136)
Off B2049 or turn up Hartsdown Road opposite Sea Bathing Hospital
One of St Augustine's Abbey's most important granges with original – but much restored – medieval buildings that include 10th-century crypt and 14th-century monks' kitchen.
Daily, May–September, 2–5.30   Small fee

Minster: Minster Abbey
Minster, near Ramsgate (0843 821254)
On B2047
Founded in AD 670, destroyed by Danes in 840, restored in 1027; now belongs to hard-working Benedictine nuns. 2 wings of old building, Norman crypt, old brewhouse, ruin of church tower. (Agricultural museum in grounds.)
All year: Monday–Saturday, 11–12. May–September: Monday–Saturday, 11–12, 2–4.30; Saturday, 3.30–5. Closed Sunday   Donation

Minster: Minster Abbey Church (St Mary and St Sexburga)
Minster, Sheppey
One of the oldest places of Christian worship in England. Remarkable for being 2 churches in one, and with fine views of 4 major waterways. Unusual sculpture, brasses and effigies. Minster Gatehouse (museum) adjoins.
                                                                Donation

CASTLES

The following are 'castles' in the strict sense of the word. Other castles, originally fortified to a greater or lesser degree but now known best as 'Historic Homes', are shown in that section, p.134, e.g. Allington, Hever, Leeds, Lullingstone and Lympne.

Bodiam: Bodiam Castle (NT)
Bodiam, near Robertsbridge, Sussex (058-083 436)

Historic Buildings

Signposted from A21 (Hurst Green), A229 (Hawkhurst) and A228 (Sandhurst, Kent)
Built 1386, 'slighted' in 17th century, but its walls and towers are still magically reflected in its wide moat. Splendid views. In Sussex – but shouldn't be missed. Museum, audio-visuals on armour and castle life. NT shop, cafeteria, Castle Inn opposite, picnic areas.
April–October: daily, 10–6; November–March: Monday–Saturday, 10 to dusk. Open GF; closed 25–27 December

Deal: Deal Castle (EH)
Deal Castle Road, Deal (0304 372762)
On the front, near town centre
Unusual and splendid fort in the shape of a Tudor rose. Built in 1540, it was the largest of Henry VIII's coastal defences, with 119 gun positions. There are cannons on the battlements; a photographic and print exhibition in the keep; prehistoric, Roman and Saxon items in the gatehouse.
EH Standard times

Dover: Dover Castle (EH)
Castle Road, Dover (0304 021628)
E side of Dover, above docks
Set high on the famous White Cliffs, the 'key to England' was also the principal royal residence. The extensive curtain walls enclose a splendid keep, with walls 17–21 feet thick, which houses a fine collection of arms and armour, an exciting Battle of Waterloo model and the Queen's Regimental Museum. Within the bailey are the Roman pharos (lighthouse) and a Saxon church, St Mary in Castro. Shop, restaurant (summer only).
D – grounds only, some steep slopes
EH Standard and Sunday mornings

Eynsford: Eynsford Castle (EH)
Eynsford, near Farningham
6 miles S of Dartford just off A225 in Eynsford
Ruins of the 12th-century castle of a Norman knight set above the River Darent. Only the lofty and imposing curtain walls remain standing. D
EH Standard times   Free

Rochester: Rochester Castle (EH)
By Rochester Bridge on A2
Second only to the Tower of London as an example of Norman military architecture. The keep (125 feet high) is the tallest in England and was built *c.* 1130 within curtain walls following the line of old Roman defences, alongside the Medway. Splendid view of the river and shipping. Spacious gardens and riverside esplanade. Souvenir shop.
EH Standard and summer Sunday mornings

Tonbridge: Tonbridge Castle and Grounds
Castle Street, Tonbridge
On riverside, off High Street
Massive 13th-century gatehouse, one of the finest in England, in pleasant landscaped gardens overlooking the River Medway in the very centre of the town. The motte still survives to its original commanding height.
Weekends only: June–mid July. Daily in school spring and summer holidays: 11.30–1, 2–5.30

Upnor: Upnor Castle (EH)
Frindsbury Extra, near Rochester (0634 78742)
Off A228 in Frindsbury onto unclassified road down to the River Medway
Elizabethan fort on the bank of the Medway built to defend Chatham Naval Dockyard opposite. Interior contains displays relating to Dutch incursion in 1667. In grounds, cannons from ships sunk in that encounter.
EH summer season, standard times

Walmer: Walmer Castle and Garden (EH)
Walmer, Deal (0304 364288)
On B2057, 1 mile S of Walmer
Like Deal Castle, built in Tudor rose shape by Henry VIII. It has, since the 18th century, been the official residence of the Lords Warden of the Cinque Ports. Among the latter was the Duke of Wellington, who died here. His furnished rooms, including camp-bed and boots, are preserved as he left them. The present Lord Warden is the Queen Mother. Also attractive gardens overlooking the Channel.   D
EH standard hours but closed Monday (not BHM) and when the Lord Warden is in residence

CATHEDRALS

Canterbury: Canterbury Cathedral
Canterbury (0227 472727)
City centre, junction of Sun Street, Mercery Lane and Burgate
England's premier cathedral and scene of Thomas à Becket's martyrdom. Splendid Perpendicular nave, soaring Bell Harry Tower, ancient and modern stained glass, Black Prince's tomb, largest Norman crypt in the world, chapter house, cloisters ... and other glories. Shop.   D
All year. Daily: summer months, 8.45–7; winter months, 8.45–5   Offering

Rochester: Rochester Cathedral
The Precinct, Rochester (0634 43366)
Off the High Street near the castle
Second oldest see in England, consecrated in AD 604 by Justus, St Augustine's right-hand man. Rebuilt by Norman Bishop Gundulf in 1080. Small but a treasure-house of architectural styles from 11th–20th century. Outstanding: Romanesque west front, Norman nave, 200 assorted heads on corbel and boss, elaborate Chapter House doorway, Wheel of Fortune pillar-painting and fine 13th-century crypt.
All year. Daily: January–March and November–December, 8–5; April–October, 8.30–6   Offering

CHURCHES

This comparative handful has been selected for beauty of setting, architecture and ornament, and for special interest and character. Together, large and small, urban and rural, they offer a cross-section of Kent's great heritage of churches.

Due to vandalism and theft, a growing number of churches have to be kept locked. Enquiry nearby or a notice on the church door will generally reveal the whereabouts of the key-holder, seldom very far away.

Obviously all are 'Free' but an offering, however small, does help with ever mounting church expenses.

Appledore: Horne's Place Chapel (EH)
Off B2080, 1½ miles N of Appledore
Charming but tiny 14th-century domestic chapel with undercroft once attached to the manor house, set on the edge of Romney Marsh.
Wednesday only: 10–5

Barfreston: St Nicholas
Barfreston, near Dover
Turn off A2 at junction with A260; then 2 miles NE
Hill-perched in gentle downland country, it is one of the finest Norman churches in England. Superb south doorway, splendid wheel-window, zigzag in plenty, arcading: all in under 50 feet length.

Brookland: St Augustine
Brookland, near Rye
On A259, 4 miles NE of Rye
Much photographed for its belfry – set *on the ground* in the churchyard! Georgian pews, medieval wall-painting, unique 12th-century font, rare tithe scales and graveside 'hudd' (shelter).

Canterbury: St Martin
North Holmes Road, Canterbury
Off the A257 Sandwich road, ½ mile E of the cathedral, immediately after HM Prison
Possibly the oldest church in England, with part of the chancel built of thin Roman brick. Queen Bertha prayed here; St Augustine preached here; King Ethelbert was probably baptized here – all nearly 14 centuries ago.

Chatham: St Bartholomew's Chapel
High Street, Chatham
Opposite Sir John Hawkins Hospital
Even in the midst of the vast enterprise of building Rochester Cathedral and Castle, Bishop Gundulf made time to found a leper hospital (1078) of which this is the chapel (1124).

Chevening: St Botolph
Off B221 at Chevening Cross to Chevening Park, 3 miles N of Sundridge

A 13th-century church on the Pilgrims Way, at the gates of Inigo Jones' Chevening Park, with wooded Downs as backcloth, should be enough for anyone. But additionally, and unforgettably, there is the Stanhope Chapel, rich in splendid monuments, and a contrastingly simple one by Chantry of Lady Frederica contentedly cradling the baby whose birth brought about her death.

Cobham: St Mary Magdalene
Cobham, near Rochester

Main street Cobham (on B2009) opposite Leather Bottle pub

The beautifully proportioned 13th-century chancel holds a superb tomb chest and probably the finest collection of brasses in the world, clearly showing medieval dress and armour. The College of Priests adjoining, built in the 14th century by Sir John de Cobham, is now delightful almshouses.

Cooling: St James
Near Cooling Castle

3 miles N of Strood, turn off B2000 at West Street for 1 mile

Complete 14th-century ragstone church with banded tower and tiny vestry decorated with thousands of cockleshells. Scene perhaps of Pip's meeting with escaped convict Magwitch in Dickens' *Great Expectations*. Unusual grouping of 13 small lozenge-shaped tombstones by the south porch may include those of 'Pip's five brothers and sisters'.

Cranbrook: St Dunstan
Off the High Street

The 'Cathedral of the Weald'! Handsomely towered and battlemented church near Cranbrook School: Father Time, chandelier, Royal Arms, Roberts' helms, tabard and banderoles, 16th-century stained glass, monuments, 13th-century Green Men carved bosses.

Dover: St Edmund's Chapel
Priory Road, Dover
Off High Street opposite town hall
A tiny chapel consecrated by the Bishop of Chichester four days before he died in 1253. Dissolved in 1544; used as barn, dwelling and forge; now restored and reconsecrated. Mass celebrated at 10 a.m. on Saturday

Fairfield: St Thomas à Becket
Fairfield, near Appledore
Off minor Brookland–Appledore road, from A259
Loneliest, smallest, wettest, largely timber church in Kent. In times of flood worshippers came by boat; today there is a pleasant grass causeway. Box pews, 3-decker pulpit, crown-post roof, 17th-century font, shingled bell-cote: '... a sweet sight' says Newman. (Key at Becket's barn Farmhouse nearby.)

Faversham: St Mary of Charity
Church Road, Faversham, near brewery
Impressive for its size, aisled transepts and distinctive, 152-foot crown spire; interesting for brasses, grotesque misericords, richly emblazoned tomb, 14th-century frescoed, octagonal pillar and pedigree Norman west bay of nave.

Folkestone: St Mary and St Eanswythe
Church Street, off Sandgate Road, near town centre
Founded by King Ethelbert's young daughter as the first 'monastery for women' in England. Its predecessors were destroyed by cliff erosion, fire, pillage and plunder but her bones rest in the present building. Also churchyard cross, brasses, tombs and memorials, carved rood beam, murals of Stations of the Cross – and a magnificent Kempe window honouring Folkestonian William Harvey who discovered the circulation of the blood.

Goudhurst: St Mary
A 14th-century hill-top church perched above the charming tiled and weather-boarded village straggling steeply below it. Some 15th-century glass, magnificent

Historic Buildings

Culpepper monuments, chandelier. From the sturdy 17th-century tower is seen one of the widest views in Kent: from Romney Marsh to North Downs – and, it is said, encompassing 51 other churches!
Church: daily, 9–5. Tower: May–September, Thursday 1–5; Saturday 11–5; also during July and August, Tuesday 1–5

Gravesend: St George
Off High Street, Gravesend
¼ miles S of Town Pier
Built in 1731, to replace church destroyed in town fire, with imposing tower and obelisk-like spire. Charming statue and details of Red Indian Princess Pocahontas who died and was buried here.

Herne: St Martin
On A291, 2 miles S of Herne Bay
Rich in monumental brasses and with a magnificent NW tower that Ruskin described as 'one of the very few perfect things in the world'. Chair and statue of Nicholas Ridley, who made St Martin's the first church in England in which the Te Deum was sung in English.

Hythe: St Leonard
Hythe, near Folkestone
Steep passageway from near town hall in main street
Splendid hill-perched Early English church with magnificent chancel, Salviati mosaic pulpit, huge reredos and a charnel house where thousands of medieval skulls and bones are high-piled. Grave of Lionel Larkin, inventor of lifeboats, in the churchyard.

Isle of Harty: St Thomas
Isle of Sheppey
5 miles SE of Eastchurch, off A250 in marshland
Solitude and simplicity; remotest church in Kent. The oil-lit church, with wooden bellcote, contains intricately carved Flanders Kist dredged up from the Swale, recently stolen – and recovered; also unusual table.

Kilndown: Christ Church
Kilndown, near Goudhurst
Off B2079, 3 miles S of Goudhurst
'A whole of colour, such as is to be seen in no other church in England.' Red and yellow tiles; walls painted up to the windowsills with patterns in red, blue and gold; stained glass, from King Ludwig of Bavaria's factory, in glowing orange and gold, regal turquoise and purple, is a back-drop that is rich but never strident. And, elsewhere, subtle touches of more colour: on angels' wings and crucifix, on font and high-perched pulpit, even on a splendidly moustached St George and his Dragon.

Little Chart: St Mary
Off B2077, 3 miles S of Charing
2 churches here! One, a mile from the village, picturesquely demolished by a flying bomb; the other (1955), opposite the village inn, plain and pale of brick with severe Gothic tower. Darell tombs and Saracen's Head from the old are now in the new.

Lower Halstow: St Margaret
Lower Halstow, near Gillingham
Off A2 at Newington
Only a grassed embankment separates this Saxon church from the Medway waters: unique 12th-century lead font, Jacobean pulpit, 18th-century brass chandelier and suspender, 14th-century wall-painting.

Lydd: All Saints
Lydd, Romney Marsh
Centre of town
'The Cathedral of the Marshes' is the longest parish church in Kent (199 feet) with a splendid tower (132 feet), commissioned by Cardinal Wolsey, giving spectacular views. Suffered a direct hit in World War II but proudly and beautifully restored: 14th-century knight in armour, many brasses, hatchments and Royal Arms.

Maidstone: All Saints
Next to the Archbishop's Palace by the river-front

Historic Buildings

Archbishop Courtenay's splendid Early Perpendicular church, (AD 1396) high, wide and airy, is Kent's largest parish church, able to hold a congregation of 1500. Full of interest: Royal West Kent's Chapel, carved misericords, Astley monument, Beale brass (showing six generations), sumptuous sedilia and reredos, ornate roof beams.

Mereworth: St Lawrence
On A228, 3 miles S of West Malling
High-handedly, in 1740, the Earl of Westmorland demolished Mereworth's medieval church and replaced it, nearly a mile away, with this appetizing 'goulash' of London church styles. In the Neo-Classic interior don't be fooled by *painted* columns and ceiling. There is much more to see and be seen in the golden glow of splendid east lunette window.

Nettlestead: St Mary
Nettlestead, near Paddock Wood
Just off B2015, 3 miles N of Paddock Wood
A tiny church, sheltering between charming cricket ground and River Medway. It was conceived, like Sainte Chapelle in Paris, as a framework for glowing stained glass. Much destroyed by great storm of 1763 but enough remains to make a visit very worthwhile.

Northfleet: St Botolph
Just off square in town centre on A226
An impressive early 14th-century church dramatically perched above huge Thames-side quarry through which tiny goods trains trundle. Sedilia, chancel screen, east window, brasses, monument and tablets.

Ramsgate: St Augustine
St Augustine's Road, behind the Regency Hotel
'One man's gift to his faith': the finest Gothic Revival work of the creator of the Houses of Parliament, A.W. Pugin. He was its paymaster as well as its architect. Rich in atmosphere, texture of stone, tile and wood, and stained glass. Towering font – but no spire: Pugin's money had run out.

Tudeley: All Saints
On B2015, 1½ miles E of Tonbridge
Unusual in its farmyard approach, and red brick tower with tiled spirelet. Remarkable for east window – the only one in England by Marc Chagall: Christ crucified, with angels, and a rider on a scarlet horse above; a drowned girl in a trough of realistically heaving waves below. It commemorates Sarah d'Avigdor-Goldsmid, drowned in a sailing accident.

Tunbridge Wells: King Charles the Martyr
London Road, Tunbridge Wells
Opposite The Pantiles
Externally a simple, square building (chequered red and blue bricks, clock-turret and cupola), seemingly unworthy of its high-sounding dedication. But inside is probably the finest plaster ceiling in Kent: partly by John Wetherel, partly by Henry Doogood, who worked for Sir Christopher Wren in St Paul's. Best seen from the unusual galleries. Before boundary revision, it was said the altar was in Tonbridge, the pulpit in Speldhurst and the vestry in Frant!

FORTS

For Canterbury's Westgate Towers, see the chapter 'Museums', p.149.

Chatham: Fort Amherst
Barrier Road, off Dock Road, Chatham (0634 47747)
Five minutes walk from town hall and bus station. Opposite Heritage Centre.
A most unusual fortress built in 1756 to protect the dockyard below. 14 acres of redoubts, ditches, embankments, gun emplacements, bastions – and a twisting labyrinth of tunnels and caves hewn out of chalk by French POWs. Museum and recreated barrack-room. Cannons fired first Sunday of month in season; on second Sunday French infantry storm the fort. Snacks.
April–June: Wednesday, Saturday, Sunday, 12–4.30 (LA);

July–September: all week, 12–4.30 (LA); October: Wednesday, Saturday, Sunday, 12–4.30 (LA)

Dover: The Grand Shaft
Snargate Street, Dover (0304 201066)
Follow signs from Snargate Street to Military Road
A unique 140-foot triple staircase, superbly designed and cut through solid chalk cliffs. A short-cut so that during the Napoleonic Wars troops could be moved quickly from the Drop Redoubt, on the Western Heights, to the town below.
Last week May–mid-September: Saturday and BHM, 2–5 (The remarkable Drop Redoubt may also be seen on BH weekends.) Small fee

Dymchurch: Martello Tower No. 24 (EH)
Dymchurch, near Hythe (0303 873684)
On sea-front, just S of Dymchurch, on A259
One of the 74 small but sturdy towers built between 1805 and 1812 along the south-east coast as far as Seaford to repel the threatened Napoleonic invasion. Exhibition.
EH summer season standard times Small fee

Gravesend: New Tavern Fort
Gravesend
W end of Gordon Promenade, ½ mile from railway station and Gravesend-Tilbury ferry terminal
Situated on Gravesend's riverside, New Tavern, crossing its fire with Tilbury Fort on the Essex shore, blocked the way to London for an enemy fleet for 150 years. Display of guns and emplacements and of underground magazines with exhibits – and ghost!
Gun emplacements and gardens: daily morning to dusk.
Magazines: April–September, Monday–Saturday, 10–4.30, Sunday 10–12 noon; Public Holidays, 2–4.30 Free

West Malling: St Leonard's Tower (EH)
1 mile S of West Malling on side of A228
A sturdy Norman tower built by Bishop Gundulf, architect of Malling Abbey and Rochester Cathedral. It is believed to have been part of his own fortified house. On a knoll,

and with small grassed area below, it makes an excellent picnic site and 'I'm King of the Castle' playground for young children.

En route to Nettlestead church and Mereworth church
Open daily   Free

HISTORIC HOMES

Most 'Historic Homes' have beautiful gardens and small specialist museums or displays, as well as the usual splendid furniture, interior decoration and pictures. All three attractions are shown under this heading.

See also the section Museums, p.144, for Goudhurst (Finchcocks), Margate (Tudor House), Rochester (Eastgate House), Smallhythe (Smallhythe Place) and Westerham (Quebec House).

Allington: Allington Castle
Allington, near Maidstone (0622 54080)
Off A20, 2 miles W of Maidstone, opposite Tudor Garage
Romantic 13th-century moated castle with gatehouse and picturesque inner courtyard on banks of River Medway: former home of Tudor poet Sir Thomas Wyatt. Fine collection of furniture and art.
All year: daily, 2–4. Closed XD and BD

Ashford: Godinton House and Garden
Godinton Park, near Ashford (0233 20773)
2 miles NW of Ashford, off A20 at Potters Corner
A Jacobean house rich in fine carving and panelling particularly in the hall and on the staircase. Porcelain, portraits and furniture. Formal 18th-century garden with topiary.
Easter holidays: 2–5. June–September: Sunday and BHM only, 2–5, tour by appointment

Birchington: Quex House and Garden
Quex House, Birchington (0843 42168)
Turn off A28 at Square into Park Lane, opposite church
Regency home of the Powell-Cottons for nearly 200 years.

Historic Buildings

Fine collection of period furniture, glass, silver, porcelain, pewter, miniatures and paintings. Cannons and other armaments in pleasant garden. Tea-room (summer only). See also Powell-Cotton Museum adjoining.
April–September: Wednesday, Thursday, Sunday and BH (also Fridays in August) 2.15–6 (LA 5)

Boughton Monchelsea: Boughton Monchelsea Place
Boughton Monchelsea, near Maidstone (0622 43120)
From Maidstone take Hastings road to Linton; turn left along B2163; Boughton Monchelsea is down minor road to right
Battlemented Elizabethan-Regency manor with fine Wealden views. Displays of haberdashery, carriages, old vehicles and early farm implements. Landscaped garden, deer park. Interesting church adjoins. Attractive tea-room.
Easter–mid-October: Saturday, Sunday and BH (July–August, also Wednesday, 2.15–6

Burwash: Bateman's (NT)
Burwash, Sussex (0435 882302)
½ mile S of Burwash (A265) from W end of village
Well worth the 8 extra Sussex miles! An imposing 17th-century ironmaster's house, once home (and now museum) of Rudyard Kipling of *Just So Stories* fame. Watermill grinds corn (Saturday 2); one of oldest water-driven turbines in world; Rudyard Kipling's 1928 Rolls Royce; spacious, self-designed garden. Café, picnic area, NT shop.
April–October: Saturday–Wednesay (including GF and BHM), 11–6 (LA 5)

Chiddingstone: Chiddingstone Castle
Hill Hoath Road, Chiddingstone, Edenbridge (0892 870347)
S of Bough Beech Reservoir, off B2027
Gothic-style Georgian 'castle' near National Trust's famous Chiddingstone village. Japanese lacquer and metal work, Stuart memorabilia, Buddhist art, Egyptian antiquities. Lakes (excellent fishing), caves. Tea-room.   D
April–end of September: Wednesday–Saturday, 2–5.30;

Sunday and BH, 11.30–5.30. Mid-July–mid-September: Tuesday also. October: Saturday–Sunday, 2–5.30

Cobham: Cobham Hall
Cobham, near Rochester (0472 823371)
4 miles W of Rochester, off the A2
Beautiful and historic Elizabethan mansion with later additions. Splendid interiors by Inigo Jones, Adam Brothers and Wyatt. 50-acre park – a favourite haunt of Dickens. Cafeteria.
Now a girls' public school, so opening times are restricted to occasional dates in spring and summer holidays, generally Sunday, Wednesday and Thursday, 2–5.30 (LA 5)

Cobham: Owletts (NT)
Cobham, near Gravesend (0474 814260)
At W end of Cobham village; B2009, 2 miles from A2
Charming though modest Carolean red-brick house with fine staircase and ornate plasterwork. Former home of architect Sir Herbert Baker who helped Luytens design the imperial splendour of New Delhi. Small but homely walled garden.
April–September: Wednesday and Thursday only, 2–5 (LA 4.30) Small fee

Eynsford: Lullingstone Castle
Eynsford (0322 862114)
1 mile W of Eynsford on cul-de-sac road beyond Roman villa
Family mansion rather than castle but behind its massive gatehouse it is splendidly set amid sweeping lawns and a lake, with a gem of a family chapel. Tudor Great Hall, Grand Staircase (shallow steps to help overweight Queen Anne) barrel-vaulted State Drawing-Room, library filled with calf-bound tomes. Furniture, porcelain, portraits etc. Teas.
April–October: Saturday, Sunday and BHM, 2–6

Hever: Hever Castle
Hever, near Edenbridge (0732 865224)
2 miles E of Edenbridge

Historic Buildings

Double-moated 13th- to 15th-century castle, once home of Anne Boleyn. Superbly renovated and furnished by American millionaire Waldorf Astor. Magnificent furniture and portraits. 'Henry and Anne' Exhibition. Spectacular gardens, including Italian garden with much Roman statuary, maze and lake, gift shop, cafeteria, restaurant, adventure playground.   D
April–October, daily. Gardens 11–6; castle 12–6 (LA 5)

Hollingbourne: Eyhorne Manor
Hollingbourne, near Maidstone (0622 780514)
400 yards N of A20 on B2163 opposite Great Danes Hotel
An outstanding 15th-century manor house with 14 rooms on show. All contain herbs to drive away evil spirits! Models show evolution of house; unique laundry museum. Intimate garden planted with aromatic herbs and old-fashioned roses. Tea and cakes available.
GF–September: Saturday and Sunday, 2–6; August: daily, except Monday and Friday, 2–6. Also BH

Ightham: Ightham Mote (NT)
Ivy Hatch, Ightham, near Sevenoaks. (0732 810378)
From A25 (Ightham) take A227 S, turning right after 2 miles for Ivy Hatch
One of the finest small medieval moated manors in England, in secluded woodland clearing: courtyard; Great Hall, undercroft, Tudor chapel, drawing-room with Jacobean frieze and Chinese wall-paper. NT shop. Small but pleasant garden, lakelet and streams, lawns, flowers and trees.
April–October daily, except Tuesday and Saturday, 11–5. Open GF and BHM

Leeds: Leeds Castle
Leeds, near Maidstone (0622 65400)
Junction of A20 and M20, 4 miles E of Maidstone
'Loveliest castle in the world' is its claim. Fairy-tale medieval castle built on two small islands in middle of lake in 500 acres of parkland. Beautifully furnished. Gardens, duckery, aviaries, greenhouses, vineyard, golf course, Dog Collar Museum. Gift and plant shop, restaurant, cafeteria.

Also major annual events: ballet, music, fireworks, hot-air balloons etc. D
All year. April–October: daily, 11–6 (LA to grounds, 5). November–March: Saturday and Sunday only, 12–5 (LA to grounds, 4)

Lympne: Lympne Castle
Lympne, near Hythe (0303 67571)
Off B2067, 3½ miles W of Hythe in Lympne Old Village, or 1½ miles from Newingreen on A20
Small 14th-century castle, with a Great Hall flanked by Norman and medieval towers. Splendidly sited on former 'cliffs' overlooking Romney Marsh and Channel. Garden, exhibition of toys and dolls, reproduction of medieval brasses, costume display, church adjoining, Shepway Cross nearby, remains of Stutfall Castle (Roman Lemanis) below.
June–September: daily (including all BHs), 10.30–6

Lympne: Port Lympne Mansion and Gardens
Lympne, near Hythe (0303 64646)
3 miles W of Hythe, off B2067; Exit 11 off M20
Unusual Dutch Colonial style mansion designed in 1912 by Sir Herbert Baker for millionaire Sir Philip Sassoon. Superb interior decoration includes Rex Whistler's 'Tent Room'; also wildlife subjects in ceramics, bronze, ivory and silver, and paintings etc. Huge wildlife mural and Moorish patio. Set in 15 acres of varied and terraced gardens with panoramic views of Marsh and Channel. Also zoo safari park, cafeteria, gift shop.
All year, daily (except XD), 10–5 or dusk (LA)

Northiam: Great Dixter House and Garden
Northiam, near Rye, Sussex (079-74 3160)
½ mile off A28, Tenterden–Hastings road, in Northiam
Superb oaken manor hall-house (1450) with magnificent Great Hall restored by Luytens, who also designed garden, which includes topiary, yew hedges, flower borders, orchard and meadow. Displays of antiques and needlework.
April–mid-October, daily (except non-BHMs) 2–5. Garden

Historic Buildings

also open late May, July and August, Sunday and BHM from 11

Penshurst: Penshurst Place
Penshurst, Tonbridge (0892 870307)
On B2176; off A26, 3 miles N of Tunbridge Wells
Home of the Sidneys for 400 years. A palace of a building of varied architectural styles highlighted by superb 14th-century Great Hall. Furniture, portraits and *objets d'art* are in keeping. Magnificent walled and terraced gardens of equal variety. Restaurants, picnic area, adventure playground, toy and farm museums. A full day out! D
Open every afternoon (except Monday) 1 April–30 September. Also BHM in season. Grounds 12.30–6. House 1–5.30 (LA 5)

Rolvenden: Great Maytham Hall
Rolvenden, near Cranbrook (0580 241346)
1 mile SE on minor road to Wittersham
A Saxon estate with an early 18th-century house encased in a huge Neo-Georgian one by Luytens (for Margot Asquith). Walled garden on which Frances Burnett Hodgson, who lived here, based *The Secret Garden*.
May–September: Wednesday and Thursday, 2–5
Small fee

Sevenoaks: Knole (NT)
Sevenoaks (0732 450608)
On A225, S end of Sevenoaks
One of the largest and finest English stately homes. Set in a huge deer park with tree-lined avenues. Magnificent State Rooms with vast range of portraits, tapestries, hangings, silver and 17th-century furniture. NT shop. Splendid walled gardens with bird-house folly.
April–October: Wednesday–Saturday (including GF) and BHM, 11–5; Sunday, 2–5 (LA 4). Additional rooms may be viewed on Fridays. Guided tours every Tuesday except after BHM. Gardens: May–September, first Wednesday in each month only

Sevenoaks: Riverhill House and Gardens
Sevenoaks (0732 452557)
Off A225, 1 mile S of Sevenoaks
Small country house with 450 years of interesting family memorabilia, panelled rooms, portraits, books etc. Teas and ploughman's lunches. Mature hillside garden with fine trees.
House: Mid-April–August, BH Sunday and Monday only, 2–5.30. Gardens: April–August, Sunday–Monday, 12–6

Westerham: Chartwell (NT)
Westerham (0732 866368)
Take B2026 eastbound from Westerham, then fork left after 1½ miles
Beautifully sited home of Sir Winston Churchill. Two rooms are evocative museums of England's great war-time leader; the remainder left exactly as when he was alive. NT shops, restaurant, cafeteria. Splendid hillside gardens including studio, wall, lakes and black swans, rose garden, lawns, streams, trees etc.
March and November: Saturday, Sunday, Wednesday, 11–4. April–October: Tuesday, Wednesday, Thursday, 12–5; Saturday, Sunday, BHM, 11–5. Closed Tuesday after BHM and GF   D

Westerham: Squerryes Court
Westerham (0959 62345/63118)
Just off A25 to W of Westerham
Attractive William and Mary manor house with superb collection of Old Masters, tapestries, furniture and porcelain. Background setting for Paul Daniels' TV *Murder by Magic*. Formal gardens, woodland walks, lake. Refreshments.
March: Sunday only. April–September: Wednesday, Saturday, Sunday and BHM, 2–6 (LA 5.30)

OTHER HISTORICAL BUILDINGS

See also the chapter 'Museums', p.144, for Canterbury (Poor Priests Hospital), Chatham (Chatham Dockyard),

Cranbrook (Union Mill), Maidstone (Archbishop's Stables), Milton Regis (Court Hall), Ospringe (Maison Dieu) and Rochester (Guildhall).

Canterbury: Eastbridge Hospital
25 High Street, Canterbury (0227 451767)
In main street past GPO and near King's Bridge and weavers' houses
Founded in 1190 as a hospital for poor travellers making the pilgrimage to the shrine of St Thomas à Becket in the cathedral. Now 9 almshouses, but the 12th-century undercroft, refectory with 13th-century wall-painting and upper chapel may still be visited.
All year, (except GF, XD and BD): Monday–Saturday, 10–1, 2–5; Sunday 11–1, 2–5   Free

Chatham: Sir John Hawkins Hospital
High Street, Chatham
Opposite St Bartholomew's Chapel
Quaint group of houses for 'poor decayed mariners and shipwrights' round a tiny square with central pump, and steps leading down to the Medway. Originally built by ruthless slaver Sir John Hawkins in 1592; restored, in red brick, in 1789.
External viewing only   Free

Fordwich: Fordwich Town Hall
Fordwich, near Canterbury
Turn off A28 in Sturry
Smallest in England on River Stour quay where Caen stone was unloaded for the building of Canterbury Cathedral. Some exhibits and ducking-stool. Old prison cell.
June–September: Weekdays, 11–4; Sunday, 2–4   Small fee

Faversham: Abbey Street
Faversham contains some 400 listed buildings! Centrally situated, Abbey Street is particularly rich in delightful 16th-century buildings of historical and architectural interest, including Arden's House (scene of 16th-century murder), Globe House and St Stephen's Gatehouse. See

also West Street.
External viewing only, except during Faversham's annual Open House Scheme (July) — Free

Gravesend: Milton Chantry (EH)
E of central Gravesend, off A226 (0474 321520)
14th-century chapel of leper hospital and chantry of the Earl of Pembroke. In 17th century became an inn and later part of coastal defence works. Now houses exhibitions of local art and crafts.
EH Standard times — Small fee

Otham: Stoneacre (NT)
Otham, near Maidstone (0622 861861)
3 miles SE of Maidstone, off A20
A gem of a half-timbered manor house, mainly late 15th-century, with Great Hall and crown-post roof, and several smaller rooms. Exhibition of embroidery. Tiny garden. Several other houses nearby, almost equally splendid.
April–September: Wednesday and Saturday, 2–6 (LA 5)

Plaxtol: Old Soar Manor (NT)
Plaxtol, Borough Green
2 miles S of Borough Green, up narrow lane from Plaxtol
Solar block of a 13th-century knight's dwelling. Exhibition.
April–September: daily, 9.30–6.30 — Free

Reculver: Reculver Towers (EH)
Reculver, near Herne Bay (0227 66444)
3 miles E of Herne Bay, off A299
On the very edge of the sea and within the walls of a 3rd-century Roman shore fort, there are remains of a Saxon and Norman church. Its twin towers are a famous landmark for seafarers. Can be reached by road or pleasant cliff path. EH Standard times, June–August
— Small fee

Rochester: Six Poor Travellers' House
97 High Street, Rochester (0634 45609)
Almshouse founded in 1579 to give 'six poor travellers not

being common Rogues or Proctors' one night's accommodation and 4 pence when they left. Roman pottery, clay pipes, historical documents and items, original bedrooms.
March–October: Tuesday–Saturday, 2–5 Free

Strood: Temple Manor (EH)
Knight Road, Strood, Rochester (0634 78743)
Off A228
Great chamber on vaulted undercroft built in 1240 by Knights Templar, an order of celibate soldiers established during the Crusades.
April–September: Monday, Wednesday, Thursday and Saturday, 9.30–6.30; Tuesday 9.30–1; Sunday, 2–6.30
Small fee

MUSEUMS

The following 'Historic Homes' (p.134) also incorporate small museums: Boughton Monchelsea (old vehicles and farm implements), Chartwell (Churchill memorabilia), Chiddingstone (Egyptian antiquities and Stuart memorabilia), Eyhorne Manor (laundry equipment), Leeds Castle (dog collars), Lympne Castle (toys, dolls and medieval brasses) and Penshurst Place (toys and farm implements).

See also 'Farms', p.104, Beltring (Whitbread Hop Farm).

Museums dealing with transport are detailed in that section, p.160.

AGRICULTURAL

Brook: Wye College Agricultural Museum
Wye College, Brook, near Ashford (0233 812401)
In Brook, 2 miles NE of Willesborough
Superb black weather-boarded 14th-century tithe barn and 19th-century oast-house. Comprehensive collection of farm tools and implements including wagons.
May–September: Wednesday, 2–5; August: Wednesday and Saturday, 2–5   Free

Sandling: Museum of Kent Rural Life
Lock Lane, Cobtree Manor Park, Sandling, Maidstone (0622 63936)
Off Forstal Road from Running Horse Roundabout on A229, 2 miles N of Maidstone
Indoor display in oast-house. 'Live' exhibits outdoors

include hop garden, farmyard, donkey paddock, orchard, apiary, herb and market gardens etc. Picnic area, cafeteria D
April–mid-October: Monday–Tuesday, Thursday–Friday, 10–4.30; Saturday–Sunday, 12–4.30 Small fee

Staplehurst: Brattle Farm Museum
Brattle Farm, Five Oak Lane, Staplehurst (0580 891222)
Off A229, 1½ miles W of Old Manor in Staplehurst
Bygone days in rural setting. Agricultural tractors and machinery, horse-drawn and hand implements and tools, blacksmith's and wheelwright's shop, vintage motorcycles and cars. D
Easter to end October: Sunday and BHM, 9.30–6.30

ARMY, NAVY AND AIR FORCE

Ashford: Intelligence Corps Museum
Templer Barracks, Ashford (0233 25251)
On A20, 1 mile NW of Ashford
Story of British Military Intelligence from the reign of Elizabeth I to that of Elizabeth II. Documents, maps, photos, weapons, flags and personal items.
All the year, daily (except Saturday–Sunday): 10–12, 2–4.
Report to guard-room Free

Brenzett: Aeronautical Museum
Ivychurch Road, Brenzett, Romney Marsh (0679 206061)
Squadrons were based on this advanced landing-ground to combat V1s and help with D-Day build-up. Engines, armaments (including a 4½-ton Dambuster bomb designed by Sir Barnes Wallis) and other World War II memorabilia. Also Women's Land Army graffiti!
Easter–September: Sunday and BH, 11–5; July–August: Tuesday, Wednesday, Thursday, 2–5.
Small fee (non-profit making)

Canterbury: Buffs Regimental Museum
Royal Museum, Library and Art Gallery, 18 High Street, Canterbury (0227 452747)

Nearly opposite the GPO
The proud history, from 1572 until absorption into The Queen's Regiment in 1967, of Kent's famous regiment, 'The Buffs', is brought to life by a wealth of exhibits ranging from uniforms and medals to silverware, pictures and battle dispatches. Excellent booklet.
All the year: Monday–Saturday, 10–5   Free

Chatham: Dockyard Museum
Dock Road, Chatham (0634 448917)
In historic dockyard
Work representative of a wide range of crafts from riggers to divers, and coopers to wheelwrights, has been returned from Greenwich National Maritime Museum to early 19th-century lead and paint mill.
Summer: Wednesday–Sunday, 10–5.45; winter: Wednesday, Saturday and Sunday only, 10–4.15   Small fee

Chatham: Historic Dockyard
Dock Road, Chatham (0634 812551)
On Brompton Road from town hall
Made redundant after 400 years of 'National Service', the birthplace of HMS *Victory* is fighting back. Splendid Georgian buildings, Commissioner's Garden, towering covered slipways, working ropery, historical centre, church, craft museum, midget submarine, high-speed minelayer – and much more. *Kingswear Castle* cruises sail from here. Refreshments, shop.   D
All year: November–March, Wednesday, Saturday, Sunday only, 10–4.30; April–October, Wednesday–Sunday and BH, 10–6

Chatham: Royal Engineers Museum
Brompton Barracks, Prince Arthur Road, Chatham (0634 44555: ext 312)
Off A2 between Gillingham and Chatham
Splendid displays in impressive buildings do the Sappers full justice. Wide variety of exhibits range from Caesar's assault bridges to a German heavy-water cell, and come from all five continents. Special rooms for Gordon and

Kitchener, of course.
All year: Tuesday–Friday and BHM, 10–5; Sunday, 11.30–5

Dover: Queen's Regiment Museum (EH)
Dover Castle, Castle Hill, Dover
An exciting blend of uniforms and medals, weapons and scenarios that recall the history of a famous regiment.
EH Standard and Sunday mornings

Hawkinge: Battle of Britain Museum
Hawkinge Airfield, Aerodrome Road, near Folkestone (0303 893140)
Off A260, 3 miles N of Folkestone
Nearest World War II fighter station to France, heavily bombed and shelled. It displays in original buildings (Fighter Control, Armoury, and Dowding Memorial Hangar) comprehensive collection of recovered remains of British and German aircraft that fought in the Battle of Britain. The hangar contains Spitfire, Hurricane and Me109e. Also armaments, uniforms, insignia, equipment, vehicles, searchlights etc.
Easter–October: Sunday and all BHs, 11–5.30; July–October: Monday–Saturday, 11–5 June: daily, 2–5
All profits ploughed back

Headcorn: Lashenden Air Warfare Museum
Headcorn Aerodrome, Headcorn (0622 890226)
Off A274, 1 mile S of Headcorn
Miscellaneous items of German and British engines, wartime equipment, radios etc and a V1 flying bomb. Pleasure flights available. Aerodrome canteen.
Easter–October: Sunday and BHM, 10–6   Free

Maidstone: Queen's Own Royal West Kent Regiment Museum
St Faith's Street, Maidstone (0622 54497/56405)
St Faith's Street runs between Week Street and Fairmeadow
Newly restored museum does full justice to the proud tradition of one of Kent's famous regiments. Uniforms, medals, weapons, pictures and artefacts.
All year: Monday–Saturday, 10–5.30   Free

Manston: Spitfire Memorial Pavilion
RAF Manston, near Ramsgate (0843 89351: ext 202)
Off A253 about 4 miles W from Ramsgate, opposite RAF main entrance.
This famous World War II fighter station houses the best-preserved Spitfire Mk XVI in the country, credited with 4 kills. Also absorbing display of World War II exhibits and memorabilia. The pavilion is flanked by a Canberra, Gloster Javelin and Hurricane. Souvenir stall. D
Daily: 10–5   Fee for car-park; pavilion, free

Westerham: Quebec House (NT)
Westerham (0959 62206)
On A25 in Westerham (E)
17th-century red-brick, multi-gabled house containing portraits, prints and memorabilia of General Wolfe. Vivid display of Battle of Quebec in the Tudor stable-block. Small garden.
April–October: Sunday–Wednesday, Friday, BHM and GF, 2–6 (LA 5.30)

GENERAL INTEREST

Biddenden: Bettenham Manor Baby Carriage Collection
Biddenden (0580 291343)
1 mile W of village; off A262, 4 miles NW of Tenterden
Victorian prams, 18th-century stick-wagons, Edwardian bassinettes, 20th-century coach-built prams and Victorian mail-carts displayed in an oast-house near the 15-acre garden of a 15th-century country manor.
By appointment only   Donation for upkeep

Birchington: Powell-Cotton Museum
Quex Park, Birchington (0843 42168)
Turn off A28 at The Square into Park Lane, opposite church
9 galleries of breathtaking dioramas of African wildlife, native arts and crafts from Africa and Asia, Oriental fine arts including porcelain, Thanet archaeology. See also Quex House and Gardens adjoining. Tea-room (summer

Museums

only).   D
April–September: Wednesday, Thursday, Sunday and BHs, also Friday in August, 2.15–6 (LA 5); also October–March, Sunday afternoon (LA 4.30)

Broadstairs: Bleak House
Fort Road, Broadstairs (0843 62224)
Cliff top
Charles Dickens' holiday home, perched above harbour, where he wrote parts of *David Copperfield* and planned other novels. Living-rooms and bedroom on show. Also Maritime and Smuggling Museums.   D
Mid-April–end of June and October–mid-November: daily, 10–6; July–September, 10–9

Broadstairs: Dickens' House Museum
Broadstairs (0843 62853)
On main sea-front
Lovely old house whose owner was model for Dicken's famous eccentric, Betsey Trotwood. Parlour exactly as described in *David Copperfield*; memorabilia, Victoriana and costumes, prints of Dickensian interest.
Mid-April–end of October: daily, 2.30–5.30. July–September: Tuesday–Wednesday, 7 p.m.–9 p.m. also
Small fee

Canterbury: Westgate Towers Museum
St Peter's Street, Canterbury (0227 452747)
¼ mile NW of the cathedral, down continuation of High Street
A collection of arms, armour and other exhibits in Canterbury's only remaining fortified gatehouse (and prison). Panoramic views from the tower battlements over city and neighbouring beautiful Westgate Gardens.
All year: daily, except Sunday April–September 10–1, 2–4; October–March 2–4

Deal: Costume and Accessories Museum
18 Gladstone Road, Deal (0304 361471)
Off the Strand by Deal Castle
The Salter collection of original costumes and accessories (1785–1935)

April–September: Monday–Tuesday, 2–7; Sunday, 3–6
Small fee

Deal: Deal Victoriana Museum
Blackburn Hall, Middle Street, Deal (0304 373184)
Off N end of High Street
Victorian dolls, china, pewter, fans and bygones. Model gypsy caravan.
Easter–October: Thursday, Friday and Saturday, 2.30–5
Small fee

Downe: Darwin Museum
Down House, Luxted Road, Downe, near Orpington (0689 59119)
On minor road to Cudham, off A233, 2 miles S of Farnborough
The 18th-century house where Charles Darwin lived for 40 years and wrote *On the Origin of Species*. Interesting items and pictures including relics from the voyage of the *Beagle*. Attractive gardens include the famous 'sandwalk'.
Daily, except Monday and Friday but open on BHM, 1–6
Small fee

Goudhurst: Finchcocks
Goudhurst (0580 211702)
Off A262, 1½ miles W of Goudhurst
Fine Baroque Georgian manor, garden and parkland. Contains collection of keyboard instruments actually played in musical demonstration tours.
D
Easter–end September: Sundays and BHM; also daily in August, except Monday and Tuesday, 2–6

Kingsnorth: Kingsnorth Museum
Halfway Bungalow, Kingsnorth, near Ashford (0233 21609)
On B2070, 1½ miles S of Ashford beside workshops of Kingsnorth Trailer Company
A row of cannons 'welcomes' you to this incredible collection of 'anything and everything' amassed by Joe Ripley in 50 years of magpie collecting. Exhibits range from a one-string fiddle to a 1914 Harley Davidson

motor-cycle, and from Queen Mary's 1916 National Savings card to a horse-bus.
All year, daily: January–March and October–December, 9–4.30; April–September, 9–6   Small fee

Lamberhurst: Mr Heaver's Noted Model Museum and Craft Village
Forstal Farm, Lamberhurst (0892 890711)
Just ½ mile off A262, just before B2162 crossroads
Illuminated and animated models and dioramas (Victorian London, fairground, World Wars I and II, Rome etc). Craft shops in village street setting. Puppet workshop. Tea-room, picnic area, farm shop.   D
Daily: 10–6   Small fee

Maidstone: Tyrwhitt Museum of Carriages
Mill Street, Maidstone (0622 54497)
Near Archbishop's Palace by the River Medway
Wide-ranging collection of over 50 carriages (the largest in England) displayed in the 14th-century Archbishop's Palace stables. A Russian droshky too!
Throughout the year: Monday–Saturday, 10–1, 2–5; April–September: also Sunday, 2–5; BHM, 11–5

Ramsgate: Model Village
Westcliff, Ramsgate (0843 592543)
On cliff-top promenade above ferry terminal
A charming reproduction of England's most beautiful countryside and buildings in miniature. Visited by Royalty. A 'must' for children.
Good Friday–October: daily, 9.30 to dusk

Rochester: Dickens Centre
Eastgate House, High Street, Rochester (0634 44176)
A fascinating award-winning centre in the annexe of a finely turreted and gabled 16th-century house with timber framing and brick nogging. Tableaux with sound and light, life-size model characters, miniature theatre sets, biographical displays, first editions, memorabilia. Famous Swiss chalet in garden.
All year: daily, 10–12.30, 2–5.30. Closed Christmas holiday period, NYD and GF

Sandwich: Precinct Toy Museum
38 Harnet Street, Sandwich
Off Strand Street at Junction with The Butchery
A lifetime's collection of toys, dolls, dolls' houses and miniatures spanning the last 120 years.
Easter–September: Monday–Saturday, 10–5; Sunday, 2–5.
October: Saturday and Sunday, 2–5   Small fee

Smallhythe: Smallhythe Place (NT)
Smallhythe, near Tenterden (0580 62334)
On B2082 to Rye, 2 miles SE of Tenterden
A gem of a 16th-century half-timbered house (one of a perfect grouping) holds memories of the great actress Dame Ellen Terry who lived here for nearly 30 years. A fascinating collection of costumes, pictures and memorabilia both personal and theatrical. Small attractive garden.
April–October: Saturday–Wednesday, 2–6 or dusk if earlier (LA: ½ hour before closing)

INDUSTRIAL

Chatham: Brook Pumping Station
Solomon's Road, Chatham (0634 362847)
Rear of multi-storey car-park in The Brook
A scheduled Ancient Monument houses a unique pair of early Diesel engines, pumping machinery and other equipment representative of local industry and public services.
Saturday, 9.30–1.30; Tuesday, 7.30–9.30   Small fee

Dungeness: Dungeness 'A' Power Station
CEGB, Dungeness, Romney Marsh (0679 20461: ext 238)
4 miles SE of Lydd
Modern atomic power station: turbo generators, machines and gas circulators can be seen working. Also control room, fuelling and pile cap. Short film. Tea/coffee and lunches available.
By appointment, all year: daily, 9–7.30

Faversham: Chart Gunpowder Mills
Westbrook Walk, Faversham (0795 534542)
Off Stonebridge Way
Well-restored 18th-century water-mills and grinding mechanism once part of a Royal Gunpowder Factory which supplied Nelson and Wellington. Gunpowder made here for 400 years.
Easter – end of September: 2.30–4   Free

Northfleet: Blue Circle Heritage Centre
The Creek, Northfleet, near Gravesend (0474 323598)
Down College Road or Grove Road off A226 Gravesend–Dartford road
Nothing like as 'dry' a subject as it might seem! Cement, so often taken for granted, comes into its own in an area where it's been made for over 100 years. Well-known Blue Circle tell a fascinating story with a cooperage, a re-constructed cement laboratory, tool and sack displays, an impressive model railway, sailing-barge story, cements that built the pyramids – and illustrations by that 'Old Master' of the comic, Heath Robinson.
All the year: Thursday, 11–4   Free

Tonbridge: Milne Museum
The Slade, Tonbridge (0732 364726)
No fewer than 5,000 items of historical equipment, books and records dealing with the history of that taken-for-granted servant, electricity. Gordon Gallery has working models with background clearly displayed. Fittingly housed in Tonbridge's former generating station.
All year: Monday and Wednesday, 9–5; Tuesday, 9–1   Free

Tunbridge Wells: David Salomon's House
Broomhill Road, Southborough, near Tunbridge Wells (0892 38614)
Designed by Decimus Burton and first house in Britain to use electricity domestically. Family memorabilia of two brothers: the elder, a leader of the 19th-century campaign for Jewish Civil Rights; the younger, an inventor of international standing.
All the year: Monday, Wednesday and Friday, 2–5   Free

LOCAL AND HERITAGE

Canterbury: Canterbury Centre
St Alphege Lane, Canterbury (0227 457009)
Off Palace Street, 2 minutes from cathedral
12th-century redundant church of St Alphege converted into a permanent centre for exhibitions connected with Canterbury, past, present and future. Models, slide/tape shows and video, book stall, refreshments.
All year: Tuesday–Saturday, 10.30–5   Free

Canterbury: Heritage Museum
Stour Street, Canterbury (0227 452747)
Off St Peter's Street, by GPO
A magical time-walk through Canterbury's 2,000-year-long history. Set on the banks of the River Stour in the beautiful medieval Poor Priests' Hospital. Presented with modern artistry.
All year: Monday–Saturday, 10.30–4

Canterbury: Pilgrims Way Time-Walk
St Margaret's Street, Canterbury
Off the High Street, opposite Boots the Chemists; 3 minutes from the cathedral
In the redundant medieval church of St Margaret, you can travel with Chaucer's pilgrims from the Tabard Inn to Becket's shrine. A selection of Chaucer's famous tales is presented by audio-visual means and life-like models. A blend of art, literature and architecture that reflects the pilgrimage history, the Chaucerian influence and Canterbury's own charm. The visit takes approximately one hour.
All the year, daily: April–October, 9–7; November–March, 9–5.30 (LA: ½ hour before closing)

Canterbury: Royal Museum and Art Gallery
18 High Street, Canterbury (0227 452747)
Small museum of local and general interest; art gallery which stages periodic exhibitions and displays its own paintings, including those by Canterbury's Sidney Cooper, who specialized in huge pastoral scenes.
All the year: Monday–Saturday, 10–5   Free

Canterbury: Tabor Barns
11 All Saints Lane, Canterbury (0227 462570)
Off St Peter's Street, near King's Bridge
Museum with a difference! 30-minute audio-visual presentation of the history of Canterbury told by a monk and a Tudor housemaid.
Easter–September: Monday–Friday, 11 and 2   Small fee

Chatham: Medway Heritage Centre
Dock Road, Chatham (0634 407116)
5 minutes walk from town hall. Opposite Fort Amherst
Highlights the story of the Medway from Sheerness to Allington. It is variously and well displayed in the locally much-loved landmark of now redundant 13th-century St Mary's which stands sentinel above the river.
April–October: Wednesday–Saturday, 10–4; Sunday, 2–5.
November–March: Wednesday, 10–4; Sunday, 2–4
    Small fee

Cranbrook: Cranbrook Museum
Carriers Road, Cranbrook (0580 713497)
Intriguing Boyd Alexander collection of birds, and items of local historic interest, including World War II exhibits, in a fine 15th-century timbered building.
March, October and November: Wednesday, Thursday, Saturday, 2–4.30. April–September: Tuesday–Saturday, 2–4.30   Small fee

Dartford: Dartford Borough Museum
Market Street, Dartford (0322 343555)
At entrance to Dartford Central Park
Lively museum stages temporary and permanent exhibitions telling the story, through archaeology, history, natural history and geology, of Dartford and district from Roman times to present day. Exhibits include 'Darenth Bowl', a priceless Christian relic from the Dark Ages; also a reconstructed draper's shop.
All year, daily: Monday–Friday (except Wednesday), 12.30–5.30; Saturday, 9–1, 2–5   Free

Deal: Deal Archaeological Collection
Deal Library, Broad Street, Deal (0304 374726)
First turn S of the pier
Local archaeological treasures spanning 5,000 years.
All year: Monday, Tuesday and Thursday, 9.30–6; Wednesday, 9.30–1; Friday and Saturday, 9.30–5   Free

Dover: Dover Museum
Ladywell, Dover (0304 201066)
Off High Street, beside Maison Dieu
History and natural history of Dover including Victoriana, fine ship models, clocks and watches, Cinque Ports banner, ceramics – and a huge polar bear.   D
All year, daily (except Wednesday and Sunday), 10–4.45   Free

Dover: Maison Dieu
Town Hall, Biggin Street, Dover (0304 201200)
Centre of town at seaward end of High Street (A2)
Founded by Richard de Burgh in 1221 for 'maintenance of poor and infirm pilgrims' travelling to or from the Continent. In its magnificent interior are stained glass windows, flags, regalia, armour, portraits of some of the Lords Warden of the Cinque Ports, and the Dover Patrol Book of Remembrance.   D
All year, daily: Monday–Friday, 9–4.30; Saturday, 9–11.30   Free

Dover: Old Town Gaol
Dover Town Hall, Biggin Street, Dover (0304 281066)
Lies between High Street and Pedestrianized shopping precinct in the centre of the town
The fascinating world of a Victorian court and prison brought to life by the latest animation and audio-visual techniques.
Daily: inc BHs: 10–5

Dymchurch: New Hall
Dymchurch, Romney Marsh (0679 872142)
Near St Peter and St Paul's Church
Although built in 1580, this court-room of the Lords of the

Level is still known as 'New'. Displays and exhibits connected with bailiffs and jurats of Romney Marsh.
Office hours   Free

Faversham: *Fleur de Lis Heritage Centre and Museum*
Preston Street, Faversham (0795 534542)
Award-winning information centre in 15th-century building. Displays, some audio-visual, run gamut from breweries and brickfields to World Wars I and II. Admirable local effort. Bookshop.
Monday–Saturday, 9.30–1 and 2–4 (Easter–end of September, 4.30). Closed Thursday and BH   Small fee

Folkestone: *Folkestone Museum and Art Gallery*
Grace Hill, Folkestone (0303 578583)
Off main street down to harbour
Museum of local, natural and social history and archaeology. Adjoining art gallery shows a variety of temporary exhibitions.
All year: Monday, Tuesday, Thursday and Friday, 9–5.30; Wednesday, 9–1; Saturday, 9–5   Free

Gravesend: *Gravesend Museum*
High Street, Gravesend
High Street, leads down directly to Town pier
Houses a collection of local historical items dating back to prehistoric times. Also an especially interesting section of items excavated from the Roman site at nearby Springhead.
Weekdays (except Wednesday), 2–5; Saturday, 10–1   Free

Hythe: *Local History Room*
Oaklands, Stade Street, Hythe (0303 66152)
A fascinating display on the history of one of the original Cinque Ports, the Confederation itself, defence of the Channel coast and smuggling on Romney Marsh. Also exhibits of local archaeological and everyday interest.
All year, daily (except Wednesday, Sunday and BH): Monday, 9.30–1, 2–6; Tuesday and Thursday, 9.30–1, 2–5; Friday, 9.30–1, 2–7; Saturday, 9.30–1, 2–4   Free

Lydd: Lydd Town Museum
Town Hall, Queen's Road, Lydd, Romney Marsh (0679 20366)
Local interest exhibits connected with smuggling and unusual kettle-net fishing, farm implements, period costumes, an 1890 manual fire-engine and a station horse-bus.
June–September: Wednesday, Saturday, Sunday, 2.30–5   Small fee; under-16s free

Maidstone: Maidstone Museum and Art Gallery
St Faith's Street, Maidstone (0622 54497)
Beautiful Elizabethan Chillington Manor, in garden setting, houses collection of natural history and local industry, costumes, ceramics and furniture, paintings and Japanese art.
All year: Monday–Saturday, 10–5.30   Free

Margate: Old Town Hall Museum
Market Place, Margate (0843 225511)
Off Marine Drive, near harbour
Paintings, prints, photos and memorabilia trace Margate's development from fishing village to rumbustious seaside resort of drinking, gambling and duelling before Victorian prudery took over. Then modern seaside resort beloved of theatrical celebrities and East Enders' 'knees-up' outings. Also 19th-century police station and court-room. See also Tudor House Museum (below) 2 minutes walk away.
May–September: Tuesday–Saturday, 10–1, 2–4   Small fee

Margate: Tudor House and Museum
King Street, Margate (0843 225511)
Opposite harbour mole
Oldest and most beautiful domestic building in Margate, dating from first quarter of the 16th century, restored to original state. Exhibits and graphics vividly recreate life in Thanet from neolithic times to 17th century. See also Town Hall Museum (above), 2 minutes walk away.
May–September: Tuesday–Saturday, 10–1, 2–4   Small fee

Museums

Milton Regis: Court Hall Museum
High Street, Milton Regis (0795 22162)
Mid-15th-century timbered building with chequered career as court, school and gaol. Small museum of well-displayed local interest.
April–September: every Saturday, 2.30–5.30   Small fee

Minster: Minster Abbey Gatehouse
Minster, Sheppey (0795 872303 during opening hours or 0795 872903)
Adjoining Abbey Church
Sturdy medieval gatehouse of one of Kent's earliest Benedictine nunneries (sacked by the Danes in AD 835). Now a museum of Island history. Spectacular roof-top view.
GF, Easter and Spring BH weekends, 2–5. Mid-July–September, daily, except Thursday, 2–5   Small fee

Ospringe: Maison Dieu (EH)
Canterbury Road, Ospringe, near Faversham (0795 762604)
In Ospringe on A2, ½ mile W of Faversham
Early 16th-century timber-framed building incorporates what was once a medieval hostel for pilgrims (and kings) *en route* to Canterbury. 3 rooms contain Roman pottery, Saxon artefacts and displays by go-ahead Faversham Society.
EH summer season, standard   Small fee

Rochester: Guildhall Museum
High Street, Rochester (0634 48717)
200 yards from bridge
Finest 17th-century civic building in Kent, designed by Wren, with magnificent plaster ceilings given by 'from-powder-monkey-to-admiral' Cloudesley Shovel. Wide range of local exhibits from arms and armour to model boats, and from dolls and toys to model Short's flying-boats.
All year, daily: 10–12.30, 2–5.30 (Not XD or GF)   Free

Sandwich: Guildhall Museum
Cattle Market, Sandwich (0304 617197)
Conducted tours of Guildhall and original panelled court-room; Victorian photos, moot horn, thumbscrews, begging-bowl and other artefacts.
Monday and Thursday: tours at 10.45, 11.45, 2.15, 3.15   Small fee

Sevenoaks: Sevenoaks Museum
Buckhurst Lane, Sevenoaks (0732 452384)
Off High Street
The story of Sevenoaks is told through an interesting variety of 18th- to 20th-century domestic objects, photographs, Roman artefacts, local geology etc and a special section dealing with local trades and industries.
Monday–Wednesday and Friday: 9.30–5.30; Thursday: 9.30–7; Saturday: 9–5 (closed BH)   Free

Tenterden: Tenterden & District Museum
Station Road, Tenterden (0580 64310)
Off W end of High Street
1,000 years of Wealden history, in maps, pictures and exhibits, includes Cinque Ports story, oasts, railways and William Caxton.
All year, January–Easter and November–December: Saturday and Sunday, 2–4. June–September: Sunday–Thursday, 2–5, Friday–Saturday, 10–5. Easter–May and October: daily, 2–5   Small fee

Tunbridge Wells: Tunbridge Wells Museum and Art Gallery
Mount Pleasant, Tunbridge Wells (0892 26121: ext 171)
At top of main street, next to town hall.
Tunbridge ware, dolls and toys, domestic bygones; local natural history, geology and archaeology collections.
All year: Monday–Friday, 10–5.30; Saturday, 9.30–5. Closed BHs, Easter Saturday and Tuesday after spring and summer BHs.   Free

TRANSPORT

Ashford: Railway Research Room
Church Road, Ashford (0233 20649)

From post office, down Tufton Street, then left into Church Road
Ideal browsing ground for railway spotter and fanatic alike, on vast range of material accumulated during Ashford's heyday as a huge Southern Railway workshop.
All the year (except BHs): Monday and Tuesday, 9.30–6; Wednesday, 9.30–5; Thursday and Friday, 9.30–7; Saturday, 9–5   Free

Broadstairs: Crampton Tower
High Street, Broadstairs (0843 62078)
Railway museum dedicated to the work of Thomas Russell Crampton, the eminent Victorian railway engineer, a native of Broadstairs.
May–mid-September: Sunday, Monday, Tuesday & Friday, 2.30–5   Small fee

Canterbury: Motor Museum
11 Cogans Terrace, Canterbury (0227 451718)
Off Wincheap, A28 Ashford road, via Victoria Road
Veteran and vintage cars, motor cycles, carts, prams etc; also signs, petrol globes and other automobilia. 1920s general store being developed.
Monday–Friday: 9–5. Weekends please telephone   Free

Deal: Maritime and Local History Museum
22 St George's Road, Deal (0304 362896)
Off High Street
Original boats, models, photos, charts, 15th-century sailing-ship relics and items of Deal history.
Spring BH to September: daily, 2–5   Small fee

Deal: Time-Ball Tower
Victoria Parade, Deal (0304 360897)
On sea-front
Handsomely restored 19th-century semaphore tower houses fascinating museum of signalling, satellite and maritime communication, time telegraphy etc with working models. Greenwich-actuated time-ball drops at 1 p.m. precisely.
Last week May–September: Tuesday–Saturday, 12–5
    Small fee

Dover: Dover Transport Museum
Connaught Pumping Station, Connaught Road, Dover (0304 204612)
Off Castle Hill Road on way to Deal
Local transport history: displays, vehicles, models, pictures, relics and Triple Expansion Worthington Simpson. Snacks.
Easter–end September: Sunday (except last in June) and BHs, 11–5 Small fee

Dover: Port of Dover Tours
Dover Harbour Board, Harbour House, Dover (0304 240400)
A chance to see the working of England's busiest passenger port.
By appointment (contact Mr P. Youden). All year, daily Free

Ramsgate: Maritime Museum
Pier Yard, Royal Harbour, Ramsgate (0843 587765)
4 galleries: Smeaton, Island, Rennie and Goodwin. Items of harbour interest, maritime history of Thanet, relics from Goodwin Sands wrecks, RNLI memorabilia; also harbour trail.
October–March: Tuesday and Thursday only, 11–4.
April–September: Tuesday–Friday, 11–4; Saturday and Sunday, 2–5 Small fee

Ramsgate: Ramsgate Motor Museum
Westcliff Hall, Ramsgate (0843 581948)
On cliff top above Sally Line terminal
125 Veteran-Classic cars and motor-cycles that range from Bentley and Berry de Dion to Vincent and Zedal. Also memorabilia and cinema.
Easter–30 November: daily, 10.30–6. Only Sunday in winter

Ramsgate: Viking Ship Hugin
Pegwell Bay, near Ramsgate
On A256 to Sandwich, 2 miles SW of Ramsgate
Full-size replica of a typical Viking ship which was

actually rowed and sailed from Denmark to Thanet in 1949 to celebrate the 1,500th anniversary of traditional landing of Hengist and Horsa. St Augustine's Cross nearby records an even more famous landing.
Permanent open display at all times   Free

Rochester: Kenneth Bills Motor Cycle Museum
144 High Street, Rochester (0634 814165)
Motor cyclists' mecca! Over 100 racing bikes and memorabilia collected by former TT rider. Ranging from 1912 500cc TT Model Triumph to 1977 Golden Jubilee Bonneville.
All year: Monday–Saturday, 9.30–5

Rolvenden: C.M. Booth Collection of Historic Vehicles
Falstaff Antiques, 63-7 High Street, Rolvenden (0580 214234)
Rolvenden: 2 miles SW of Tenterden on A28
10 Morgan 3-wheelers, 1913–35, only known Humber Tri-car of 1904, a 1929 Morris van and various cycles and motor-cycles. Toy and model cars and memorabilia.
All year: Monday–Saturday, 10–6. Closed most Sunday and Wednesday afternoons

Sittingbourne: Dolphin Yard Sailing Barge Museum
Crown Quay Lane, Sittingbourne (0795 24132)
On Milton Creek, 1 mile N of Sittingbourne
Former queens of the Medway, russet-sailed Thames barges, can be seen here undergoing restoration. Excellently displayed photos and exhibits in original forge and sail loft. Snacks, souvenir shop.
Mid-April–mid-October: Sunday and BHM, 11–5
                                                              Small fee

WINDMILLS AND WATERMILLS

Cranbrook: Union Mill
Stone Street, Cranbrook (0580 712256)
At west end of main street

One of the largest and finest working smock-mills in England. Original frame, built in 1814, but giant sweeps restored by local generosity. 'Union' Mill because it was owned by partnership of Cranbrook tradesmen.
Easter–September: Saturday and BHM, 2.30–5   Donation

Edenbridge: Haxted Watermill Museum
Edenbridge (0732 862914)
1½ miles W of Edenbridge
Restored watermill driving old mill machines. Mill picture gallery. Taped commentary. Restaurant, tea-room.
April–May, weekends: 12–5. June–September, daily: 12–5

Frant: Bartley Mill
Bells Yew Green, near Frant
On B2169, 2 miles SE of Tunbridge Wells
A step over the Sussex border – but too good to be missed! Once a hop farm, now milling organic wheat for the first time since 1900, thanks to working restoration of mill. Farm shop, teas, museum
Daily: 10–5   Small fee (OAPs free)

Herne: Herne Windmill
Herne, near Herne Bay (0227 363345)
Just off A291 at Herne
Built in 1789, this early Kentish smock-mill has been restored and is now working with its original machinery.
Early April–end September: Sunday and BHM, 2–5   Small fee

Lower Mersham: Swanton Mill
Lower Mersham, near Ashford (0233 72233)
3 miles SE of Ashford, off A20
17th-century weather-boarded watermill on the East Stour and the original Domesday site. Its restoration, in 1975, gained it a well-merited European Architectural Award. In working order, it grinds organically grown wholemeal flour which can be purchased. Exhibition of mills and milling. Garden, 3-acre nature reserve with lake. Shop, museum.
April–October: Saturday and Sunday, 3–5

Margate: Draper's Windmill
St Peter's Footpath, off Millmead Road, Margate (0843/291696)
Last remaining of three built in 1850. Restored as operational windmill by Mill Trust.
End of May–mid-September: Sunday, 2.30–5 July and August: Thursday, 6.30–8 Small fee

Meopham: Meopham Windmill
The Green, Meopham, near Gravesend (0474 812110)
Centre of Meopham, A227, 4 miles S of Gravesend
An unusual hexagonal smock-windmill, built 1801, with imposing sweeps and fantail renewed. Looks down onto famous village green and cricket ground.
July–mid-September: Sunday, 2.30–4.30 (LA 4.30) Small fee

Sandwich: White Mill and Folk Museum
Sandwich (0304 612076)
1 mile W of Sandwich on A257
A 1760 smock-mill with machinery intact and exterior (including 4 new sweeps) completely restored. Also small local folk museum.
Easter–mid-September: Sunday and BHM, 2.30–5.30
Small fee

Smeeth: Evegate Mill
Smeeth, near Ashford (0233 72234)
5 miles SE of Ashford, off A20
Now an antique shop, this beautifully situated 17th-century watermill (not working) is open to mill enthusiasts by appointment. Straight out of Constable!
Donation

Stelling Minnis: Stelling Minnis Windmill
Stelling Minnis (0227 720358)
8 miles S of Canterbury just off Stone Street, B2068
In pleasant rural surroundings, this smock-mill, 1866, on site of former mill, is in full working order.
April–September: Sunday, GF and BH Saturday and Monday, 2–5 Small fee

Wateringbury: Brattles Mill
Mill Lane, Wateringbury, near Maidstone (0622 812363)
4 miles SW of Maidstone
18th-century watermill (not working) on site mentioned in Domesday Book. Can be seen from road.
By appointment with owner　　　　　　　　　　Donation

Westwell Watermill
Westwell, near Ashford (0233 712500)
Turn S off A252 from Challock Lees down delightful lane. Situated just beyond the church
Everything a watermill should be – including a mill-pond lapping at the upstairs sitting-room window! *Not* open to the public but worth viewing even at a distance – and you *might* find the very jolly miller in expansive mood.　　Free

Wittersham: Stocks Mill
Wittersham, near Tenterden
Beside B2082, 1 mile E of Wittersham
A picturesque and well-preserved post-mill (1781) in private hands. Machinery removed but interior and exterior fully renovated.
June–September: Sunday and BH, 2.30–5. Also Easter and May BH weekends　　　　　　　　　　　　　　Small fee

Woodchurch: Woodchurch Windmill
Woodchurch, near Ashford (0233 86701)
Off B2067, between Tenterden and Ham Street; opposite the church
In poor repair after World War II, it has had to be completely dismantled. The tower is now bravely re-built and mill machinery has been installed. Photographic exhibition.
April–September: Sunday, 2.30–4.30　　　　　Small fee

Seaside Attractions

AMUSEMENT PARKS AND ARCADES

Dymchurch: Phoenix Amusements
Dymchurch, near Hythe
Alongside sands, off A259
A family fun park (next to splendid sands) that includes Olde Tyme Fairground Favourites as well as modern rides and indoor amusements area. Take-away refreshments.
March–May: Weekends. Late May–late September: daily.
Admission free

Folkestone: Rotunda
Marine Parade, Folkestone
Just W of the harbour
Big fairground and amusement arcade, novelty putting course and boating pool. Huge Sunday market held adjacent.
Daily: summer season
Admission free

Margate: Bembon Brothers Theme Park
Marine Terrace, Margate (0843 227011)
On sea-front to W of harbour
Europe's most breathtaking 'white knuckle' rides: Britain's tallest Big Wheel, Looping Star, Mary Rose Swing Boat, Zeppelin Tower, Ghost Train, Scenic Railway and many others. Also rides specially for younger children. Barbecue and picnic areas, 4 cafeterias, kiosks.
Mid-April–end-May: Saturday–Sunday, 10.30–6.30. June–mid-September: Monday–Friday, 10.30–6; Saturday and

Sunday, 10.30–6.30
Inclusive fee covers all rides   (under-5s free)

Ramsgate: Pleasure Park
Marina Esplanade, Ramsgate (0843 591080)
Just N of the harbour
Thanet's answer to Blackpool's Golden Mile! Largest amusement arcade in Kent: pool tables, videos, fruit machines etc. Also Pleasure Park with dodgems, ghost trains etc. Soft play area (25,000 balls), Galaxy Space Ride and Honda Mini Bikes for under-10s. Snack bar and café, gift shop.
All the year, daily, 10–10. Rides etc only Easter–September
Admission free

BEACHES AND COASTAL TOWNS

TT indicates that a Town Trail leaflet is available from the local Tourist Information Centre.

Barton's Point
Recreation and picnic area features: a lake with boats, pitch and putt, croquet, outdoor bowls, BMX bikes, children's adventure playground. If wet, try Sheerness.

Birchington
Unspoilt entrance to the Isle of Thanet and to its ever-growing urban conglomeration of seaside resorts that, unbroken, stretch through Margate to Broadstairs and Ramsgate. Birchington sets the Thanet pattern of low, grass-topped chalk cliffs, protected by sea-wall and buttresses; with sandy bays sometimes separated by barriers of seaweed-covered rocks. It has four such bays:
  Minnis Bay: wide expanse of sand makes it the most popular. Putting.   Parking fee
  Grenham Bay: short walk to sand with rocks at east end.   Parking fee
  Beresford Gap: reserved largely for power-boats and water-skiing etc.
  Epple Bay: prettiest of the four, its sandy bay,

surrounded by chalk cliffs, is penetrated by steps and ramp.
Cliff-top walks. Powell-Cotton Wildlife and Ethnographic Museum.

Broadstairs
Pleasantly unsophisticated. Has no fewer than 7 sandy chalk-cliffed bays: Dumpton, Louisa, Viking, Stone, Joss, Kingsgate (steps, some rocks) and Botany. All have comparatively easy access.
 Viking Bay, sheltered by 16th-century jetty, with cliff-lift, bandstand and gardens above, is perhaps the most popular – especially with children, for its donkey rides, Punch & Judy, trampolines etc. Lifeguards and patrol boat. TT
North Foreland Lighthouse and Kingsgate Castle; Dickens House Museum; Crampton Tower Railway Museum; Dickens' Bleak House.

Camber
Magnificent dune-backed beach – miles of it. Even big holiday camp and urbanization at its worst cannot detract from the spaciousness. In Sussex – but never mind! Cafés, souvenir shops, amusement arcade.

Cliftonville
A Hove to Margate's Brighton. Equally good sands here but steps or cliff-lift down to them. Wide range of amusements, cafés etc, including bandstand, The Oval and an aquarium/dolphinarium; putting, table tennis, pitch and putt.

Deal
Of the sea rather than the seaside. Its steeply shelving shingle beach and modern 1,000-foot pier are ideal for anglers; bathers, however, should stay close to the shore and keep an eye open for the hoisting of the red flag (lifeguards). Boat trips to the notorious Goodwin Sands ('Shyppe Swallower'). TT
 Caesar's landing-place, Deal Castle, Time Ball Tower and Cinque Ports golf course. Also maritime, local history, costume and Victoriana museums.

Dover

Castle dominated and alive with maritime interest. Magnificent 'White Cliffs' stand sentinel to either side of Eastern and Western Docks, as busy with ships as a bus station with buses.

On the cliffs: Blériot Memorial at North Fall Meadow near the magnificent Norman castle ('the Key to England'), Saxon church and Roman pharos. Dazzling docks views from terraced car-park off minor road to St Margaret's Bay. And for good measure, in the town below, the Roman Painted House and Maison Dieu. From the Prince of Wales Pier (café and angling) there are exciting views of Hovercraft arrival and departure.

Interesting and sweeping inner harbour promenade drops down to steeply shelving shingle beach: ideal sheltered water for canoeing and sailing. Kiosks.

Dungeness

A waste of steep sloping shingle – and desolation. A world of its own!

Swirling currents make swimming *dangerous*. But Dungeness has a wind-surfing lake, the Romney, Hythe & Dymchurch Railway (one-third scale), railway terminus, a lifeboat, 2 nuclear power stations, a bird reserve, 3 lighthouses – one converted, one redundant and the third magnificently stentorian in swirling mist.

For the rest, shacks and shanties – but one pub, The Pilot, and much fresh fish for sale.

Atmospheric! Eerie!

Dymchurch

Kent's finest and safest sand beach, backed by its most massive, Roman-based sea-wall, necessary to prevent the flooding of low-lying Romney Marsh behind it – and 7½ feet below it! Safe bathing except at south end.

In the town, shades of the notorious smuggler-cum-clergyman, Dr Syn, and his gang.

More practically, cafés, Phoenix amusement arcade and fairground, pub, fish-and-chips and 'all the usual seaside razzamatazz'. Also, refurbished, No. 24 Martello Tower (a circular, Napoleonic coastal defence fort) and 'Lords of the

Level' New Hall, an 18th-century law court.

Folkestone
Still Queen of the South-East, a happy dichotomy of popular and select.

Directly east of the harbour are splendid sands (rocks at the other end can be dangerous). Crazy golf, fish-market, souvenir shops, cafés, kiosk. Above, built round the Martello tower, is the East Cliff open-air leisure complex (tennis, bowls, pitch and putt). Café. Huge, grass, cliff-edge car-park – ideal for a lazy day.

Further east still, vast, overgrown landslip of The Warren through which the Folkestone–Dover line burrows dramatically. Mainly sandy beach with some rocks. Kiosk. Splendid sea-wall walk beneath majestic 'White Cliffs' half-way to Dover.

To the west is the Rotunda, fairground and amusement arcade, boating and open-air swimming-pools. Shingly beach with groynes.

Huge Sunday market. Famous cliff-top Leas, Leas Cliff Hall, bandstand and New Metropole Arts Centre are reached lazily by water-operated lift or more energetically by shady cliff paths. TT

Greatstone-on-Sea
Scene of war-time Operation PLUTO (Pipeline Under the Ocean). Splendid sandy beach – but depressing and drear ribbon development. At low tide, sections of D-Day Mulberry Harbour are visible. Seldom crowded. Pub, shops.

Romney, Hythe & Dymchurch Railway nearby. Footpath on sea-wall to St Mary's Bay.

Herne Bay
Has known hard times but is having a face-lift.

Seven miles of safe but varying beaches, from Swalecliffe to Minnis Bay, come under its sway. Stands high in the National Sunshine League! Gardens, 80-foot clock-tower and bandstand are a reminder of its high 19th-century aspirations. Its mile-long pier (second only to Southend's), ravaged by storm, rust and fire, is sadly truncated but now carries imaginative leisure centre where, amongst other sports, top-class roller-hockey is still played. Trampoline, helter-skelter, roundabout and 'amusements' nearby.

Best bathing, off shingle sloping to sand, lies to west between pier and Hampton. There is a power-boat channel between Hampton and Swalecliffe.

Eastwards: amusement arcades, bandstand, cafés, pubs, restaurants, near promenade-side parking. Kings Hall in summer season offers shows and café.

East Cliff walk along grassy Downs and on to picturesque Bishopsbourne Glen: picnicking, sun-bathing but steep wooden steps to beach.

East again loom sailors' landmark, the twin Reculver Towers. A few steps down to rocky beach. Pleasant sea-wall walk still further east to Plum Pudding Island and Minnis Bay TT

Hythe
Sleepy but charming country town once a famous Cinque Port and still well worth exploring – especially St Leonard's church with its high-stacked 2,000 skulls and 8,000 thigh bones.

The sea, ½ mile distant, has deserted it. Steep, shingle beach leads to some sand at low tide. There's always the shady Royal Military Canal (angling, boating).

Intriguing Malthouse Arcade.

Kingsdown
Fishing village now partly urbanized. Steep shingle beach – and to the south, a firing-range (so look out for the red flag!). Rising cliffs, with golf course, make inviting walks with fine views of Straits of Dover shipping. Walmer and Deal offer 'if wet' facilities.

Langdon Bay
Tiny bay, dramatically cliff-sheltered, near Dover. Accessible only from cliff-top by steep, vertiginous but railed path. Gloriously uncivilized. No amenities whatever.

Leysdown
A weekend 'beside the seaside' is the *raison d'être* for this stretch of 'caravan 'n chalet' country on Sheppey. Easy access to sandy beaches. Coastal park has nature trail, picnic areas, pitch and putt, kiosks and toilets. If wet: Bingo, amusement arcades, cafés and pubs.

Littlestone-on-Sea
It has, thankfully, forgotten its early 1900s 'big-time' ambitions. A quiet, old-fashioned resort. Safe bathing on sandy beach. Fine golf course, putting, cafés, children's playground.
    New Romney well worth a visit.

Lydd-on-Sea
A mile or more from the interesting town with its airport and imposing 'Cathedral of the Marsh' church. Sand, backed by a shingle bank. More bungalows – and the Romney, Hythe & Dymchurch Railway. Safe swimming, wind-surfing.   TT from New Romney TIC

Margate
Brash and boisterous. Splendid Marine Sands (backed by shops, cafés, amusement arcades and Bembons' huge Amusement Park) are wide and safe for bathing unless red flag is flying. Can be very crowded in season.
    Caves and grotto, Tudor House Museum, Salmestone Grange, Draper's Mill, Winter Gardens, harbour jetty.   TT

Minster in Sheppey
Abbey Gatehouse and Minster stand on clay cliffs above a sand and mud beach, scattered with stones. It makes amends with rich hauls of cockles and fossils. Lifeguards patrol at weekends. The Leas afford fine views, grassy areas for games and picnics, and footpath to Warden Point.

Palm Bay
Sand but with some pebbles. Pitch and putt and Margate nearby.

Pegwell Bay and Cliffsend
Sand and mud beach with marshy grass behind. Viking Ship *Hugin* and picnic site, St Augustine's Cross, lavender farm, golf course, Richborough and Sandwich quite near. Sea disappears at low tide.

Ramsgate
Combines an almost Riviera marina with bustling commercial docks, and Victorian elegance with modern amusements.

Below splendid Royal Esplanade on cliff-top, there is a sandy beach. To the east of the harbour is a smaller beach of good sand, with adjoining fairground, amusement arcade, café and casino. Harbour Trail.

Sally Line offers day trips to Dunkirk, Bruges, Ypres and even the Stella Artois Brewery.

Motor Museum, model village on esplanade, Spitfire Museum at RAF Manston, autumn 'Festival of Light' illuminations, Pugin's St Augustine's church.

St Margaret's Bay
Its shingle and rocks haven't deterred numerous Channel swimmers from heading out to sea for France from here. Encircling cliffs make it extremely picturesque but rocks, cliffs and groynes militate against carefree swimming. Splendid cliff walks: to the north, Dover Patrol Monument; to the south, lighthouses and windmill. Excellent pub mentioned in *The Scarlet Pimpernel*, on promenade. Pines Gardens nearby. Kiosk.

St Mary's Bay
A sandy beach divided by wooden groynes with a holiday camp across the road. Romney Marsh mystery and lanes inland.

Sandgate
Can be reached on foot or by car from Folkestone along seaside toll road almost reminiscent of the Riviera.

Beach, backed by promenade and busy Hythe road, is still shingle. Splendid in winter storms when south-easters send spray fountaining over H.G. Wells' Beach

Cottage – and others – into main road. Shops, pubs, cafés.

Sandwich Bay
Rather bleak and isolated, 2 miles from town. Access by footpath or toll-road with beach-side parking. Sloping beach of sand and shingle. Mobile refreshments-van.

Sandwich Bay Nature Reserve, Gazen Salts Nature Reserve, two famous golf courses – St George's and Prince's, Naturist beach among dunes at rear; and, of course, Sandwich itself and Roman Richborough Castle.

Seasalter
Romans enjoyed its shellfish; salt was once made here – and it had a mention in the Domesday Book. Now largely caravan and chalet territory with roadside parking. Shingle beach with rocky outcrops, and mud flats across which the sea disappears at low tide. Rock pools. Whitstable nearby.

Sailing Club. 9-hole golf course. Mount Ephraim gardens nearby. Pubs and cafés.

Sheerness
Where the Nore Mutiny started against inhuman Navy conditions (1797) and where Nelson's body was brought from Trafalgar (1805). Today, above a sand and shingle beach, there is a massive mile-long sea wall with wide views of Essex, the Thames Estuary and its shipping. Lifeguards patrol at weekends but bathing near the Swale estuary is to be avoided.

Leisure centre with open-air swimming pool, children's play area including 'Galleon Adventure Complex', sea-front gardens, picnic areas, traditional amusements.

Car/passenger ferry to Flushing.

Shell Ness
Accessible on foot. Strictly for Naturists and bird-watchers. Further along this Sheppey coast is Kent's most isolated church, at Harty.

The Swale
Both the south Sheppey and north Kent shores are largely

marshland put to good use as nature reserves: King's Hill Farm, Elmley Marshes, Shell Ness, South Swale Nature Reserve. Ideal for birdwatchers, walkers and lovers of the isolated. The Saxon Shore Way runs its length.

Tankerton
Genteely trim and quiet. Separated from Whitstable by a tree-covered hill, crowned by a ship's mast and cannon. Street parking behind pleasant grass slopes and promenade. Groynes; shingle beach gently slopes to low-tide sand. Kiosk.

One-mile finger of shingle and sand ('The Street' or 'Street Stones') juts out from beach. Uncovered at low tide to reveal a wealth of shells – but watch the tide, *and* swimming can be dangerous.

Walmer
Deal's still quieter twin. Again easy access to steeply shelving shingle. Walmer Castle, official residence of the Lords Warden of the Cinque Ports, stands on adjacent coast road. Fishing-boats and the *Hampshire Rose* lifeboat are launched excitingly down steep incline.

Putting, paddling and crazy golf on big expanse of Walmer Green.

Warden Point
'Warden' here means 'watch-hill'. Splendid views of Thames Estuary shipping, war-time off-shore forts, and tricks played by slithering cliffs – on which care should be taken. Sand and even muddier beach. Leysdown amenities near to hand.

Westbrook
Gently shelving sand with rocks on either side. Putting, bowls. Margate round the corner.

Westgate-on-Sea
Offers easy access and gently shelving sandy beach at both St Mildred's Bay and West Bay, though the latter has some rocky outcrops. Putting, table tennis, kiosk. Lively Margate nearby.

Whitstable

Still synonymous with oysters, though now on miniscule scale due to pollution and storm. West beach is main area. Groynes; shingle slopes down to sand at low tide. Unspoilt – but strongish tide.

Interesting small harbour (from which first steamer left for Australia) and in-shore lifeboat station. Off Island Wall and Middle Wall picturesque alleys of white weatherboarded fishermen's cottages, and black-tarred boat and sail sheds. Ideal yachting centre with power-boat channel that helped the rise to fame of world champion water-skier Liz Hobbs. Kiosk.

LIFEBOATS AND LIGHTHOUSES

Lifeboats other than those listed below can be seen afloat at Dover, Ramsgate and Sheerness.

There are also two lighthouses on the South Foreland; one is redundant, and the other is likely to become so. Neither is open to the public but they are still well worth a pleasant walk – with a camera.

Broadstairs: North Foreland Lighthouse
North Foreland, Broadstairs (0843 61869)
Off B2052, 1½ miles N of Broadstairs
Oldest (1691) working lighthouse in England. 62 feet high and 180 feet above sea-level, it affords fine views over the bay.
Easter–September: daily, 1 p.m. to one hour before sunset (operational duties permitting) Free

Dungeness: Dungeness Lifeboat
Dungeness, Romney Marsh (0679 20276)
Near the Pilot Inn
Virtually unsinkable *Alice Upjohn*, (vital statistics: 37 feet 6 inches, 11 feet 6 inches, 13 tons) has saved 23 lives. Souvenir shop. Illustrated history available.
In the season: daily Donation

Dungeness: Dungeness New Lighthouse
1 mile S of the Pilot Inn on minor road from Lydd across Denge Marsh and Beach

Splendid, slim-line, modern lighthouse, 140 feet high and black-and-white banded. Built in 1961 of 12-foot diameter pre-cast concrete rings, with a xenon electric arc-light that ranges over 23 miles, and a bull-voiced foghorn that it is well worth waiting to hear in misty weather. Fourth in line, it magnificently maintains the Dungeness lighthouse tradition dating back to 1615.
Sadly, *not* open to the public

Dungeness: Dungeness Old Lighthouse
Dungeness, near Lydd (0679 21300)
By-roads, 4 miles SE of Lydd
Old lighthouse with 167 steps to the top, where the Great Lens weighs 3 tons. Demonstration of how lantern was worked and cleaned. In eerie setting of desolate shingle banks. Near New Lighthouse, Dungeness Atomic Power Station and terminus of Romney, Hythe & Dymchurch Railway (narrow gauge).
April–September: 9.30–5.30   Small fee

Margate: Margate Lifeboat
The Rendezvous, Margate Harbour (0843 221613)
Lifeboat *Silver Jubilee*, Inshore Rescue Boat and many other items pertaining to the RNLI's work. Souvenir shop, 'lifeboat' kiddie ride, overhead viewing platform.
Mid-May–end September: daily, 10–1, 2–5   Donation

Walmer: Walmer Lifeboat
Walmer, Deal (0304 375816)
On the sea-front at Walmer Green, 1 mile N of Walmer Castle
RNLI's *Hampshire Rose*, named in honour of single-handed, round-the-world yachtsman Sir Alec Rose. Poised on the shingle beach ready for a dash to 'shyppe-swallower' Goodwin Sands. It is one of only 2 'beach-launches' in the United Kingdom.
All the year   Donation

SHOPPING CENTRES

Even amid the rising tide of inflation, window shopping, be it at auction or arcade, antique shop or craft display, market or supermarket, is still *free*.

ANTIQUES

Canterbury: Coach House Antiques
Duck Lane, St Radigund's, Northgate, Canterbury (0227 63117)
Opposite car-park and near Beggars' Roost pub, off Northgate, opposite the Jolly Sailor
'Unusual' is the keynote! A wide and individual variety of collectors' bric-à-brac items – packed into 2 floors of constantly changing stock – 'at very reasonable prices'.
All the year: Monday–Saturday, 10–5

Canterbury: Conquest House
17 Palace Street, Canterbury (0227 464587)
Nearly opposite the Archbishop's Palace
In Canterbury's 'Little Chelsea' next to the cathedral. A house with an 11th-century Norman undercroft on a Roman site and, above it, a 14th-century hall-house fronted by a picture-book 17th-century black-and-white house with handsome, projecting bay windows. No mean setting for an extensive collection of fine antiques! For good measure: its massive beams were once ship's timbers; Becket's murderers armed here; and pilgrims slept on straw in its gallery.
Monday–Saturday, 9–6

Canterbury: Revivals
19 Cobden Place, Canterbury (0227 459882)
At the far end of Palace Street
Sandwiched between two huge wall murals and with King's School's leaning, half-timbered shop opposite, Revivals is well worth a visit. Antiques and bric-à-brac, prints and china, oil paintings and cricket bats rub shoulders.
Monday–Saturday, 9–6

Folkestone: Folkestone Antiques Centre
136 Sandgate Road, Folkestone (0303 55800)
In centre of Folkestone on Hythe road
18 stands
All year: Monday–Tuesday, Thursday–Saturday, 10–5

Rolvenden: Falstaff Antiques
63-7 High Street, Rolvenden (0580 241234)
Adjoining Motor Museum
General antiques, furniture, small items and reproductions.
Daily: 9–6 but closed Wednesday p.m. and most Sundays

Sandgate: Peckwater Antiques
99 High Street, Sandgate, Folkestone (0303 49600)
On the A259 in the middle of Sandgate High Street
Georgian and Victorian furniture is a speciality.
Monday–Saturday, 10–5.30

Sandgate: Sandgate Antiques Centre
61-3 High Street, Sandgate, Folkestone (0303 38987)
In centre of town on Folkestone–Hythe road, A259
7 showrooms
All year: Monday–Saturday, 10–6; Sunday, 11–6

Sutton Valence: Sutton Valence Antiques
Sutton Valence, near Maidstone (0622 843333)
Opposite King's Head
Antiques with a view! 14 showrooms in Sutton Valence and 5,000 square feet of display space at the nearby Park Wood Industrial Estate (A274). Its wares range high, wide

Shopping Centres 181

and handsome. 4½-foot-high doll's house or 14-foot expanding Victorian table? Overwhelming German dresser-cum-sideboard or ventriloquist's careworn dummy?
  Daily: 10–5.30 (except Sunday and BHs); 9–5.30 at warehouse

Tunbridge Wells: Mission Antiques Centre
Old Methodist Church, Camden Road, Tunbridge Wells (0892 45858)
Off Mount Pleasant Road, via Monson Road, near town hall
8 stands
All year: Monday–Saturday, 9–5

Tunbridge Wells: Sawdust and Lace
100 Camden Road, Tunbridge Wells (0892 43246)
Off Mount Pleasant Road, via Monsoon Road, near town hall
Dolls from 1700s to 1960s; Teddy bears, 1915 upwards; rocking-horses, dolls' houses, prams etc
Saturday, 10–4, by appointment. Longer hours in summer, Thursday and Friday

Westerham: Dunsdale Lodge Antiques
Brasted Road, Westerham (0959 62160)
Ceramics: Early Staffordshire pottery, 18th- to 19th-century porcelain figures, lustre, Toby jugs, Stafford portrait figures.
Daily: 9–6

ARCADES

Ashford: Tufton Centre
Bounded by Apsley Street, Queen Street, Bank Street and Lower High Street
Pleasing blend of ancient (Middle Row, with its narrow 16th-century passages and overhung alleyways) and modern (the recently opened Tufton Centre, a paved pedestrian area with open squares and covered walk-

ways). In the heart of the town with splendid St Mary the Virgin Church and its peaceful 'close' just a step away.

Broadstairs: Westwood Hypermarket
St Peter's, Broadstairs
On B2053
RA Co-op has a vast range of 'bargain price' foods and household commodities. Also almost equally huge DIYs.

Canterbury: Marlowe Arcade
Rose Lane, Canterbury
Off The Parade in town centre
Spanking new arcade – with wishing-well. Revives memories of London's Burlington Arcade. Large British Home Stores and many other well-known and often trendy shops. Restaurant. Bands and choirs perform occasionally.

Chatham: Pentagon Centre
High Street, Chatham
Spacious modern centre that plays host to 91 units (including C & A on two floors and largest Boots in the south) spread roomily over 500,000 square feet.

Dartford: Blue Water Park
Off the A226 on the outskirts of Dartford
Still awaiting full planning permission. It is planned as an 'out-of-this-world' Shopping Arcade-cum-Leisure Centre to be sited in a former quarry – and to include three attractive stretches of open water! Opening Date: 1990? Worth waiting for!

Gillingham: Hempstead Valley Shopping Centre
Hempstead Valley, near Gillingham
Lies off Hoath Way, A278 between A2 and M2 (Exit 4)
In 1980 it won the title 'European Shopping Centre of the Year'. Lush greenery and water feature. Sainsbury and British Home Stores, Savacentre Hypermarket and 35 other shops. Exhibition centre, restaurant, novel fast-food area.
Monday, 10–6 (Savacentre opens 8.30); Tuesday, Wednes-

day, Thursday, 8.30–8; Friday, 8.30 a.m.–9.p.m.; Saturday, 10–6

Hythe: Malthouse Arcade
High Street, Hythe (0303 60103)
SW end of High Street
37 varied 'shops' in ancient brewery building: antiques, militaria, crafts, books, pictures etc. Garden café.
Friday, Saturday, BHM, 10–6

Maidstone: Stoneborough Centre
Pads Hill, Maidstone (0622 691130)
Behind King Street and Gabriel's Hill in city centre, off A20 from Ashford
Modern shopping complex with wide variety of shops on 3 levels and under cover.

Rochester: Fagin's Alley
23 High Street, Rochester
Almost opposite the cathedral
12 shops under one roof, largely antiques and crafts. Refreshments.

Tunbridge Wells: The Pantiles
The Pantiles, Tunbridge Wells
At S end of town at foot of London Road and beside the common
Kent's most elegant shopping centre (18th-century). Bath House, Musick Gallery, bandstand, broad, paved terraces, fine trees, shops and cafés (open-air in summer) make it an ideal place for leisurely shopping.

AUCTIONS

Canterbury: Worsfold Fine Art
40 Station Road West, Canterbury (0227 68984)
Opposite Canterbury West railway station
Fine arts and antiques, furniture, clocks. Specialist sales: books and pictures.
First Saturday each month plus regular monthly auctions

(500 lots), Thursday. Preview: well before sale, and Fridays

Chatham: Baldwin & Partners
26 Railway Street, Chatham (0634 400121)
Antiques and other effects
Monthly, first Wednesday Preview: Saturday and Tuesday before sale

Folkestone: Michael Shortall
Bayle Place, 11 Bayle Parade, Folkestone (0303 45555)
Off central shopping precinct
Fine arts and antiques and house contents
Every 2 months. Preview: day before sale

Hythe: Lawrence Butler & Co
Butler House, High Street, Hythe (0303 66022)
Auction rooms at Marine Walk Street, Hythe
Antique furniture and effects, silver, paintings etc.
Monthly: Wednesday. Preview: Monday before sale

Margate: Stewart, Gore
102 Northdown Road, Margate (0843 221528)
Auction rooms at Clifton Place, Margate.
Antiques and modern effects.
Every 4–6 weeks. Thursday, 9–2. Preview: day before sale

Sevenoaks: Parsons, Welch & Cowell (SOFAA)
49 London Road, Sevenoaks (0732 451211)
Salerooms at Argyle Road, Sevenoaks
Fine art sale of good-quality antiques and collectors items (approx. 1,000 lots). Buyer's premium 10 per cent.
Every 6 weeks: Wednesday. Preview: day before sale

Tunbridge Wells: Bracketts
27-9 High Street, Tunbridge Wells (0892 33733)
Auction rooms at Royal Sussex Assembly Rooms, The Pantiles, Tunbridge Wells
Antiques and modern effects.
Weekly: Friday. Preview: day of, and morning before, sale

CRAFTS

Ashford: Ashford School of Spinning and Weaving
Gregory, Prentis & Green, Woolstaplers, Mace Lane, Ashford (0233 20084)
Handspinning, handweaving and grading. Demonstrations, shop.
Contact Mr J. Morfee. All year: Monday–Friday, 8–5.30; Saturday, 8–4

Aylesford: Aylesford Friary Pottery
The Friary, Aylesford, near Maidstone (0622 77272)
3 miles NW of Maidstone off A229
Hand throwing of stoneware pottery. Demonstrations, shop, tea-rooms. In the grounds of the beautifully restored Friary. (See p.121)
All year: daily 10–5

Beltring: Whitbread Hop Farm Crafts
Beltring, Paddock Wood, near Tonbridge (0622 872068)
On B2160 midway between Paddock Wood and East Peckham
In converted oasts of huge hop farm: pottery, patchwork, soft furnishings, toys and mobiles, brass, copper, silver and woodwork items and pressed flowers. Demonstrations by arrangement, purchases, tea-rooms, nature trail.
April–October: Tuesday–Sunday and BHMs, 10–5.30
  Fee includes admittance to hop farm and museum (p.104)

Bethersden: Stevenson Bros Rocking-Horses
The Workshop, Ashford Road, Bethersden, near Ashford (0233 82363)
On A28, 5 miles W of Ashford
Fascinating renewal of nursery joys in the restoration and creation of splendid rocking-horses and carousel-horses; hand carving, painting, fitting with leather, hair – and time capsule. Demonstrations, purchases.
All year: Monday–Friday, 8.30–5.30; Saturday, 8.30–12.30

Biddenden: House for Pure Wool
20 High Street, Biddenden, near Ashford (0580 291339)
On A274 in village centre
In a beautiful village long famed for its weaving. Spinning and make-up of pure wools into stoles and other knitwear garments. Demonstrations, purchases.
All year: Tuesday, Thursday–Saturday, 9–5.30; Wednesday, 9–1

Brookland: Foster House Studio
Brookland, Romney Marsh (06794 219)
On A259, 4 miles NE of Rye
Making of ecclesiastical and domestic stained glass, batik and heraldry. Demonstrations, shop.
All year: by appointment (Mrs Heskett)

Brookland: Philippine Village Craft Centre
Old RAF camp, Brookland, Romney Marsh (06794 616)
On A259, 4 miles NE of Rye
A vast range of crafts, the largest in England, from the 'Land of the 7,017 Islands', the 'Pearl of the Orient': cane furniture, clothing, embroidery etc. Tea bar, children's play area. See the Jeepney: a multi-coloured minibus with 12 mirrors, nodding cockerels and chrome horses. Philippine Festival last weekend in June.
Whitsun–September: 10–6; winter: weekends and Wednesdays

Chartham: The Master Makers
Howfield Lane, Chartham, near Canterbury (0227 730183)
On A28, 2 miles SW of Canterbury immediately after Milton Bridge over railway and river
Silk screen printing on fabric and pottery, and a wide variety of other work by master craftsmen. Demonstrations, purchases, special exhibitions, refreshments.
All year: Monday–Saturday, 9.30–6

Chilham: Chestnuts
The Oast, Hurst Farm, Chilham, near Canterbury (0227 730109)
Minor road (Mountain Street) from Chilham Square

Rocking-horses! A heart-warming place to visit for all lovers of craft, children and horses. Creation of the new, to their design or your specification; rejuvenation of the old and weary.
Monday–Saturday, 10–5.30

Dover: Gaskin Bros (Glass)
59 London Road, Dover (0304 207548)
Cutting and leading glass for stained glass windows, leaded lights and lamps, copper foil work and hand-painting of ceramic tiles. Demonstrations. Small items can be purchased.
All year: Tuesday–Friday, 9.30–2. By appointment

Faversham: Shepherd Neame Ltd
17 Court Street, Faversham (0795 532206)
Off the market-place
A chance to see how the nation's favourite drink (beer?) is made. Shop.
By appointment: Mid-January–mid-December: Monday, 2.30–4; Tuesday–Thursday, 10.30–12, 2.30–4

Folkestone: Rowland Rock (Confectionery) Factory
17 Old High Street, Folkestone (0303 54723)
A chance to see how that essential seaside holiday souvenir, a stick of rock, is made – through a viewing window into the factory.
March–September: daily (except Wednesday and Sunday), 9–6. Shop open all the year.

Hernhill: Hernhill Crafts Centre
Mount Ephraim Gardens, Hernhill, near Faversham (0227 751204)
3 miles E of Faversham, off either A299 or A2
Wide variety of crafts: spinning, forge work, rush-cane seating, glass-engraving, basketwork and bellows-making. Demonstrations, purchases. Tea-rooms.
May–mid-September: Sunday and BHM, 2–6

Hildenborough: Frank Berry Pottery
120 Tonbridge Road, Hildenborough (0732 832225)
Hand-made earthenware and stoneware pots can be seen

being produced, as well as speciality oast-house models.
All the year: Tuesday–Saturday, 9–5.30

Northbourne: Paul Harrison, Silversmith
New Mill, Northbourne, Deal (0304 373460)
Off A256, 1½ miles W of Deal
Design and manufacture of goods in precious metals and fine woods. Occasional exhibitions. Purchases.
By appointment. All year

Rochester: Castle Gallery
Castle Hill, Rochester (0634 406878/718520)
Off Esplanade, Boley Hill, or off High Street through Two Post Alley
The gallery, a listed building, set in an idyllic garden, lies through a small archway in Rochester's Norman wall. It presents the work of established and emerging artists and craftsmen in a wide field of sculpture, ceramics, jewellery, silverware, furniture and pottery.
Weekdays: 10–4.30, except Saturday, 10.30–4. Variable Sundays

Sellindge: Sellindge Pottery and Crafts
Barrow Hill, Sellindge, near Ashford (0303 812204)
Next to lay-by on A20, E of Swan Inn
A working pottery and craft shop that specializes in handmade arts and crafts.
All the year: Monday–Saturday, 10–5

Stourmouth: Theobalds Barn Cider
Heronsgate Farm, Stourmouth (0227 722275)
On B2046, 3 miles N of Wingham
Kentish apples into Kentish cider! Pressing, pasteurizing and bottling according to season. Orchard walk. Shop.
By appointment: July–December, daily 10–5
Free. Small fee only for sampling

Tonge: Old Mill
Old Mill, Tonge, near Sittingbourne (0795 78300)
Off A2 at Bapchild, 2 miles NE of Sittingbourne
Embroidery, macramé, pottery, painting, calligraphy and

batik are crafts carried on here, in delightful old building. Tea-shop, cream teas, purchases. Dog park in yard.
Mid-March–Christmas: Monday–Friday, 1.30–5; Saturday, 10–5. Gardens: Monday–Saturday, 1.30–5

West Malling: Mill Yard Craft Centre
Swan Street, West Malling (0732 843484)
Just off main street in town centre
Silversmiths, toy- and doll-makers, tailor, seamstresses, knitwear designer, florist and ceramics artist. Purchases.
All year: Monday–Saturday, 9–4.30   D

Whitstable: Harbour Gallery
39 Harbour Street, Whitstable (0227 264842)
Between Sea Street and High Street
Selection of jewellery, glass, ceramics and turned wood from 30+ British artists. Together with gold and silver jewellery made on the premises.
Daily: Monday–Saturday, 9.30–5.30

Yalding: Ju Du Crafts
The Old Granary, New Barns Farm, Benover, Yalding (0892 73474)
On B2162, 2 miles S of Yalding
Batik, enamelled goods, oils, watercolours, knitted goods and machine embroidery, according to work being undertaken at time of visit. Demonstrations, purchases.
By appointment: May–October: Monday–Saturday, 10–4

MARKETS – GENERAL

Ashford

Elwick Road	cars	Monday: 8.30–3
Elwick Road	livestock	Tuesday–Wednesday: 8.30–3.30
Elwick Road	general	Saturday: 9–3.30
Elwick Road	livestock/farm machinery	Friday 8.30–3.30

Elwick Road	furniture	One Thursday each month, from 10
Elwick Road	horse sale	Periodic Thursdays: March, May, June, September, November
Elwick Road	farm machinery	Periodic Thursdays: January, March, May, June, August, November
Lower High Street	general	Tuesday and Friday: 9–4

Canterbury

Ivy Lane	bric-à-brac	Monday–Saturday: 9–5.30
Kingsmead Road	livestock	Monday: 6–4
Kingsmead Road	general	Wednesday: 8–4
Sidney Cooper Centre, St Peter's Street	antiques crafts	Saturday: 9–4

Chatham

The Brook	indoor market	Monday–Saturday: 9–5

Dartford

Priory Shopping Centre car-park, Instone Road	general	Thursdays: 8.30–3.30
High Street	general	Saturday: 8.30–4

Deal

Corner of High Street/Union Road car-park	general	Saturday: 9–4
Indoor Market, High Street	general	Friday and Saturday: 9–4

Dover
Indoor Market, Bench Street	general	Tuesday, Thursday–Saturday: 9–5
Market Square	fruit and veg	Saturday: 7.30–4.30

Edenbridge
Market Yard car-park	general	Thursday: 8.30–3

Faversham
Guildhall, Market Place	general	Tuesday, Friday and Saturday: 8–5

Folkestone
Jenners car-park, Middleburg Square	general	Thursday: 8.30–3
Rotunda, Marine Parade	general	Sunday: 10–4

Gillingham
Hempstead Valley Shopping Centre	crafts	One Sunday each month: 10–4
High Street	general	Monday: 9–2

Gravesend
Between High Street and Queen Street	indoor, general	Monday–Tuesday and Thursday–Saturday: 9–5; Wednesday: 9–1
Adjacent to High Street	outdoor, general	Saturday: 8–5

Herne Bay
King's Road/Beech Street	general	Saturday: 9–4

Maidstone
Lockmeadow	livestock	Monday: 10.30–1
Lockmeadow	general	Tuesday: 8–2
Lockmeadow	furniture/bric-à-brac	Thursday: 10.30–4.30

Lockmeadow	produce	Friday: 10.30–3.30
Margate		
Lido, Cliftonville	general	Monday: 9–4 (April–September)
Old Market Place	general	Saturday: 9–5
Ramsgate		
Dumpton Stadium	general	Friday: 8.30–4
Rochester		
Corporation Street	flea/antiques	Saturday: 9–1
Corporation Street	general	Friday: 7–3
Sandwich		
Cattle Market	general/plant and veg auction	Thursday: 8–1
Sevenoaks		
Cattle Market, near Station	livestock/produce	Monday: 8–3
Cattle Market, near Station	general	Wednesday: 8–4
Cattle Market, near Station	produce	Thursday: 8–2
Sheerness		
Bridge Road	general	Tuesday: 9–3
Bridge Road	general	Sunday: 9.30–3 (Mid-May–August)
Sittingbourne		
Bull Ground Football Club, off Roman Square	general	Friday–Saturday: 9–4
Strood		
Car-park behind shops in High Street	general	Tuesday: 9–4

Tenterden
Station Road — general — Friday: 8.30–4

Tonbridge
Angel Centre — fleamarket — Friday: 9–1
Bank Street — general — Saturday: 9–4

Tunbridge Wells
Drill Hall, Victoria Road — antiques, secondhand furniture — Wednesday
Victoria Road behind Marks & Spencers car-park — general — Wednesday: 9–3 (9–4 summer)

Whitstable
Gorrell Tank — general — Thursday: 8–3.30 (8–4 summer)

MARKETS – WI

Virtually everything on offer is home-produced, and goods for sale may include toys and dolls, knitted and embroidered articles, plants, cut flowers and vegetables, cakes, cheeses, preserves etc.

Ashford
Elwick Road — Saturday: 8–1.30
Willesborough WI Hall — Friday: 8.30–11.30

Bearsted
WI Hall, The Street — Saturday: 10–11

Borough Green
Village Hall, High Street — Thursday: 2.15–3.15 (March–December)

Canterbury
St Peter's Methodist Church Hall, St Peter's Street — Friday: 9.30–11.30

Charing
1 Palace Farm Cottages,
Market Place   Friday: 2–3.30

Dover
UR Church Hall, High
Street   Thursday: 9–11

East Peckham
Methodist Church, Curran
Hall   Thursday: 10–11 (February–
                                December)

Faversham
Methodist Church Hall,
Preston Street   Friday: 2.15–4

Folkestone
United Reformed Church
Hall, Radnor Park   Friday: 9.30–11.30

Hawkhurst
Dunk's Hall, Rye Road   Thursday: 10–11

Ide Hill
Village Hall   Wednesday: 11–12.30
                                (March–December)

Longfield
Jubilee Hall, Main Road   Friday: 10.30–11.30

Maidstone
United Reformed Church
Hall, Week Street   Thursday: 12–2

New Romney
Scout Hut, Church Lane   Friday: 10–12 (March–
                                December)

Rochester
Gordon Hotel, High Street   Thursday: 12.30–2

Shopping Centres

Sandwich
Cattle Market   Thursday: 8–1

Sevenoaks
King's Hall, Bligh's Hotel,
High Street   Thursday: 10–11.30

Sittingbourne
Masonic Hall, Albany Road   Friday: 9–11

Tenterden
Glebe Hall, Church Road   Friday: 10–11

Tonbridge
Scouts Hut, River Walk   Friday 10.15–12

Tunbridge Wells
TOC H Hall, Little Mount
Sion   Thursday: 10.15–11.30

Whitstable
Primary Room, Methodist
Church, Argyll Road   Friday: 10–11.45

SPORT

ANGLING

Kent offers a wide variety of coarse and game fishing, with Bewl Water providing perhaps the finest trout angling in the South.

Those wishing to fish Southern Water rivers (Medway, Tiese, Beult, Royal Military Canal and Stour) must have the usual now combined trout and coarse fishing licence and be a member of an angling club or purchase a day or period ticket. Such waters must be kept unpolluted, and its environs free of litter and discarded tackle.

There is, however, *free* fishing (but licence still necessary) at the following: upstream from Yalding Sluice, 220 yards south bank; from East Farleigh to Maidstone, north bank (except mooring area); high-level railway bridge in Maidstone to tidal limit at Allington Lock.

Any enquiries should be addressed to Kent Fisheries Officer, Southern Water Authority, Luton House, Capstone Road, Chatham (0634 46655), who issue an excellent free booklet, or to the Secretary named below.

The coarse fishing season extends from mid-June to mid-March; that for trout fishing from 3 April to 31 October.

Appledore: Ashford & District Angling Club
Mrs B. Thomsett, c/o Ashford Sports, 14 North Street, Ashford (0233 31377)
Coarse fishing: Royal Military Canal, Iden Lock to Appledore; Appledore to West Hythe (S bank only)

Ashurst: Crowborough & District Anglers' Association
Coarse fishing: ¼ mile stretch of Medway (railway bank side) at Ashurst, 4 miles W of Tunbridge Wells on A264
Day tickets, during opening hours, from adjacent Bald Faced Stag

Chartham: Griffin Lake
Off A28, 4 miles SW of Canterbury
Large numbers of small tench (1½–2 lb) can be taken, as well as bream, rudd, roach and pike.
Day tickets from Griffin Garage or bailiff

Chatham: Capstone Country Park
Capstone Road, Chatham (0634 812196)
Coarse fishing in country park on outskirts of Chatham and near Walderslade.
Tickets available on site

Chiddingstone: Chiddingstone Castle Lake
Off B2027, 1 mile W of Leigh (0892 870347)
Coarse fishing. Day tickets for fishing 3-acre lake from adjacent castle

Cowden: Scarletts Lake
J. Jackson, Scarletts Farm, Furnace Lane, Cowden, near Edenbridge (0843 52924)
Coarse fishing: off A264, 4 miles E of East Grinstead

East Peckham: Medway
R. Edmunds, 31 Allington Gardens, Wateringbury, near Maidstone (0622 812904)
Coarse fishing: off B2160, 6 miles SW of Maidstone
Day membership from local tackle shops

Folkestone: Radnor Park
Off A20 in Folkestone, near railway station
Tickets available on site

Larkfield: Johnson's Lakes, Larkfield
New Hythe Lane, Larkfield
Off A20, 3 miles NW of Maidstone
Temporary membership available from bailiff on bank

Lamberhurst: Bewl Water Reservoir
The Manager, Recreation Office, Bewl Water, Lamberhurst, near Tunbridge Wells (0892 890352)
Bewl Water, off A21, 1 mile S of Lamberhurst
Tackle shop, visitor centre, boat hire, fly-casting course, trout fishing. Other facilities for family. (See Leisure Centres, p.217). Parking fee

Lamberhurst: Hoathly Fishery
Near Lamberhurst, Tunbridge Wells
Trout fishing: permits from Hoathly Farm, Clay Hill Road, Hick Green, Lamberhurst (0892 890235)

Little Bayham: Bartley Mill Stream
Mr Bulman, The Garage, Little Bayham (0892 890201)
Off B2169 and A21, 1½ miles W of Lamberhurst. Permits from above
Coarse fishing: Bayham Estate, Little Bayham, near Lamberhurst

Luddenham: Luddenham Trout Fishery
Luddenham, 2 miles NW of Faversham
Phone S. Wetherley (0795 533188) or C. Hales (0795 533903)

Maidstone: Mote Park Lake
Coarse fishing in splendid lake off A20, 2 miles E of Maidstone
Permits from A & R Dept, The Old Palace, Mill Street, Maidstone (0622 602169)

Minnis Bay: Dykes between Herne Bay and Minnis Bay
Access off A299
Roach and possibly biggest tench (6 lb) in area.
Nearest farmer's permission, subject to observance of Country Code, is generally given.

Monkton: The Stour
From Plucks Gutter to Grove Ferry
Both off A28, for Grove Ferry at Upstreet; for Plucks Gutter near Monkton

Good catches of bream and roach can be taken; best in summer, at dawn or dusk.
Canterbury & District Angling Association permits obtainable from bailiffs or N.S. Stringer, 14 Mill Road, Sturry, near Canterbury (0227 710830)

Oare: Faversham Angling Club
Mr A.P. Baldock, 5 Kennedy Close, Faversham
Coarse fishing: lake at Oare, 1 mile N of Faversham

Pluckeley: Lambden Trout Fishery
Home address: Orchard View, Ladds Corner, Eastcourt Lane, Gillingham (0634 56537)
Fishing: Off Station Road in Pluckley (on B2077, 2 miles SW of Charing), past the Black Horse and down Lambden Road
Fly-fishing on small still-water lake and stream regularly restocked with Rainbows and Browns: average weight 1½ lb, and up to 10 lb. Restricted bookings.
March (weather permitting) to October   Also cost of fish

Reculver: River Wantsum
Between Reculver and Sarre and Plucks Gutter
Once a seaway, now little more than a dyke, but fishing can be very good, with tench and roach as main quarry. Bream, carp, perch and pike are also present.
Day tickets obtainable from bailiff or Wantsum Angling Association (0843 291653) or Vic's Tackle & Bait, 86-8 King Street, Ramsgate (0843 52924)

Richborough: Betteshanger Colliery Angling Society
Mr A. Herbert, 'Alanda', 58 Celtic Road, Deal (0304 364179)
Coarse fishing: River Stour at Minster and Richborough

Rolvenden: The Lake at Pooh Corner
Mr I. Thomson, Pooh Corner, Rolvenden, Cranbrook (0580 219)
Trout fishing

Saltwood: Brockhill Country Park
Coarse fishing at country park near Saltwood, Hythe

Off A20, or from Hythe
Day tickets available on site

Sandwich: Stonar Lakes
Alongside A256, Sandwich–Ramsgate road
A large saline gravel pit stocked in 1984 with carp and rudd. Carp up to 10 lb can be taken, and naturalized bream up to 9 lb.
Obtain tickets first, from local Thanet tackle shops, as charges on the bank are double: Fisherman's Corner, 6 Kent Place, Ramsgate (0843 582174)

Sandwich: Rope Walk
Behind Guildhall and market   Free

Sandwich: Sandwich & District Angling Association
D.W.R. Daniels, 48 Hazelwood Meadow, Sandwich (0304 613658)
Coarse fishing: River Stour; Reed Pond, Sandwich; North and South Streams, Lydden. Temporary membership from J. Vranci, Newsagent, The Butchery, Sandwich, or club bailiff on bank.

Seabrook: Royal Military Canal
J.B. Walker, Fishing Tackle Ltd, 84 Stade Street, Hythe (0303 66228)
On A259, midway between Sandgate and Hythe
Coarse fishing from Seabrook to West Hythe Dam. Tickets from above; Romney, Hythe & Dymchurch Railway, Hythe; or bailiff on bank.

Seabrook: Seabrook Trout Farm
Horn Street, Seabrook, Hythe (0303 30657)
Follow signs from M20, Junction 12, midway between Sandgate and Hythe
Excellent trout fishing in pleasant surroundings. Rods for hire.
All the year

Sellindge: Heminge Farm Fly Fishing Centre
Heminge Farm, Sellindge, near Folkestone (0303 813134)
Off the A20, near Sellindge

A 4-acre reservoir which is stocked with brown and rainbow trout. Rods available for hire.
Country pub nearby.
Mid-April–mid-October: 8.30 a.m. to lighting-up time

Stowting: Stowting Trout Lake
C. & C. Cole, Water Farm, Stowting, Ashford (0303 862401)
3 miles NE of Sellindge on A20 or from B2068 (Canterbury–Hythe road) at 3 miles N of Newingreen
A clear, spring-fed 2-acre lake below the North Downs.
A secluded haven for the discerning fly fisherman. Evening, half- or full-day permits; fish taken to be paid for. Open throughout the season by appointment; opening and closing times vary according to season

Teston Bridge: Picnic Site
J. Perkins, 33 Hackney Road, Maidstone (0622 29047)
Entrance on B2163, between level-crossing and river, off Maidstone-Tonbridge Road, A26
24 acres of pleasant water-meadows and a splendid medieval bridge offer a fine setting for not-too-absorbed anglers.
Medway tow-path yields delightful rural riverside walks. Small car-parking fee. WC

Tenterden: Coombe Farm
B. Evans, Coombe Farm, Tenterden (0580 63201)
Permits. Theory and casting tuition available.

Tonbridge: Tonbridge & District Angling Society
A.S. Wolfe, 59 Hunt Road, Tonbridge
Coarse fishing: River Medway in Tonbridge area. Day tickets available from bailiffs on bank.

Tunbridge Wells: Court Lodge Down
Court Lodge Down, Nevill Golf Course, Tunbridge Wells (0892 892388)
Day tickets available on site

BADMINTON

There are badminton courts at all leisure and sports centres (see p.211). Equipment may generally be hired. Advance booking advisable. See also p.221.

BOWLS (INDOOR)

Bowls are booming! As fast as indoor centres are built, the demand increases. It is, therefore, almost impossible to get a 'spur-of-the-moment' game. Prior enquiry is a wise precaution to find out (a) rink availability; (b) slack periods (if any!); (c) if open in the summer; (d) prescribed dress, if applicable; (e) time of sessions. Other centres exist but are often 'Members Only'.

Ashford: Stour Centre
Tannery Lane, Ashford (0233 39966)
Turn left off Ring Road, 150 yards past bus station
4 rinks: 38 yards × 14 feet. Greengauge.
All the year. Daily: 9 a.m.–11 p.m.

Chatham: Medway Indoor Bowls Club
3 Riverside, Dock Road, Chatham (0634 41287)
6 rinks: 35 yards × 13 feet. Scapagrene. Slips and woods may be hired. Refreshments.
October–April: daily, 10 a.m.–10.30 p.m. (not XD or BD)

Folkestone: Shepway Indoor Bowls Club
Folkestone Bowls Centre, Radnor Park Avenue (0303 52162)
Turn off Cheriton Road (A20), ¼ mile after station roundabout
7 rinks: 42 yards × 17 feet. Scapagrene. Bar, snacks (a.m. only)
All the year, daily, 10 a.m.– 11 p.m.

Hoo: Rochester Indoor Bowls Club
Deangate Ridge, Four Wents, Hoo (0634 250537)
From A2, NE on A228; signposted from Went Cross Road

6 rinks: 40 yards × 16 feet. Scapagrene. Slips and woods may be hired. Bar.
October–April: daily, 10 a.m.–10.30 p.m. (not XD or BD)

Stone: *Dartford Stone Lodge Indoor Bowls Club*
Cotton Lane, Stone, near Dartford (0322 74111)
Off A226, 2½ miles E of Dartford
7 rinks: 40 yards × 14 feet. Scapagrene. Woods and overshoes may be hired. Refreshments, bar.
October–May: 9 a.m.– 11 p.m.

Tonbridge: *Tonbridge Indoor Bowls Club*
Angel Centre, 90 Vale Road, Tonbridge (0732 771200)
Off High Street, just N of railway station and opposite public library.
6 rinks: 40 yards × 15 feet. Scapagrene. Bar, snack bar.
All the year: daily, 9 a.m.–10.30 p.m.

Tunbridge Wells: *Royal Tunbridge Wells District Indoor Bowls Club*
Highwoods Lane, Hawkenbury, Tunbridge Wells (0892 23498)
Near St Peter's Church. Signposted
6 rinks: 40 yards × 15 feet. Greentex. Bar, snack bar.
All the year: daily, 9.30 a.m.–10.30 p.m.
Must play with a member.

Whitstable: *The Oyster Indoor Bowls Club*
The Harbour, Whitstable (0227 277692)
A290, High Street, leads into Harbour Street
8 rinks: 40 yards × 17 feet. Greengauge. Bar, snack bar.   D
Daily: 9 a.m.–10 p.m., in 2½-hour sessions
Must be member or friend of a member.

BOWLING: TEN-PIN

Cliftonville: *Cliftonville Bowl*
Ethelbert Crescent, Cliftonville, Margate (0843 228632)
12 lanes. Bar snacks.
Winter: Monday–Friday, 1–11; Saturday and Sunday, 10 a.m.–11 p.m. Summer, daily, 10 a.m.–11 p.m.

Whitstable: Whitstable Bowl
Tower Parade, Whitstable (0227 274661)
B2205, W of The Castle
10 lanes. Snack bar, bar.
All the year, daily 10 a.m.–midnight

FLYING

See Kent Gliding Club and Lashenden Aerodrome (Unusual Excursions, p.257)

GOLF

With one or two exceptions, Kent golf clubs welcome visitors without prior booking. Where indicated, proof of club membership (CM) and/or handicap card (HC) is asked for. It may well be wise to take both, whatever club is visited. At weekends, clubs obviously give first consideration to their own members, so it is essential to note restricted times for visitors, and possibly book. Fees vary according to course status.

Ashford: Ashford Golf Club
Sandyhurst Lane, Ashford (0233 20180)
On A20, 1½ miles N of Ashford
Parkland course easy on the feet and the eye. Narrow fairways and meanly bunkered greens offer a challenge.
18 holes. SSS 70. 6,246 yards.
Visitors welcome weekdays: after 11.30 a.m. on Saturday, Sunday and BH

Bearsted: Bearsted Golf Club
Ware Street, Bearsted, Maidstone (0622 38198)
E of Maidstone, between A20 and M20
Parkland course offering good views.
18 holes. SSS 70. 6,253 yards.
Visitors welcome Monday–Friday; weekends only with a member. CM HC

Broadstairs: North Foreland Golf Club
Convent Road, Kingsgate, Broadstairs (0843 62140)

4 miles N of Ramsgate, off 'coast' road
Where Thames meets the North Sea, the breeze can be tricky but the fairways are soft underfoot. Also a Par 3, 1,752 yards, approach and putt course (CM not obligatory).
18 holes. SSS 69. 6,132 yards.
Visitors welcome except on competition days. CM HC

Canterbury: Canterbury Golf Club
Littlebourne Road, Canterbury (0227 453532)
On A257, 1½ miles E of town centre
Undulating course where nature is eye-catching and supplies some of the hazards.
18 holes. SSS 70. 6,209 yards
Visitors welcome on weekdays; at weekends, *no* Sunday morning visitors. CM HC

Chatham: Chatham Golf Centre
Street End Road, Chatham (0634 48907)
From M2 turn off onto A229 in Chatham direction
Driving range with 30 floodlit bays. Bar, food. Pro Shop.
Daily: 10–10. No membership needed

Chestfield: Chestfield Golf Club
Chestfield Road, Chestfield, near Whitstable (0227 792365)
5 miles N of Canterbury on Canterbury–Swalecliffe road
Near to but not strictly a seaside course. Its picturesque thatched club house is probably the oldest in the country.
18 holes. SSS 69. 6,068 yards.
Visitors welcome but on Saturday not before 10 or between 1 and 2.30. On Sunday, after 2.30 only.

Dartford: Dartford Golf Club
Dartford Heath, Dartford (0322 23616)
From A2(M) take A2018 to Dartford, then first right
A mixed bag of park and heathland.
18 holes. SSS 68. 5,914 yards.
Visitors welcome on weekdays (CM); at weekends must be accompanied by a member.

Deal: Royal Cinque Ports Golf Club
Golf Road, Deal (0304 374007)
Along sea-front to N end of Deal
Famous seaside course that can be very windy but is flat and easy underfoot. In 1909, the English Open; in 1954, the English Amateur; today, the Halford Hewitt Challenge Cup is played here.
18 holes. SSS71. 6,409 yards.
Visitors with a letter of introduction welcome. CM

Deal: Walmer and Kingsdown Golf Course
Kingsdown, Deal (0304 373256)
Coastal road, 1½ miles S of Walmer
An undulating cliff-top course with splendid sea views. Approach it with bated breath, for here, in 1964, Assistant Professional Roger Game became the first golfer in Britain to hole out in one, on 2 *successive* holes, the 7th and 8th!
18 holes. SSS 71. 6,451 yards.
Visitors welcome Monday–Friday. Weekends and BH, only after 11.30

Denton: Broome Park Golf and Country Club
Denton, near Canterbury (0227 831701)
On A260, 1 mile S from junction with A2
Spanking new course in extensive rolling park of Lord Kitchener's old home. Time-share and country club amenities (including squash) also available in fine setting.
18 holes. SSS 72. 6,600 yards.
Book 24 hours in advance. CM HC

Faversham: Faversham Golf Club
Belmont Park, Faversham (0795 89251)
Off Throwley minor road, 2 miles S of Faversham (A2)
The course – and its pheasants – is part of the estate of former Lord Harris, one of Kent's greatest cricketers. Although played down heavily wooded valleys, there are excellent views.
18 holes. SSS 69. 5,965 yards.
Visitors welcome weekdays (HC); at weekends and BHs only with a member. Catering by arrangement.

Folkestone: Sene Valley, Folkestone & Hythe Golf Club
Sene, Folkestone (0303 68514)
Off A20, 2 miles N of Hythe
On the Downs behind Folkestone, so a fair amount of leg work; and from the back tees it is 7,000 yards.
18 holes. SSS 70. 6,320 yards.
Visitors welcome (HC); *wide*-wheeled trollies required. Limited catering on Mondays.

Gillingham: Gillingham Golf Course
Woodlands Road, Gillingham (0634 53017)
Off A2 at Woodlands Road, ½ mile W of Twydall roundabout
Parkland course
18 holes. SSS 68. 5,863 yards.
Visitors welcome during week (CM); at weekends must be accompanied by a member.

Gravesend: Mid-Kent Golf Club
Singlewell Road, Gravesend (0474 68035)
1 mile N of A2 along Wrotham road
A downland course with excellent greens
18 holes. SSS 70. 6,206 yards.
Visitors welcome on weekdays (HC 18 or below); weekends only with a member

Hawkhurst: Hawkhurst Golf Club
High Street, Hawkhurst (0580 52396)
On A268 Flimwell road, 2 miles W of Hawkhurst
A pleasant parkland course.
9 holes. SSS 68. 5,769 yards.
Club and course are closed to visitors on Sunday until noon

Hoo: Deangate Ridge Golf Club
Hoo, Rochester (0634 251180)
From A2, NE on A228, course signposted from Went Cross Road
A municipal, parkland course with plenty of trees and ditches.
18 holes. SSS men 70; ladies 72. Men: 6,300 yards; ladies, 5,612. Open to the public.

Littlestone: Littlestone Golf Club
St Andrews Road, Littlestone, New Romney (0679 62310)
1 mile E of New Romney, off A259
A seaside links course with classic holes at the 8th, 15th, 16th and 17th, sufficiently tricky to warrant its selection in 1985 as an Open Qualifying Course. Wind can be an added hazard. Extensive practice area. Tennis courts.
18- and 9-hole course. SSS 71. 6,417 yards.
Visitors welcome. HC. No restrictions on 9-hole course.

Maidstone: Cobtree Manor Golf Course
Rochester Road, Maidstone (0622 53276)
Off the A229 Rochester–Maidstone road
An undulating course set in parkland between Downs and Medway, with interesting views. Bar, snack and meal facilities.
18 holes. 5,700 yards.
With 48,000 rounds played annually, on a 'pay and play' basis, book a week ahead.

Maidstone: Leeds Castle Golf Course
Leeds Castle, near Maidstone (0627 80467)
Off A20 on B2163, 4 miles E of Maidstone
Delightful course in the extensive park of a magnificent stately home with moat and castle making unusual setting. 9 holes (2 tees for each). SSS 69. 6,017 yards.
Open to the public

Ramsgate: St Augustine's Golf Club
Cottington Road, Cliffsend, Ramsgate (0843 621346)
Off A266, near Viking Ship *Hugin* and Hoverport
Vikings (and St Augustine) landed nearby. Its worst hazards perhaps are dykes running across the flat course.
18 holes. SSS 65. 5,138 yards.
Visitors welcome. HC

Sandwich: Prince's Golf Club
Prince's Drive, Sandwich Bay, Sandwich (0304 612000)
From Canterbury, E on A257 then Upper Strand Street
One of Sandwich's 'Big Three': a top-class Championship course of duneland stretching along Sandwich Bay.

18- and 9-hole course. SSS 73. 6,950 yards.
Visitors welcome. (HC); at weekends only with a member. Prior booking advisable

Sandwich: Royal St George's Golf Club
1 mile from Sandwich on road to Sandwich Bay (0304 613090)
Sea, sky and the course: a world of its own. The ideal dune course. But an Eden for men only. Joint host for the Halford Hewitt Challenge Cup and frequent host for the English Open.
18 holes. SSS 72. 6,534 yards.
Visitors welcome weekdays with prior arrangement. CM

Sevenoaks: Knole Park Golf Club
Seal Hollow Road, Sevenoak (0732 452150)
Fork right at lower end of High Street, then ½ mile further on
Another stately home plays host to golfers among magnificent trees and with the possible hazards of grazing deer. Dry and delightfully situated.
18 holes. SSS 70. 6,249 yards.
Visitors welcome weekdays. CM, HC

Sevenoaks: Woodlands Manor Golf Club
Woodlands, near Otford, Sevenoaks (09592 4161)
Turn off A20 at West Kingsdown at Portobello Inn
Another parkland course but with several tricky holes. Indoor nets. Billiard table.
18 holes. SSS 68. 5,858 yards.
Visitors welcome during week, weekends after 1 p.m. with HC

Sheerness: Sheerness Golf Club
Power Station Road, Sheerness (0795 662585)
From Sittingbourne (A2) take A249 to Sheerness; turn left at first traffic lights
A seaside course, so wind adds to the hazards of numerous dykes.
18 holes. SSS 71. 6,448 yards.
Visitors welcomed by arrangement with Hon. Secretary.

Green fees, Monday–Saturday only. Full catering facilities.

Sittingbourne: Sittingbourne and Milton Regis Golf Club
Wormdale, Newington, Sittingbourne (0795 842261)
Leave M2 at Junction 5 then 400 yards N on A249
A downland course that involves a little 'collar work' but rewards it with good views.
18 holes. SSS 69. 6,121 yards.
Visitors welcome; at weekends must be accompanied by a member. Some delays on busy days.

Tenterden: Tenterden Golf Club
Woodchurch Road, Tenterden (0580 63987)
About 1 mile down Woodchurch road (B2067)
An attractive, easy-walking course, though the last 3 holes are hilly.
9 holes. SSS 65. 5,119 yards.
Visitors welcome Monday–Saturday but on Sunday only after noon

Tonbridge: Poult Wood Golf Course
Higham Lane, Tonbridge (0732 364039; for squash 0732 366180)
3 miles N of Tonbridge off A227
Woodland and parkland with water hazards. Bar, restaurant, also 4 squash courts.
18 holes. SSS Men 67; ladies 69. Men: 5,569 yards; Ladies, 5,027 yards.
Municipal course. Weekdays: 8 a.m.–sunset; weekends: 7 a.m.–sunset. Squash courts: 9 a.m.–10.20 p.m.

Tunbridge Wells: Nevill Golf Club
Benhall Mill Road, Tunbridge Wells (0892 25818)
S side of Tunbridge Wells off Forest Road
An interestingly varied and undulating course with heather, gorse, trees and a stream. Too good to miss, though nearly all of it, apart from its address, is in Sussex!
18 holes. SSS 69. 6,199 yards.
Visitors are welcome on weekdays (CM, HC)

Westgate-on-Sea: Westgate and Birchington Golf Course
Domneva Road, Westgate-on-Sea (0843 31115)
Off A28 between Westgate and Birchington
A flat course without undue hazards that plays short. Near the sea.
18 holes. SSS 64. 4,926 yards.
Visitors welcome (CM); at weekends, no visitors before 10.30

West Malling: West Malling Golf and Country Club
Addington, near West Malling (0732 844795)
On A20, 1 mile W of West Malling
Parkland course in pleasant surroundings. Also 2 squash courts.
18 holes. SSS 73. 7,029 yards.
Visitors welcome on weekdays but only after noon at weekends.

Whitstable: Whitstable and Seasalter Golf Club
Collingwood Road, Whitstable (0227 272020)
Off A229 to Oxford Street, second left to Nelson Road, then second left again.
Flat little seaside 9-holer. 9 holes. SSS 63. 5,276 yards.
Visitors welcome if CM or member's guest; at weekends must play with a member

LEISURE AND SPORT CENTRES (INDOOR)

Leisure centres generally charge spectator and player alike a small admittance fee; thereafter charges vary according to the activity undertaken.

Use of the main hall may be switched from one sport to another several times a day, facilities may be reserved for club bookings, and courts may be previously booked, so it is often advisable to phone and so avoid disappointment.

Some equipment, such as rackets and balls or shuttles, may be available on hire. Special youth or family activities are often arranged; so too is a certain amount of coaching.

Black-soled sports shoes are generally taboo, though there are no restrictions as to clothing worn.

Ashford: Stour Centre
Tannery Lane, Ashford (0233 21177)
Off Ring Road, 150 yards S of bus station
Badminton, squash, weight-training, swimming, sauna, solarium, keep-fit, outdoor tennis, bowls etc. Set in 20 acres of land between Great and East Stour, it caters for 14 different sports, as well as being used for art exhibitions and general entertainments.
All the year, daily, 9 a.m.–11 p.m.

Canterbury: Canterbury Sports Centre
Military Road, Canterbury (0227 763723)
Off A28 (Canterbury–Margate road), 1 mile from town centre
A new use for the former Garrison Theatre. Table tennis, badminton, roller-skating etc.
Monday–Friday, 10–10; Sunday, 9–noon, badminton only. Facilities reserved for schools and clubs at very varied times, so booking is advisable.

Chatham: Lordswood Leisure Centre
North Dane Way, Walderslade, Chatham (0634 682862)
Multi-sport hall that offers table tennis, badminton, judo, basketball, trampolining, popagility, short tennis, 50+ Club etc.
All year: Sunday–Friday, 10 a.m.–10.30 p.m.; Saturday, 10–4. Programme advisable as activity timetables are very varied.

Dartford: Downs Sports Centre
Green Road, Dartford (0322 21768)
Facilities for badminton, cricket nets, basketball and volleyball, gymnastics etc.
All the year: Tuesday–Friday, 7 p.m.–11 p.m.; Saturday, 1–11; Sunday, 10 a.m.–11 p.m.

Dover: Dover Sports Centre
Townwall Street, Dover (0304 201145)
Near junction of Marine Parade and A20, ½ mile from ferry terminal
Swimming-pool with giant water-slide, spiral and chi-

canes. Squash courts, sports hall (badminton etc), weight-training.
All year, daily. Sports Hall: 9 a.m.–10 p.m. Pool: varied times

Folkestone: Folkestone Sports Centre
Radnor Park Avenue, Folkestone (0303 58222/58223)
Signposted off Cheriton Road, ½ mile beyond railway station
Swimming-pool, main sports hall (badminton, table tennis, roller skating etc), tennis, dry ski slope, squash courts. Restaurant, bar, shop.
All the year, daily: 9 a.m.–10 p.m. (Sunday 8 p.m.). Not XD and BH

Gillingham: Black Lion Sports Centre
Mill Road, Gillingham (Enquiries: 0634 53784: Bookings: 0634 54972)
Lies off Brompton Road at W end of High Street
Splendidly equipped modern sports centre. 3 pools: main, diving and teaching. Main hall: badminton, tennis, basketball etc. 6 squash courts. Rifle range. 2 practice halls (table tennis, trampolining etc). Weights room. Cafeteria, bar, crèche   D
All the year, daily, 9 a.m.–10.30 p.m. Swimming pool: Monday–Friday, 9–8, except Tuesday and Wednesday until 9 p.m.; Saturday and Sunday, 9–6

Gillingham: Priestfield Sports Complex
Gordon Road, Gillingham (0634 576828)
Going N, off Gillingham Road, just before railway station
Brainchild and farsighted project of Gillingham Football Club. Tennis and squash coaching, 5-a-side soccer, gymnasium, short tennis, badminton, tennis
Monday–Saturday, 9 a.m.–11 p.m.; Sunday, 9 a.m.–10.30 p.m.

Gravesend: Thong Lane Sports Centre
Thong Lane, Gravesend (0474 337471)
E of Gravesend, off A226 Rochester road or A2/M2 Dover road

Badminton, squash, table tennis. Additional courses, such as trampolining, tap-dancing, yoga, aerobics, gymnastics and judo at various set times.
All year, daily, 9.30 a.m.–11.p.m.; weekends until 10 p.m.
Crêche: Monday, Tuesday, Wednesday and Thursday mornings

Herne Bay: Pier Pavilion Sports Centre
Herne Bay: (0227 366921)
On pier, W end of Central Parade
Badminton, bowls, squash, gymnastics, roller-skating, weight training multi-gym etc in £1 million complex. Also League Roller Hockey matches on Saturday evenings. Roller disco (Friday evenings). Solarium, bar, shop.
Varied times owing to use of facilities by different groups or activities, but generally, Monday–Saturday, 10 a.m.–10.30 p.m.; Sunday, 8.45 a.m.–10.30 p.m.

Maidstone: Larkfield Leisure Centre
New Hythe Lane, Larkfield, Maidstone (0622 79345)
Exit 4 from M20 or from A20
Sports hall with 6 badminton courts and facilities for a dozen other games; 3 squash courts, fitness suite, sauna, lagoon-shaped swimming-pool with beach entry, slide and wave machine. Garden patio, restaurant.
Daily: 9.30 a.m.–11 p.m.

Maidstone: Westborough Sports Centre
Oakwood Park, Tonbridge Road, Maidstone (0622 59615)
Off the A26, Tonbridge–Maidstone road, at Oakwood Road, ¾ mile
Multi-purpose hall: badminton and table tennis, 2 squash courts, multi-gym unit; also tennis courts. Vending and social area.
Shared with a school, so term time: weekdays 6 p.m.–11 p.m., weekends 10 a.m.–11 p.m.; school holidays, weekdays and weekends, 10 a.m.–11 p.m.

Margate: Hartsdown Sport and Leisure Centre
Hartsdown Road, Margate (0843 226221)
Off A28 Canterbury–Margate road, opposite Sea-Bathing

Hospital, into Hartsdown Road
Set ¾ mile from the sea-front in park surroundings, it has main and teaching pools, main hall (badminton, table tennis, roller-skating, short-mat bowls etc); solarium, burger bar, lounge area, pool tables and amusement machines.
All the year, daily. Hall: 9 a.m.–10.30 p.m. Pool: 9 a.m.–7 p.m. (except Tuesday 6.30 p.m. and Thursday 8.30 p.m.)

Northfleet: Springhead Hall Sports Centre
Springhead Road, Northfleet (0474 69746)
6 squash courts and sports hall for badminton and other activities.
All year, daily: 9.30 a.m.–10 p.m.; weekends until 11.30 p.m.

Sevenoaks: Wildernesse Sports Centre
Seal Hollow Road, Sevenoaks (0732 451437)
Off High Street by Vine Cricket Ground, at far end of Seal Hollow Road
Sports hall: badminton, table tennis, squash, tennis etc.
Monday–Friday, 6–10.30; Saturday, 1–10.30; Sunday, 10 a.m.–10.30 p.m.

Sheerness: Sheerness Sea-Front
Sheerness, Sheppey (pool: 0795 667735; leisure complex: 0795 668061)
On Sheerness Promenade
Breezy views of busy Thames Estuary shipping from 1½ mile-long promenade. Sea-front gardens, picnic area. Leisure complex offering tennis, squash, keep-fit, badminton, sauna, solarium etc. Heated indoor pool with sun deck. Bar. Children's Galleon Adventure Area.
Leisure complex: Monday–Saturday, 10 a.m.–11 p.m.; Sunday, 10 a.m.–10.30 p.m. Pool: Monday, Wednesday, Friday, 9 a.m.–8.30 p.m.; Tuesday, Thursday, 9 a.m.–6.30 p.m.; Saturday, 9 a.m.–5.30 p.m.; Sunday, 9 a.m.–4.30 p.m.

Strood: Strood Sports Centre
Watling Street, Strood (0634 723888)
1 mile NW of Rochester on A2 at junction with Gravesend Road

Multi-purpose sports hall, 3 squash courts, body-conditioning room, 3 swimming-pools. D
Daily: 10 a.m.–10.30 p.m., but swimming: Monday–Friday, 12–8 (school holidays opens at 9 a.m.). Weekends and BHs 9–1 and 2–6. (Activity programme advisable owing to wide range of activities and times.)

Tonbridge: Angel Centre, Tonbridge
Vale Road, Tonbridge (0732 359966)
Off High Street, just N of railway station and opposite public library
Badminton, table tennis, squash courts, conditioning room, solarium. Stage productions and exhibitions, shopping centre, information point, bar, cafeteria, restaurant.
All the year: daily (except XD and BD) 9 a.m.–11 p.m.

Tunbridge Wells: Tunbridge Wells Sports & 'Y' Centre
St Johns Road, Tunbridge Wells (0892 40744)
On A26 to Tonbridge
Swimming-pool, sports hall (football, badminton, netball, basketball etc), squash court, spa sauna, sun-bed.
Sports hall open 8.30 a.m.–10.30 p.m., swimming-pool from 8 a.m. but varied closing times

Whitstable: Sir William Nottidge Sports Centre
Whitstable (0227 274391 after 6 p.m.)
Bellevue Road, 1 mile SE of harbour, near railway station.
On school premises
Badminton, table-tennis, karate, aerobics, trampoline etc; also golf and cricket nets.
Monday–Friday, 6 p.m.–11 p.m.; Saturday, 1–10

LEISURE AND SPORTS CENTRES (OUTDOOR)

Admission is free but obviously a fee is payable for facilities used.

Dartford: Hesketh Park
E of Dartford town centre, on B220, Watling Street
County cricket has been played here for 250 years. Tennis

courts, bowling green, children's playground.
All the year, daily

Folkestone: East Cliff
Wear Bay Road, Folkestone
By the harbour wall is a stretch of fine sands and above it, on the cliff slopes, reached by steps, a delightful complex of bowling greens, grass tennis courts and an 18-hole pitch and putt course round a Martello tower. 2 cliff-top car-parks with splendid views. Restaurant.
Daily: summer season

Gillingham: Strand Leisure Park
Lower Rainham Road, Gillingham (0634 52907/573176)
Turn off A2 at Will Adams Memorial down Woodlands Road, onto B2004
This 27-acre park on the banks of the Medway provides open-air swimming, boating, pitch and putt, crazy golf, tennis, Santa Fe miniature railway, children's playground, donkey rides and band concerts.
April–September: dryside, 10–8; wetside, 12–6 (weekends and holidays, 10–6). October–March: dryside, weekends only, October 9.30–4.30, November–January 9.30–3.30, February and March, 9.30–4.30; wetside closed

Hoo: Deangate Ridge Complex
Hoo, near Rochester (0304 250537)
From A2, NE on A228, course signposted from Went Cross Road
18-hole golf course (6,300 yards) in wooded countryside, which has spawned an 18-hole pitch and putt course, to say nothing of a 6-rink indoor bowling green, synthetic athletics track and 3 hard tennis courts. Bar, snacks.
All the year, daily: 9 a.m.–10.30 p.m.

Lamberhurst: Bewl Bridge Reservoir
Lamberhurst (0892 890661)
Off A21, S of Lamberhurst
Largest stretch of fresh water in SE England in beautiful surroundings. Day permits for fly-fishing; board sailing (Monday–Friday), certificate of competence essential. Also

rowing, canoeing, sailing and diving: club membership needed but occasional instructional courses are held. Riding trails, nature trails, adventure playground, motor-launch cruises, visitor centre display. Refreshment kiosk, viewing and picnic areas.
Daily: 9 to sunset   Car-park fee

Maidstone: Mote Park
Ashford Road, Maidstone
Off A20 on E approach to Maidstone
450 acres of natural parkland containing a big lake which provides excellent fishing and sailing. Nature trail, miniature train rides on summer Sunday afternoons, pitch and putt, swimming-pool. Kiosks, cafeteria.
Daily

Ramsgate: Westcliff Leisure Park and Boating-Pool
Royal Esplanade, Ramsgate (0843 581999)
Indoor ball pond, soft play area, fun castle, adventure playground, arcades, kiddies' rides, cafeteria.
Daily in season

Tonbridge: Tonbridge Sportsground
Off New Wharf Road, Tonbridge
Down Castle Street and The Slade
A splendid sportsground of 50 acres encircled by the Medway and almost below the castle walls. Tennis courts, crazy golf, putting, bowling. For younger members of the family: paddling-pool, model boating-pool and (summer: Saturday and Sunday only) a miniature railway.
Easter–September daily

RIDING

Allhallows: Slough Fort Riding Club
Allhallows, near Rochester (0634 270386)
6 miles NE of Rochester (A228), near caravan site entrance
20 mounts
Hacking only: daily, except Tuesday and Wednesday 10–6

Ash: Padbrook Carriage-Driving Centre
Padbrook, Paramour Street, near Ash-with-Sandwich (0304 812574)
In Ash, turn off A257 for Ware; after 2 miles continue ahead into dead-end road
Learn to drive pony and trap, or a pair and a Steptoe 'totters' cart, or be driven luxuriously down leafy lanes (optional Black Pig and Rising Sun stops) by experienced 'whip' behind a pair of matched greys or chestnuts on nodding terms with Prince Philip at national events.
All the year, daily, 10–6. Advance phone-call advisable

Badlesmere: Deepdene Stables
Badlesmere, near Faversham (0233 74228)
On A251, 5 miles S of Faversham
20 mounts; special pub rides
Hacking and lessons: daily (except Monday) 10–6

Bridge: Bursted Manor Riding Centre
Pett Bottom, near Canterbury (0227 830568)
2 miles SW of Bridge off A2
10 mounts; indoor school.
Lessons: Wednesday and Thursday; weekends by appointment. Hacking, daily 10–6

Cranbrook: Kingsmead Stables
Biddenden (0580 291300)
Past Union Mill, 1 mile from Cranbrook on Tenterden road
15 mounts; nervous riders welcome.
Hacking and lessons: daily, but advisable to phone 10–6

Gillingham: Matthew Riding Centre
Walnut Tree Farm, Lower Rainham Road, Gillingham (0634 577131)
Near junction with Eastcourt Lane
Lessons: Monday–Saturday. Hacking: all week 10–6. It is advisable to make an appointment

Great Chart: Blue Barn Riding Stables
Blue Barn Farm, Great Chart, near Ashford (0233 22933)
Great Chart is on the A28, 2 miles SW of Ashford

20 mounts; riding for disabled; nervous riders welcomed. Group and individual tuition.
Lessons: Tuesday, Wednesday, Thursday and Saturday.
Hacking: every day 10–6

Hildenborough: Hildenborough Riding Stables
Riding Lane, Hildenborough, near Tonbridge (0732 838717)
20 mounts; indoor school; all standards.
Hacking and lessons: daily (except Monday) 10–6

Saltwood: Hayne Barn Stables
Saltwood, near Hythe (0303 60338)
Past the castle, 1½ miles up Sandy Lane
20 mounts.
Hacking and lessons: daily, 9–6

Seasalter: Alberta Riding Centre
Faversham Road, Seasalter, near Whitstable (0227 272214)
10 mounts; small indoor school; mentally handicapped groups welcomed.
Lessons. Hacking (not Monday or Friday) 10–6

Stelling Minnis: Marberdan Riding Stables
Maxted Street, Stelling Minnis, near Canterbury (0233 75308)
Off Stone Street, B2068 (Canterbury–Hythe road) at Six Mile Cottages
10 mounts; children's riding holidays.
Hacking: daily, 10–6

SKATING AND SKI-ING

Chatham: Alpine Ski Centre
Capstone Farm Country Park, Capstone Road, Chatham (0634 827979)
Signposted from Junction 4, M2; 2 miles S of Chatham on Capstone Road
200-metre dry slope with two ski-lifts able to transport 1,200 skiers per hour. Practice (must be able to do

controlled snowplough turns) and private lessons. Ski hire. Bar, restaurant, coffee shop.
All year, daily: 9 a.m.–10 p.m.

Folkestone: Folkestone Ski Slope
Folkestone Sports Centre, Radnor Park Avenue, Folkestone (0303 58222)
Signposted off Cheriton Road (A20) just beyond station roundabout. 1 mile W of town centre.
Equipment hire; private instruction.
September–March (Phone for times open to *individuals*)

Gillingham: Ice Bowl
Gillingham Business Park, Ambley Road, Gillingham (0634 388477)
On A2 at A278 roundabout. (Leave M2 at Junction 4)
Opened by the Queen in 1984 and subsequently enjoyed by 1¼ million visitors. 56 × 26 metres international-size ice pad. Wide range of activities: disco and games nights, beginners, league hockey, junior sessions, group and individual lessons, video sessions. Bar, cafeteria, shop.
Daily, generally in 3 sessions: 10–12, 2–4.30, 8–11

SPECTATOR SPORTS
BADMINTON
Gillingham: Medway Badminton Association
Castlemaine Badminton Hall, Castlemaine Avenue, Gillingham (0634 572187)
Off Woodlands Road and then Grange Road near Chalk Pit
Kent I, II and III teams all play a number of their Inter-County Championship matches here.
November–April: a number of Sundays, 2–7
Free, but limited spectator accommodation

CRICKET
Canterbury: St Lawrence Cricket Ground
Old Dover Road, Canterbury (0227 456886)
Off A2, ½ mile S of town centre, down St Lawrence Road
Historic headquarters of Kent county cricket for nearly 150

years – with a tree *within* the boundary! Stands and open seating, kiosks, cafeteria, bar, and restaurant.
County championship, one-day and international matches throughout the season. Famous 'Cricket Week' in August. Phone for fixture list and starting times.

Maidstone: Mote Park Cricket Ground
Willow Way, Mote Park, Maidstone
Off A20 on E outskirts of Maidstone
Kent County Cricket Club play occasional County Championship games here and Sunday League games. Mote CC play good-class club fixtures at weekends, and mid-week in Kent and Mid-Kent Leagues.

RUGBY
Gillingham: United Services
Brompton Road, Gillingham
On main Gillingham–Chatham Dockyard road just outside centre of the town
Closing of the dockyard has sadly reduced Naval rugby firepower but exciting play can still be seen.
Most Saturday afternoons: September–April   Free

Maidstone: Maidstone Rugby Football Club
Willow Way, Mote Park, Maidstone
Off Lower Stone Street, then down Mote Avenue
Maidstone RFC play in the Courage National League (Division III). 1st, 2nd or 3rd XV matches virtually every Saturday   Free

SOCCER
Chatham: Chatham Town Football Club
Maidstone Road, Chatham (0634 43678)
M2–A229 Chatham turn-off, follow Chatham signs for 1½ miles; ground on right, opposite garage
'Chat's in all-red strip play in the Beazer Homes (formerly Southern) League. In 1889 beat Nottingham Forest to reach the FA Cup quarter-final!
Saturday, and Tuesday mid-week games

Folkestone: Folkestone Town Football Club
Cheriton Road, Folkestone (0303 51374)
On A20 behind Presto Stores, 1 mile W of Folkestone Central railway station
Reached the third round of the FA Cup in 1965–6. Now in Beazer Homes (formerly Southern) League. The 'Amber and Black' are 104 years old!
Saturday, and Wednesday mid-week games

Gillingham: Gillingham Football Club
Priestfields Stadium, Gordon Road, Gillingham (0634 51854)
Off Gillingham Road, just before railway station
The 'Gills', although now languishing in Division III, have had greater moments of Cup glory and are well worth a visit.
Most Saturday afternoons: September–April. Ticket office open 9–5

Gravesend: Gravesend and Northfleet Football Club
Stonebridge Road, Northfleet, Gravesend (0474 533796)
5 minutes walk from Northfleet railway station
'The Fleet' have won the Kent Senior Cup 3 times and now play in the Beazer Homes (formerly Southern) League. Several players with FL experience.
Saturday, and Tuesday mid-week games

Margate: Thanet United Football Club
Hartsdown Park, Hartsdown Road, Margate (0843 221769)
Turn right at Sea Bathing Hospital just before promenade
'The Islanders', patriotically in red, white and blue strip, played before an 8,500 gate when they met Spurs in the 1972–3 FA Cup third round. Now in Beazer Homes (formerly Southern) League.
Saturday, and Tuesday for mid-week games

Tonbridge: Tonbridge AFC
Darenth Avenue, Tonbridge (0732 352417)
Off Shipbourne Road, N of Tonbridge School, at Pinnacles pub
Blue and navy 'Angels' once attracted 8,000 in 1951 FA

Cup first round v Aldershot. They play now in Beazer Homes League.
Saturday, and Tuesday for mid-week games

RACING: CARS
Fawkham: Brands Hatch
Brands Hatch Circuit, Fawkham, Dartford (0474 872331)
Off A20 at West Kingsdown
Thrills and spine-tingling noise in beautiful Downland countryside at the South's leading car-racing circuit. Surprising range of other events, from motor-cycles to vintage cars, from mammoth trucks to push-bikes and from hovercraft to skate-boards. Learn how to handle a racing car – or a skid.

Lydden: Lydden Circuit
Administrative office: 0795 71978
Off A2 Canterbury–Dover road, 4 miles NW of Dover
The exciting venue for a variety of motor-sport activities that include the thrills of rallycross, car and motor-cycle road races, kart and scooter races, 'Festivals of Motorsport'.
Meetings held on most Saturdays, Sundays and BHM from April–October, intermittently thereafter

RACING: GREYHOUNDS
Canterbury: Canterbury Greyhound Track
Kingsmead, Canterbury (0227 457245)
Off the A28 at Sainsbury's roundabout
11 races: restaurant.
In season: Monday, Tuesday, Friday and Saturday, 7.30 p.m.

Crayford: Crayford Greyhound Track
118 Crayford Road, Crayford (0322 522262)
Greyhound racing; also banger and speedway racing.
In season: Monday, Wednesday and Friday. Off season: Monday and Saturday

Ramsgate: Dumpton Park Greyhound Stadium
Dumpton Park, Hereson Road, Ramsgate (0843 593333)

Mid-way along Broadstairs–Ramsgate road, opposite railway station
Covered stands, gymnasium, squash and snooker too in leisure centre.
Bar, restaurant. (Free cabaret after Saturday racing.) 400+ stall market on Fridays.
Racing: July–September, Monday, Wednesday and Friday, 7.45 p.m.; October–June, Wednesday and Saturday, 7.30 p.m.

RACING: HORSES
Folkestone: Folkestone Racecourse
Westenhanger, near Folkestone (0444 450989/451597)
Leave M20 at Junction 11 and follow signs. Off B2068, ½ mile N of Newingreen roundabout. Railway station adjoins course. (So too do remains of Westenhanger Manor, which had a 50-foot moat, 126 rooms and the almost conventional 365 windows.)
Over the sticks? On the flat? Either way, have fun and a flutter at Kent's only racecourse.
All the year. One or more fixtures every month.
Fee, but under-16s free if with parent

RACING: POINT-TO-POINT
Aldington: East Kent Hunt Point-to-Point
Mr E. Maylam, Court Lodge Farm, Petham, near Canterbury (0227 70 273)
Street Land, Aldington: 6 miles SE of Ashford on B2069
5 or 6 races, bookies, Tote. Refreshments, bar.
Easter Monday: 2 p.m.

Aldington: West Street Hunt Point-to-Point
Mr A. Hayes, Middle Pett Farm, Pett Bottom, Canterbury (0227 830342)
Street Land, Aldington: on B2069, accessible from A20 at Smeeth or from B2067 halfway between Lympne and Ham Street
5 or 6 races, bookies, Tote. Refreshments, bar. Children's 'Fun Castle', trade stands.
May Day Monday: 2 p.m.

Charing: Ashford Valley Point-to-Point
H. Ellison, Littlefield, Smarden (023 377 594)
Palace Farm, near Charing, alongside the A20
5 or 6 races, bookies and Tote. General trade stands, side-shows, children's entertainments. Bar, refreshments.
Easter Saturday: 1 or 1.30 first race

Detling: Tickham Hunt Point-to-Point
Major P. de G.V.C. Warren, New Cottage, Manor Farm, Hollingbourne (062 780 365)
Brimbury Meadows, Detling, ½ mile from Kent Showground on A249
5 or 6 races, bookies and Tote.
General trade stands, entertainments for children. Refreshments, bar.
Generally, first or second Saturday before Easter, 12–4.30

SQUASH

There are squash courts at all leisure and sports centres except Ashford, Canterbury, Chatham (Lordswood) and Dartford (Downs). Additionally there are courts at Dartford Pool (p.227) and Hundred of Hoo Pool (p.227). Equipment may generally be hired. Booking strongly advisable for peak periods.

SWIMMING-POOLS

There are also swimming-pools at Ashford, Dover, Folkestone, Gillingham (Black Lion and Strand), Maidstone Larkfield, Margate, Sheerness, Strood, and Tunbridge Wells, listed under 'Leisure Centres' on p.211.

It should be appreciated that the pool *may* be reserved at differing times on certain days for specified categories of swimmers, e.g. OAPs, schools, disabled, etc. Most have a hoist for the latter.

Canterbury: Kingsmead Swimming-Pool
Kingsmead Road, Canterbury (0227 69818)
Off A28 at roundabout near Sainsbury's
Swimming- and teaching pools, solarium, vending

machines, spectators' gallery.   D
Daily: Monday, 9–6; Tuesday and Thursday, 9–9; Wednesday and Friday, 9–8; Saturday, 9–6; Sunday, 8–6

Dartford: Fairfield Pool
Lowfield Street, Dartford (0322 343111)
Adjoining Central Park off High Street
Unusual L-shaped pool that slopes diagonally from corner to corner to give plenty of shallow water for 'family fun'. Teaching pool, diving bay. Also squash courts, sauna and weight-training room.
Daily but differing times for each facility

Deal: Deal Swimming-Pool
Park Avenue, Deal (0304 821199)
In Victoria Park, S side of Park Avenue
Brand new £750,000 worth of leisure pool with sauna, wave pool, jacuzzi, bubble bath, flume slide, beach, gusher and mushroom fountain.

Hoo: Hundred of Hoo Swimming-Pool
Main Road, Hoo, Rochester (0634 251588)
½ mile from village centre
2 pools, main and teaching; 2 squash courts and table tennis.
All year: Monday–Friday, 12–8; Saturday, Sunday and BHs, 9–1 and 2–6. (During summer holidays weekday hours are extended to 9–8)

Hythe: Hythe Swimming-Pool
South Road, Hythe (0303 69177)
Off Stade Street, down South Road; last turn on left before Marine Parade
Main and learners' pools. Recently refurbished. Weekly 'Fun Session' – and a putting green.   D
Times too complicated for inclusion. Phone for Times Card.

Maidstone: Mote Park Swimming-Pool
Willow Way, Maidstone (0622 64631)
Off A20 (Ashford Road) at Square Hill just E of town

centre or off Hastings Road, at Mote Road
Main pool, diving-pool, 2 teaching pools. Instruction available. Sauna, solarium, hoist for disabled, small-bore rifle and pistol range. Wide range of times and activities. Snacks. D
All the year, daily: Monday and Wednesday, noon–10; Tuesday and Thursday, noon–8; Friday, noon–6; Saturday, 9–4; Sunday, 8–3. During school holidays pools open Monday–Friday, 9 a.m.

Ramsgate: Warre Swimming-Pool
Newington Road, Ramsgate (0843 593754)
On Canterbury–Broadstairs road, 10 minute walk from railway station
Heated swimming-pool, 6 hard tennis courts, grass recreation area, vending and amusement machine area, children's play area (slides etc)
All the year, daily: Monday–Friday, 9 a.m.–10 p.m.; Saturday 9–7; Sunday 9–9

Sevenoaks: Sevenoaks Pool
Buckhurst Avenue, Sevenoaks (0732 459712)
Off High Street just below bus station
25-metre pool and children's learning pool
Daily, 9 a.m.–10 p.m.

Tonbridge: Tonbridge Swimming-Pool
Lower Castle Playing Field, The Slade, Tonbridge (0732 355061)
Approached from the High Street, via Castle Street (next to castle) and The Slade
Below the castle walls, a 30-metre pool, heated to 76°F, with extensive lawns and sun-bathing area. Varied programme includes mother-and-baby sessions, learner and improver classes, even barbecues and discos. Fully supervised children's sessions. Refreshments available. Adjoining miniature railway will keep the 'dry-bobs' happy (summer, Saturday and Sunday).
May–September daily

WINDSURFING

Gillingham: Kent Windsurfing Centre
The Broadway, Featherby Road, Gillingham (0634 376350)
Off M2 at Junction 4 and down Hoath Way; or off A2 just after roundabout from M2
A day-course (8 hours) on simulator and board to qualify for RYA Boardsailing Proficiency Certificate; or additional practice. (Must be able to swim 50 metres.) Shop. Phone to book.
Daily during summer season

Lydd: Romney Marsh Windsurf Centre
Lydd, Romney Marsh (0679 21028)
Gravel lakes off Dengemarsh road, near Lydd
Caters for all levels from beginner (RYA Certificate) to advanced. Shop, hire and repair facilities.
Summer season: daily

Maidstone: London Dinghy Centre Sailsports
The Corner House, Chatham Road, Sandling, Maidstone (0622 56912)
Sailing at Larkfield Lake (near Tesco Superstore), Maidstone
Board and wet-suit hire. Day Courses: March–October

Sandgate: Windsurfing South-East
97 High Street, Sandgate, near Folkestone (0303 30110)
2 miles W of Folkestone on A259
Learn a new skill in 4 hours! Short courses include board and wet-sail hire and, hopefully, lead to the Royal Yachting Association Certificate. Higher levels catered for. Shop.
Daily: summer season

Southborough: Wind-Surfing Tuition
24 London Road, Southborough, near Tunbridge Wells (0892 28019)
Courses held at Bewl Water Reservoir, near Lamberhurst
A chance to learn a fast-growing and exhilarating sport. One-day courses: rigging a board, sailing theory, dry land

simulator, on-water practice, safety and self-rescue. Shop. Courses: summer season, daily

Whitstable: Whitstable Windsurfing
1 Beach Walk, Whitstable (0227 276566)
Off Tankerton Road (B2205), ¼ miles W of castle
Learn the thrills of windsurfing at a Royal Yacht Association Registered School or just hire a board if you are already proficient.
Daily during the summer

TOWNS AND VILLAGES

Large towns have been selected for inclusion because of their own intrinsic interest, many facilities, wide range òf attractions and historical associations; smaller towns and villages because of the beauty, individually and collectively, of their buildings and of the surrounding countryside. They offer a varied cross-section of Kent's many lovely villages and market towns.

In both cases, nearby attractions are shown.

LARGER TOWNS
(Population over 10,000)

Abbreviations: All places mentioned, except those asterisked, are described in detail in their appropriate section on other pages. 'TT' indicates that a Town Trail leaflet has been published and is available at the local Tourist Information Centre.

Ashford
A bustling, still growing town which retains something of its agricultural heyday but little of its once all-important Southern Railway workshops.

Stour Leisure Centre; Railway Research Room; Kingsnorth Museum; Intelligence Corps Museum; St Mary the Virgin Church (tombs)*; cattle market; shopping centre; Middle Row (old houses).

Nearby: Wye College of Agriculture Museum at Brook; Farm Trail at Coldharbour Farm; Crundale Downs Nature Reserve; Hothfield Common (KTNC); Godinton House.

Canterbury

'Cradle of Christianity' – England's premier cathedral city. In season, it can be a seething Tower of Babel but it still offers much, despite the havoc of German World War II 'Baedeker raids'. The cathedral, miraculously unscathed, towers superbly above the old city walls. Take your choice also of St Augustine's Abbey or St Martin's Church, Blackfriars or Greyfriars, Eastbridge Hospital or Westgate Gardens ...

For 20th-century enjoyment there is a modern Marlowe Theatre, a brand new Pilgrims Way time-walk, a recently opened Heritage Museum, to say nothing of a week's County cricket and three weeks of autumn international festival. And theatre-in-the-round at the Gulbenkian on the University's hill-top campus. TT

Nearby: Fordwich; Wickhambreux; Bishopsbourne; Blean Woods; Bigbury Fort; Howletts Zoo Park; Blean Bird Park; Whitstable; Herne Bay.

Chatham and Gillingham

Siamese twins; two sprawling urban agglomerations. The former for nearly 500 years played a major role in British Naval history until its huge dockyard (with 8,000 men) was declared redundant and reduced to a (fascinating) museum-piece. The latter nurtured Will Adams, founder of the Japanese Navy! Now only a few gems and museums act as a reminder of their faded glory.

Chatham: Historic Dockyard; Heritage Museum; Fort Amherst; Capstone Country Park; St Bartholomew's Chapel; Sir John Hawkins Hospital; Great Lines Naval Memorial*.

Gillingham: Black Lion Sports Centre; Royal Engineers Museum; Will Adams memorial*; Strand Open Air Leisure Centre; Eastcourt Meadows Country Park.

Nearby: Rochester; Upnor Castle; Bluebell Hill picnic site; *Kingswear Castle* pleasure cruises; Lower Halstow; Kits Coty.

Dartford

Pilgrims on Watling Street, Canterbury bound, and Spenser's 'Silver Darent' seem a far cry from this busy

industrial town with cement and paper, engineering and petro-chemical works. Still, Dartford, heath and marsh surrounded, has a tiny soft centre of park and museum, two historical hostelries, a grimy church with fine brasses and splendid tomb to the wife of Sir John Spielman, Queen Elizabeth I's jeweller and founder of Dartford's paper-making industry (1617).
Nearby: Blue Circle Heritage Museum; Stone Lodge Farm; St John's Jerusalem (NT); Dene Country Park.

Faversham
Bypassed – and the better for it! A cheerful, historic market town: its former 'star', a vast abbey long since obliterated, has been replaced by an amazing 400 listed buildings 'in the wings'. Orchards and blossom to the south; sea and shipyard creek to the north. Two breweries add delicate aroma. TT

Fleur de Lis Heritage Centre; West, Court and Abbey Streets; Guildhall – and pump; Arden's House*; Old Grammar School*; St Mary of Charity Church; Shepherd Neame Brewery; The Creek*.

Nearby: Chart Gunpowder Mills; Ospringe Maison Dieu and Museum (EH); Swale Nature Reserve; Hernhill, Ephraim Gardens and Orchard Trail; Davington Priory*; Blean and Perry Woods; Preston Church*.

Gravesend
'A grey town on a grey river'? But with its sweeping views of Thames and Thames shipping, it still holds some of the maritime romance of its heyday as 'Gateway to the Port of London', the Tilbury Ferry and the mecca of Victorian East Enders out for a 'knees-up'. And in the background are the fascinating figures of Pocahontas and Gordon of Khartoum. TT

Milton Chantry; 'Three Daws'; Royal Terrace Pier*; St George's Church; Pocahontas and Gordon Memorials; New Tavern Fort; Gravesend Museum; Gordon Promenade and Gardens; Windmill Hill Viewpoint*.

Nearby: Cooling Castle, and St James' Church; Tilbury Fort*; Northfleet's St Botolph's Church and Blue Circle Heritage Museum; Chalk Old Forge (*Great Expectations*)*.

Maidstone

'Busy, noisy and largely ugly' ... 'haphazard and incoherent'. Hardly the praises you would expect of a county and market town, set in lovely countryside, astride a fine river. Especially one that has an 'iguanadon proper collared gules' (red) as supporter for its crest which includes a horse's head 'gorged with a chaplet of Hops fructed proper'! For all that, it is worth visiting though its delights, except for one superb grouping, are widely scattered. TT

Archbishop's Palace and Stables (Carriage Museum), College of Priests*, All Saints Church, Gatehouse: all together in riverside gardens; Mote Park and lake; Chillington Manor Museum and Art Gallery; Bank and Earl Streets*; river trips.

Nearby: Allington Castle; Aylesford Friary; Museum of Kent Rural Life; Cobtree Manor Park; Bluebell Hill picnic site; Kits Coty (EH); Westborough Sports Centre; Teston Bridge picnic site; Yalding; Loose (Wool House, NT); Leeds Castle and Aviaries; Boughton Monchelsea Place; Stoneacre Place, Otham.

Rochester

Too long regarded as Canterbury's poor relation, this compact old walled city, superbly sited on the Medway, offers proof that 'small, too, is beautiful'. Didn't Dickens, who is the Spirit of Rochester, confirm it through the mouth of Mr Jingle: 'Fine place ... glorious pile ... old Cathedral too'? Rochester has recently had a face lift. TT

Cathedral; castle (EH); Bridge Chapel*; Royal Victoria & Bull Hotel*; Guildhall Museum; Old Corn Exchange*; Watts Charity; Dickens Museum in Eastgate House; The Vines*; Minor Canons' Row*; La Providence*; Jasper's Gate*; Satis House*; Kingswear Castle Steamer Trips; Strood Leisure Centre.

Nearby: Chatham; Cooling Castle; Upnor Castle; Temple Manor (NT); Cobham; Camer Country Park; Black Lion Sports Centre; R.E.s' Museum.

Sandwich

Kent's answer to Rye! A quiet town of narrow streets and

still narrower alleys packed with medieval buildings. Once a prosperous Cinque Port; now distanced from the sea by dunes. World famous in golfing history.

St George's and Prince's Golf Clubs; Guildhall*; Strand Street*; Fisher Gate*; Barbican*; Rampart Walk*; St Clement's and St Peter's Church*; Dutch House*; St Bartholomew's Hospital*; Precinct Toy Collection.

Nearby: White Mill; Richborough Castle (EH); Richborough Amphitheatre (EH); St Nicholas Vineyard; Viking Ship *Hugin*; Pegwell Bay picnic site; St Augustine's Monument*; Ramsgate; Deal.

Sevenoaks
Comfortably commuterized but still with underlying charm and character – and, of course, incomparable Knole ('a town rather than a house') and Kent's cricket heritage, The Vine. Breezily and cheerfully sited on the north slopes of the Greensand Hills and within sight of the Downs and the delectable Darent Valley. TT

St Nicholas Church*; Sevenoaks School*; Manor House*; Market House*; Old Post Office*; The Red House*.

Nearby: Crockham*, Toys and Ide Hills (NT) (walks and viewpoints)*; Tonbridge; Ightham Mote (NT); Otford; Shoreham; Westerham; Kemsing; Hever Castle; Penshurst Place; Riverhill House.

Sittingbourne
Desolate Swale to the north: smiling Downland villages and blossom orchards to the south. Once an important staging-post for pilgrims and, later, stage-coaches. Now, few tourists stroll its two-mile long High Street which holds only vestiges of its Georgian prosperity. Today's wealth lies in unlovely but lucrative paper-mills, cement works and industrial estates. Its suburb, tiny, once proud *Milton Regis*, is now the magnet. TT from Swale Council Office

Tree-lined Avenue of Remembrance*; St Michael's Church*; Sittingbourne & Kemsley Light Railway; Dolphin Yard Sailing Barge Museum.

Nearby: Milton Regis: Holy Trinity Church*, Old Court Hall Museum, and Bradley House*; Lower Halstow;

Borden*; Bredgar*; Milstead; Elmley Marshes Bird Reserve.

Tenterden
Once merely a pasture ('den') for swine, hewn out of the forest; today still showing the breeding and elegance, never *over*-played, bequeathed it by the Weald's wealthy ironmasters and weavers. The single, broad High Street, tree- and grass-lined, cottage-garden flanked, is a palimpsest of façades – Tudor black-and-white, Regency bow-windowed, and Victorian tile-hung – which harmonize despite their diversity. Quality shops and tempting tea-rooms, and pubs too. With almost everything pleasing to the eye, Tenterden is a place for strolling – unruffled and carefree. TT

St Mildred's Church*; Kent & East Sussex Railway; Tenterden Museum; Tudor Rose*; Woolpack Inn*; Town Hall*.

Nearby: Tenterden Vineyard: Ellen Terry Smallhythe Museum (NT); Biddenden and Vineyard; Sissinghurst Castle and Garden (NT); Rolvenden Historic Vehicle Museum, and Windmill*; Woodchurch; Benenden.

Tonbridge
Stands astride the Medway at its limit of navigation. 'To the north, old and good; to the south, young and bad' encapsulated it for author Reginald Turnor. Towering castle motte and massive gatehouse dominate riverside walk and gardens. Black-and-white Chequers and mellow-bricked Rose & Crown beckon invitingly. Bordyke (Street) offers a pleasant diversion. Ferox Hall and Tonbridge School, *alma mater* of Colin Cowdrey, have a fitting last word.   TT from Tunbridge Wells TIC

Nearby: Tunbridge Wells; Matfield; Brenchley; Whitbread's Beltring Oast Houses; Ightham Mote (NT); Sevenoaks; Knole (NT); Dene Country Park; Riverhill House; Penshurst Place.

Tunbridge Wells
'Royal' by act of Edward VIII, 'The Wells' seesawed from the vice of the profligate 17th-century Society which

flocked there to the strait respectability of 19th-century Victorians. Not even the infuriated trumpeting in *The Times* of reactionary 'Disgusted' has disturbed its quiet gentility.

Today, it is a pleasant, hilly town with wide, tree-lined avenues and streets, soaring office blocks, a breezy common, a rhododendron-ringed County cricket ground, the Baroque splendour of King Charles the Martyr Church and, dignified but faded, the Decimus Burton Calverley Park.   TT
And, of course, shades of 'Beau' Nash in Kent's most elegant shopping mall, tree-shaded and colonnaded, The Pantiles.

Nearby: High Rocks; Groombridge; Bayham Abbey; Lamberhurst, and Vineyard; Owl House Garden; Scotney Castle; Penshurst Place; Hever Castle; Finchcocks Keyboard Museum; Bewl Bridge Reservoir; Mr Heaver's Craft Village; Whitbread's Beltring Oast Houses; Matfield; Brenchley; Tonbridge; David Salomon's Museum.

SMALL TOWNS AND VILLAGES

Aylesford
3 miles N of Maidstone, off A229 or M20
'Cradle of English History'! A 600-year-old humpbacked bridge crosses the Medway near where the British slew the Saxon invader Horsa. There is a splendid groupiing of church (with two magnificent tombs) and gabled and tiled houses above it.

The 13th-century Friary, lovingly and recently restored by Carmelites, and with a breathtaking open-air shrine, is an oasis of peaceful beauty. George Inn and Chequers are both worth admiring – and the Little Gem claims to be England's smallest pub. Almshouses, too.

Nearby: Allington Castle; Kits Coty (EH); Larkfield Leisure Centre; Rochester Castle (EH) and Cathedral; Tyrwhitt-Drake Carriage Museum, Maidstone; Chatham; Rochester.

Benenden
On B2086, 5 miles W of Tenterden

Lies snugly in rolling Wealden countryside. Huge Victorian 'Elizabethan' mansion, now a school, set in fittingly vast grounds, dominates the village – and is the Princess Royal's *alma mater*.

Below, tile-hung cottages look interestedly (and interestingly) at the vast, sloping green-cum-cricket-ground, flanked by a lively village school (with two cheeky turrets) and crested by the pale sandstone of St George's which, sadly, lost its 134-foot-high *detached* belfry in a 1672 tempest!

The windmill just outside keeps up the interest. So too does Hole Park Garden.

Nearby: Cranbrook Union Mill; Kent & East Sussex Railway; Tenterden; Sissinghurst Castle and Garden (NT); Hemsted Forest.

Biddenden
On A262, and A274, 5 miles NW of Tenterden

Owes part of its fame to the Biddenden Maids, Siamese twins for thirty-four years, whose charity still provides an annual 'dole' of embossed cakes on Easter Monday. Most of it, to a near-perfect main street: church at one end, village green at the other; brick and tile one side; half-timbered, with vast sloping roofs opposite. Paved with Bethersden marble too. A magnificent Old Cloth Hall with splendid gables could – but mustn't – be missed.

Nearby: Headcorn; Sissinghurst Castle and Garden (NT); Lashenden Air Warfare Museum: Cranbrook Union Mill.

Bishopsbourne
Off A2, 3 miles SE of Canterbury

Peacefully tucked away below the Downs at the bottom of a splendid tree-lined avenue. It has a tiny green, war memorial cross and huge chestnut tree beside the church that honours a former rector, Elizabethan theologian Richard Hooker. Add to that an old forge, pretty cottages and 'Oswalds', where Polish sea-captain Joseph Conrad wrote impeccable English prose. A literary pilgrimage that delights the eye.

Quiet lanes lead to parkland and mansion, both east and west, at Bourne Park and Charlton House.

Nearby: Canterbury Cathedral, St Augustine's Abbey (EH) etc; Howletts Zoo Park; Wickhambreux.

Boughton Malherbe
On minor road 3 miles SE of Harrietsham on A20
Pronounce it 'Mallerby'. A mere hamlet – but a tiny church packed with interest; a former school house owned by a former 'Dr Who'; a magnificent Boughton Place (sadly not open to the public), the home of 16th-century adventurer, diplomat, wit, poet and scholar, Sir Henry Wotton – and, to cap it all, a superb view.
Nearby: lovely Quarry Hills countryside; Lenham; Leeds Castle; Charing; Headcorn.

Brenchley
Off B2160, 2 miles S of Paddock Wood
It can hardly be faulted! Kent's tiniest village green? With church, yew and views, to say nothing of splendid black-and-white timbered buildings crowding round it. They range from butcher's shop to Old Palace and back again to Kent's most splendid Wealden council house! Hop- and orchard-surrounded too. Worth anyone's Sunday afternoon.
Nearby: Whitbread's oast house complex; Horsmonden church; Tunbridge Wells; Lamberhurst Vineyard; Owletts Garden; Tonbridge.

Charing
At the junction of A252 and A20, roughly mid-way between Canterbury and Maidstone
Above it, the Pilgrims Way, a windmill, a hill-top restaurant (once sponsored by Canterbury's 'Red Dean'), a panoramic view, and, possibly, Challock gliders overhead.

Charing's picturesque High Street of black-and-white and 18th-century houses neatly sidesteps both the A20 and A252 traffic. Off it, in a charming cul-de-sac, lies an interesting church whose shingled roof was ignited by the discharge of a fowling-piece; a community centre that started life elsewhere as a barn, and an archbishop's palace, now a farm, that knew the majesty of Henry VIII's

Field of the Cloth of Gold retinue.
Nearby: Westwell; Challock Forest; Lenham; Eastwell Park; Hothfield Common; Boughton Malherbe.

Chiddingstone
Off the B2027, at Bough Beech, 5 miles W of Leigh
Chilham's rival for Kent's 'most visited village' title.
Unique perhaps in that the whole village is owned by the National Trust – and is only half a street plus church. But what a street! Almost untouched 16th- and 17th-century three-storey houses of timber, tile and brick-nogging, with pargeting and bargeboards, overhang and bay ... St Mary's tall tower with crocketed pinnacles on the other side completes the picture – or nearly, for there is a castle and lake, obscured by trees, at the end of it.
Nearby: Hever Castle; Penshurst Place; Penshurst Vineyard; Bough Beech Reservoir

Chilham
Off A28 and A252, 6 miles SW of Canterbury
Hollywood's picture of England! Four lanes, each with its quota of attractive buildings climb up to a square completely surrounded by lovely half-timbered and tiled houses, none of which puts a foot wrong. Church and inn are companionably side by side at one end; castle and gardens, where falconry and jousting are held, at the other.
Nearby: Chartham church, containing England's finest brass*; Canterbury Cathedral, St Augustine's Abbey (EH); St Martins' Church etc; Perry Woods.

Cobham
On B2009, 1 mile off A2, 3 miles W of Rochester
Probably packs more interest into (or just off) one narrow High Street than half-a-dozen others could if rolled into one!
It runs from superb Elizabethan hall, first home of 'The Ashes', past (if you are strong-willed) Darnley Arms (haunted and with smugglers' secret tunnels): the half-timbered Leather Bottle, Dickens to the core; St Mary Magdalene, with the finest collection of brasses in

England, and its old Priests' College, now almshouses; the village pump; and finally 17th-century Owletts, former home of architect Sir Herbert Baker, who helped Luytens design New Delhi. Throw in oasts and houses, of period and charm, to taste.

Nearby: Cobham is a day's sightseeing – and more – in a single mile, but if you must, throw in Rochester and Meopham, cricket and windmill.

Cranbrook
On the A229 (Maidstone–Hastings road), 3 miles N of Hawkhurst

A snug little market town that vies with Tenterden for the title of 'Capital of the Weald'. But St Dunstan's is unchallenged as the 'Cathedral of the Weald'.

Union Mill, Kent's tallest at seventy feet, looks down on an L-shaped main street, church, impressive 'free and perpetual Grammar School' and delightful weatherboarded or tile-hung houses.

Pleasant walks in Angley Woods and Glassenbury Park.

Nearby: Sissinghurst Castle and Garden (NT); Biddenden; Bedgebury Pinetum; Kilndown church; Scotney Castle (NT).

Elham
On B2065, 6 miles N of Hythe

Best of the dreamy valley's villages!

The Abbot's Fireside, once Wellington's HQ, is a massive half-timbered house whose overhang is supported on gorgeously ugly caryatids. The less showy Rose & Crown opposite was a welcome halt for the France-bound Scarlet Pimpernel.

The church, tall of spire, modestly occupies one side of the tiny square and yields the other three to pleasantly simple 18th-century houses and cottages. It is filled with art treasures, including an alabaster Becket triptych and a stained glass window in which David and Saul can be recognized as Carlyle and the opera singer Mme Patti – with Gladstone, Disraeli and three of Queen Victoria's daughters in attendance. By the vicar's brother!

Beyond the capricious Nailbourne are inviting walks

along leafy lanes. A rural idyll.
Nearby: Lyminge Forest; Park Gate Nature Reserve; Port Lympne Mansion, Garden and Safari Park; Hythe and Folkestone.

Farningham
Off A225 and A20, 4 miles S of Dartford
Delightful respite before London turmoil

The River Darent is the focal point; all within a pebble's throw are a 'folly' bridge with fossil tree *Metasequoia Glyptostroboides* beside it; an 18th-century manor; a coaching inn, the Lion, whose shady lawns slope down to the river; the White House, strikingly picked out in black; and, dominating all, a towering white weather-boarded mill and its handsome consort mill-house. A show-piece!

Further down the road: a brick buttressed church, with a John Nash mausoleum and a rare Seven Sacraments font; an immensely long stone barn, converted; and a village hall that does its brave bit for 20th-century architecture.

Nearby: Brands Hatch; St Johns Jerusalem (NT); Eynsford Castle (EH) – and bridge; Lullingstone Castle and Roman villa (EH).

Fordwich
½ mile off A28 at Sturry, 3 miles NE of Canterbury

Only tiny – but don't miss Canterbury's medieval port! Humpbacked bridge over a gentle Stour, old inn, houses of quiet charm, England's smallest town hall – with lock-up; ancient quayside complete with ducking-stool for nagging scolds!

Nearby: Canterbury; Stodmarsh Nature Reserve; Herne Bay; Wickhambreux; Howletts Zoo Park; Rusham Bird Park; Grove Ferry picnic site.

Groombridge
On B2188, 4 miles SW of Tunbridge Wells

One foot in Sussex – and one in Kent, but definitely not to be missed.

Its sloping, triangular green has weather-boarded cottages on one side; brick-and-tiled on the other. On the third is an unusual brick church, with gleaming and immaculate interior, built to celebrate the future Charles I's return from Spain in 1623 *without* a bride. Still better is neighbouring Groombridge Place, with wide moat and wider lake, one of the most beautiful modestly sized houses in England.

Equally bewitching is L-shaped Court Lodge, half-timbered and tile-hung – transported bodily by traction engine some thirty miles from Rye at the behest of a comic postcard 'artist', Lawson Wood, who had prospered on 'Cheeky Chimps' and 'Comic Coppers'. For all this, well worth travelling to the 'end of Kent'.

Nearby: High Rocks; Tunbridge Wells; Cowden*; Chiddingstone (NT); Hever Castle; Penshurst Place.

Headcorn
On A274, 8 miles SE of Maidstone
Medieval wool's gift to the 20th century.
Its wide dog-legged street is full of splendid half-timbered buildings: Chequers; Shakespeare House (surely straight out of Grimm's Fairy Tales?) and huge Cloth Hall. Behind the imposing church, with 15th-century battlemented tower and finely carved 20th-century rood screen, lies the Manor, an immaculate Wealden double-bay hall-house.

Outside St Peter and St Paul's west door is a thousand-year-old oak, with a hollow trunk still big and tough enough to hold twenty-seven children! Saved from the axe by local vigilantes who kept guard night and day.

Medieval St Stephen's Bridge to the south is Headcorn's last, admirable word.

Nearby: Biddenden; Sissinghurst Gardens (NT); Lashenden Air Warfare Museum, and Aerodrome; Sutton Valence; Cranbrook Union Mill.

Hernhill
2 miles E of Faversham, off either A2 or A299
Another picture-book village! Sufficiently beautiful to be Somerset Maugham's 'Ferne' in *Of Human Bondage*. It looks down on bleak Graveney Marshes from amongst encircling orchards. Lime trees shade a pocket-handkerchief green round which companionably crowd

the Red Lion, a Wealden hall-house, rustic St Michael's Cottages with gables, overhang and central arch, an intriguingly variegated Manor House and St Michael's, a complete Perpendicular church.

In its graveyard, in an unmarked grave, are buried the rabble-rouser Messiah 'Mad Thom', the self-styled Sir William Courtenay, and six of his duped and hungry victims of the strange 'Battle of Bossenden Wood'.

Nearby: Mount Ephraim Gardens; Whitstable beach; Faversham's Abbey and West Streets etc; Blean Woods; Canterbury Cathedral etc.

Hollingbourne
On B2163 off A20, 3 miles E of Maidstone

A two-part village, split by a railway bridge, that straggles delightfully up the lower slopes of tree-clad Downs.

Eythorne has a manor rescued at the last minute from demolition crowbars and picks, and pretty cottages. Hollingbourne modestly claims a church, rather dark but with fascinating Culpepper monuments, especially that of Lady Elizabeth, 'Best of Women; Best of Wives; Best of Mothers' with a 'Thoye' at her feet; a splendid manor, high of wall and higher still of gable and chimney-stack; to say nothing of picture-book mill and pond, chequered brick of King's Head Inn, timber-framed Malthouse and brick-and-flint Old Forge.

The Pilgrims Way at its best tops it all!

Nearby: Leeds Castle; Stoneacre (NT); Maidstone; Lenham; Charing.

Ightham
½ mile off A25, on A227, 4 miles E of Sevenoaks

Upstaged by its two-mile distant Mote to the south, but a delectable village with a style all its own. A widening of the road in a hollow makes an unusual village square. Tile-hung cottages clamber up one side; half-timber ones, with a very personable George & Dragon, cluster on the other. Ightham Court, a third of a mile north, and the church, on an orchard-surrounded hillock to the east, are both well worth the short walk.

The latter is rich in monuments, including those of

Dorothy Selby, who perhaps uncovered the Gunpowder Plot; two Sir William Selbys, lying one above the other; Jane, wife of the celebrated William ('Perambulations') Lambarde; Benjamin Harrison, village grocer turned international archaeologist; Adelaide Kemble, niece of actress Sarah Siddons and opera singer in her own right, and two VCs.

Nearby: Ightham Mote (NT); Ightham Vineyard; Wrotham; Sevenoaks; Knole Park; Tonbridge; Oldbury Camp (NT); Mereworth Woods and church.

Kemsing
On Otford–Wrotham minor (and delightful) road running parallel to M25

A chance to pay tribute to Kent's first Women's Institute (1915) – founded here and still going strong. Now commuter-surrounded but still with great charm. St Edith's Well, bubbling stream and war memorial are set in tiny gardens below brick and tile cottages. Bull *and* Wheatsheaf stand invitingly by. A pleasing variety of houses too, amongst which is Kent's finest village hall, complete with hopscotch court. The church, set in a 'garden' churchyard (with cheeky crinkle-crankle wall), is unusually rich in its furnishings – almost overwhelmingly so. Above it are the Downs and a fieldpath Pilgrims Way that offers bird's-eye views of the palatial mansion of St Clere in equally spacious Heavsham Park.

Nearby: Otford; Shoreham; Wrotham; Brands Hatch; Knole Park; Westerham.

Lenham
½ mile off A20, nearly midway between Charing and Maidstone

Lenham, once as famous for its watercress as notorious for its quarrelsome women, is a second Chilham, but a handsome, hardworking, rolled-up sleeves, no-nonsense farmer's wife rather than a not-a-hair-out-of-place lady of leisure.

Its market square is shaded by lime trees and surrounded by houses ranging from splendidly medieval to formal Georgian, to say nothing of a tiny lock-up and a resplendent, Royal Arms Dog & Bear.

An ancient lychgate invites entrance to a church as attractive within as without. Near the altar a tombstone records Mary Honeywood, a 17th-century Elizabeth Fry who lived through the reigns of three kings and three queens, and produced sixteen children, 114 grandchildren, 228 great-grandchildren and (in her lifetime) nine great-great grandchildren. If all that is not tempting enough, another delightful square leads to farm, pond and magnificent aisled barn.

Across the thunderous A2, the Downs rise to an unusual pine-crested ridge beneath which is carved a huge chalk war memorial cross. And a beautiful stretch of the Pilgrims Way makes this an obligatory extra!

Nearby: Charing and Boughton Malherbe, both with splendid views; Quarry Hills countryside*; Leeds Castle; Stoneacre (NT); Sutton Valence; North Downs Way; sources of the Len and Great Stour*.

Loose
On A229, 2½ miles S of Maidstone

Wisely pronounced 'Luze', it is a last bastion of beauty before urban Maidstone. Perched on a hillside, the 'Switzerland of Kent' is full of the music of little streams that dive underground, quickly to reappear, and form an unusual valley-bottom stream through which runs a raised causeway. It is a teasing maze of little streets where brick-and-tile and half-timbered houses rub shoulders. The National Trust 'Old Wool House' elegantly queens it over them all.

A striking if incongruous 19th-century viaduct strides across the valley.

Nearby: Maidstone; Mote Park; East Farleigh*, Yalding and the Medway; Leeds Castle; Linton*; Boughton Monchelsea Place.

Lower Halstow
Off A2, 3 miles W of Sittingbourne

'Lost Lands of the Medway': only for lovers of the unusual!

A salt-water creek with a jetty from which Romans

exported oysters and pottery, and near which in 1912, 18 million bricks, as well as barges, were made. Saxon St Margaret's, flint, stone and tile-flecked, crouches on the edge of the creek. Inside, fading wall-paintings, massive chandeliers, Jacobean pulpit and beautiful tub-font.

Outside, orchards and sheep to the water's edge; sea vistas across the Estuary to BP refinery's moth-balled towers at Grain; and to Deadman's Island and the one-time lazaret on Chetney Island. Boats on the low tide mud – and birds.

The village itself, inland, is undistinguished and indistinguishable from a dozen others.

Nearby: Sittingbourne and Kemsley Light Railway; Newington apple blossom*; Gillingham RE's Museum; Strand Leisure Park; Black Lion Sports Centre; waterside walks.

Matfield
On B2160, 2 miles S of Paddock Wood

A little outshone by 'black-and-white' Brenchley, of which it was once the senior partner. But it ranks high on its own quiet merits. A wide main street, with an inn at each end and white weather-boarding, is flanked by a pleasant combination of spacious village green and tiddler-sized pond. Behind it more cottages, red and blue brick, and a dignified Queen Anne manor whose clock-turreted stables urge 'Mind the Time'! Neat modern church a mile down the road.

Nearby: Whitbread's Oast House Complex; Horsmonden church; Tunbridge Wells; Lamberhurst Vineyard; Owletts Garden.

Milstead
½ mile S of M2. Best approached from Bredgar on B2163

It is tucked away at the foot of the North Downs along narrow lanes, in sight but thankfully not sound of M2. St Mary's, on its hillock, may be 'grossly over-restored' internally, but externally it peers benignly enough through Milstead's splendid trees. Among them, close clustering, are half-timbered Hoggeshaws (old post office); a huge Wealden hall-house, Milstead Manor, a gem of Elizabethan half-timbering and more recent brick, set behind protective walls in a spacious garden; and a fine old farm with water-gardens.

Nearby: Beautiful downland countryside and villages*; Bredgar*; Doddington Garden; Newnham Vineyard.

Offham
1 mile off A20, 1 mile W of West Malling

Orchards and views are its keynotes, the only remaining quintain in England its highlight. This post was once used by mounted and armoured knights to keep their hands in at tilting. May Day sees a May Queen and maypole dancing.

The church stands apart but two fine houses grace the little green.

Nearby: Great Comp Gardens; Mereworth Castle and church; Wrotham; Aylesford Friary; Allington Castle; Teston picnic site; Trosley Country Park; Coldrum Stones (NT)

Old Romney
On the A259, 1½ miles W of New Romney

Quite different! Hard to believe that it was once one of the bustling Cinque Ports. Ships used to tie up here – until the church cut its own throat by turning unproductive marsh into rich grazing – and so severed its link with the sea. Tiny in 1377 (133 souls), it is today not so much a village as a hamlet with a mere handful of cottages.

The church, on what nowhere other than on Romney Marsh could be called even a hillock, is tree-framed and sheep surrounded and has a 'higgledy-piggledy' roof line. Inside are rough-hewn beams, an altar slab buried for 400 years, clear glass windows, a minstrels' gallery and box pews once painted a surprising pink by J. Arthur Rank Films who 'borrowed' St Clements' for a 'Dr Syn' smuggling epic in 1959.

Nearby: New Romney*; ruins of Midley church*; Philippine Village; Brookland church; Brenzett Air Museum; Appledore Answer; Lydd; Dungeness Atomic Power Station; Dungeness Old Lighthouse; Romney, Hythe & Dymchurch one-third scale railway.

Otford
On A225, 3 miles N of Sevenoaks
On the Pilgrims Way, in the shadow of the Downs, and the key to the lovely Darent Valley, old Otford, despite railway electrification in 1930, has retained its charm. Its entrance roundabout is the willow-encircled village pond with early Georgian houses, Chantry Cottage and church (gleaming brass, eight funeral hatchments as well as Royal Arms, and a towering Polhill tomb) set spaciously round the green. Behind them are the scant remains of Archbishop Warham's vast palace, filched from him by Henry VIII.

The High Street too is full of interest: the Old Forge, the Bull Inn, which houses an oak settle used by Becket, silvery Darent itself and water-mill; a car-park with grandstand view of village cricket, and the best-kept loos in Kent; silver-grey beauty of half-timbered Pickmoss, a 16th-century manor and a simple church hall – by Luytens.

Nearby: a splendid valley walk to Shoreham; Chevening*; Sevenoaks; Knole; Lullingstone Roman villa and Castle (EH).

Otham
As befits a village whose spiky spired church has a tomb recording the death of 'Nobody', Otham modestly holds aloof from Maidstone. Hop- and orchard-surrounded on its Greensand hillock, it looks splendidly across the diminutive River Len to the Downs. In Stoneacre (NT), Gore Court, Synards and Wardes (scene of a 1985 murder), Otham has splendid 15th-century half-timbered houses.

Nearby: Maidstone; Leeds Castle; Boughton Monchelsea Place; Sutton Valence; Loose.

Rolvenden
On the A28 Hastings road, 2 miles SW of Tenterden
It was burned down in the 17th century but today, with rich brick, tiling and dazzling white weather-boarding, a wide, grass-verged main street and a dominant, heavily buttressed church, it runs Tenterden a fair second. In St

Mary's, the lord of the manor's elevated 'box', complete with easy chairs, table *and* curtains, is a 'must'. Hops, orchards and a post-mill keep Rolvenden's feet on Wealden agricultural ground.

Nearby: Hole Park Garden; Great Maytham Hall; Tenterden; Smallhythe Ellen Terry Museum (NT); Isle of Oxney*; Benenden; Kent & East Sussex Railway.

Rye, (Sussex)
On A259 Folkestone–Hastings road, 12 miles NE of latter
Sussex to the core … but on no account to be missed. An almost medieval town that rises from stark black warehouses and boats on the Rother through cobbled streets lined with delightful Georgian and half-timbered houses to its hill-top crowned by St Mary's Church with its ancient clock and gilded 'Quarterboys'.

Be sure to visit the Mermaid Inn and Lamb House (Henry James); arcaded town hall and ancient Landgate; Rye Museum in Ypres Tower on the Gun Garden with wide marsh and sea views; Mermaid, High and Watchbell Streets; art gallery, pottery and town model with sound and light effects.

Nearby: Winchelsea, Camber Castle and Sands; Dungeness Nuclear Power Station and Bird Reserve; Beckley Children's Farm; Ellen Terry Smallhythe Museum; Great Dixter; Brenzett Aeronautical Museum; Bodiam Castle.

Smarden
On the B2077 between Charing and Biddenden
As near perfect as they come! It has proportionately more lovely houses for its size than any other village in Kent. Not to be missed are Chessenden, Hartnup House, Thatched House, Cloth Hall, Dragon House: half-timbered, black-and-white and brown-and-ochre, white weather-board, even a Union Jack door.

The church, at the fiercesome dog-leg turn of the sole street, is approached below the over-hanging first storey of the Pent House, one of the buildings that protectively hem it in. Unflatteringly known as 'the Barn of Kent', its aisle's great width is spanned by ingenious scissor-beams.

A medieval bridge welcomes you; blossom and lambs

bid you good-bye.

Nearby: Biddenden; Headcorn; Sissinghurst Gardens (NT); Tenterden.

Sutton Valence
On the A274, 7 miles S of Maidstone

'Town Sutton' sprawls along the steep face of the Quarry Hills on three or four levels – each with a widening Wealden view. There is a tiny crumbling Norman castle not far from the gleaming Swan Inn at one end of the village. At the other, St Mary's, with a grand west tower and lofty octagonal piers, has a 'garden' graveyard in which lies John Willes. He was the first cricketer to bowl round-arm, a style learnt from his sister, who played with him in a hooped skirt that precluded under-arm action.

Between them are the bequests of William Lambe, local 16th-century boy who made good: two almshouses and a minor public school whose playing-field is known as 'Bloody Mountain' – after a Saxon battle not a rugby maul. It owns the pretty village green too – for which each year it receives one red rose.

Inns of character, houses of charm, and always *that view*! It can be enjoyed at leisure in almost traffic-free streets.

Nearby: Headcorn; Ulcombe*; Linton; Boughton Monchelsea Place; Leeds Castle.

Westerham
On A25, 4 miles W of Sevenoaks

Now spared the worst of the A25 traffic bedlam, it has regained its hill-top, market-town image. Across its 17th-century market-place, Georgian hotel faces Tudor inn; across its sloping triangular green, backs sadly towards each other, a dashing General Wolfe and an armchair-slumped Churchill.

Round the green are antique shops and tea-rooms, a modestly retiring church, with rare 14th-century octagonal timber tower-steps and a glowing Wolfe Memorial window by Burne-Jones; and, below, multi-gabled Quebec House (NT), its finely proportioned rooms discreetly filled with Wolfe memorabilia.

Nearby: Westerham Hill, highest point in Kent, and

other splendid walks*; Squerryes Court; Chartwell; Emmetts Garden; Bough Beach Reservoir.

Westwell
Off the A20, 4 miles NW of Ashford
Happily isolated beneath Downland beechwoods. It has two greens: one beside the Wheel Inn, the other by the Early English church. Scabrously rendered outside, the latter is spaciously light inside, where a forest of pillars gives it a coltish charm. Triple sedilia, carved choir stalls, stone vaulted chancel and a 13th-century Jesse window add to its interest.

Just down the road, a picture-postcard watermill, a period house, a garden rich in roses, a mill-race and, above it, a mill-pond that laps at the sitting-room windows.

Nearby: Eastwell Park: lake and ruined church*; Pilgrims Way; Charing village and former Archbishop's Palace; Hothfield Common Nature Reserve; Kent Gliding Club near Challock; Godinton Park.

West Malling
½ mile off A20 at Leybourne roundabout, 5 miles W of Maidstone
Famous for World War II fighter station and as cricketing 'home' of the 'Lion of Kent', Alfred Mynn, who played in the bruising no-pads era.

Its wide High Street is lined with the warm, red-brown brick and white stucco of early 18th-century houses of charm and individuality. Light and bright, St Mary's offerings range from a splendid Royal Arms of James II, lavishly beflowered and fruited, to an impressive Jacobean monument complete with shrouded skeleton.

Throw in for good measure Gundulf at his best: St Leonards Tower and (behind a 15th-century double-arched gatehouse) Malling Abbey Tower; and an 18th-century Manor House with lakelet.

Nearby: Allington Castle; Larkfield Leisure Centre; Mereworth church and Castle; Medway villages.

Wickhambreux
1½ miles off A257 at Littlebourne, 3 miles E of Canterbury

Perfection in miniature on the Little Stour. A village green with splendid lime and chestnut trees (until the 1987 hurricane wrought havoc) round which, uncramped, are white weather-boarded mill with undershot wheel, rectory, church with a star-spangled ceiling and dramatic, Art Nouveau east window by Rosenkrantz, manor house, village inn, crowstepped gables of the old post office and a charming river vista.

The Hooden Horse inn bespeaks morris-dancers in a village that was part of the estate of the Fair Maid of Kent, 'most beautiful ... and most loving of women'.

Nearby: pleasant circular walk via Seaton and Ickham*. Stodmarsh Nature Reserve; Littlebourne and Wingham*; Howletts Zoo Park.

Winchelsea (Sussex)
On A259, 4 miles SW of Rye

Drowned in 1287 by the Great Storm, repeatedly attacked by the French in the 14th century and finally deserted by the sea in the 15th, it became only 'a few despicable hovels'.

Today, inland and spaciously planned, it drowses peacefully on Iham Hill ('whereon formerly only coneys did dwell') full of white-walled, richly tiled and flower-festooned houses. Outstanding are Strand and Pipe Well Gates, Court Hall Museum and St Thomas's, containing many tombs, including that of Gervase Alard, first Admiral of the Fleet.

Nearby: Rye, Camber Sands and Castle; Beckley Children's Farm; Great Dixter; Bodiam Castle (NT); Pestalozzi Children's Village*.

Woodchurch
On B2067, 4 miles E of Tenterden

Cut through modern mediocrity, and Woodchurch, near the Marsh but not of it, has much to offer. An unusually spacious green is pleasantly but sparingly surrounded by charming houses, including superb half-timbered Hendon Place. The 105-foot church steeple makes a gentle show of outdoing the Leaning Tower of Pisa and contains 'fraudulent' Bethersden Marble pillars. Two pubs stand amicably side by side across the road, one the intriguingly named 'Bonny Cravat'. And behind them, an enthusiastically restored windmill, Jack, whose Jill was demolished some years ago.

Nearby: Ham Street Woods; Appledore Answer; Smallhythe Place (NT); Tenterden; Isle of Oxney*; Kingsnorth Museum; Ashford.

Wrotham
Junction of A20 and A227

Beneath the Downs, a welcome oasis of peace amid a bewildering whirlpool of traffic (A20 and M20; A25 and M25). Around its tiny square: two inviting inns (and two more in the offing), a red brick manor, a war memorial, the remains of an archbishop's palace and an unusual church, with a 350-year-old clock. An intriguing 18th-century (just) tablet on the churchyard wall records 'murder most foul'.

Nearby: Wrotham Hill viewpoint (A20); Trosley Country Park; Kemsing and Otford villages; Mereworth church; Ightham village and Ightham Mote (NT).

Yalding
On B2010, 6 miles SW of Maidstone

Picturesquely situated in the heart of the hop country and where Beult and Teise merge before joining the Medway. Twyford Bridge and Town Bridge are both splendid medieval constructions.

Fishing, picnicking, boating and tow-path walks at Yalding Lees. Peace and quiet beyond the ancient causeway in a harmonious village street that runs downhill from the grammar school (once home of poet Edmund Blunden) past war memorial, tiny green and tinier village lock-up, Georgian houses and church to the river.

Nearby: Benover, a tiny village of great charm*; Whitbread's Hop farm; Nettlestead church.

TOWN TRAILS

Most major towns now have published at least one 'Town Trail'. Their use ensures that all the major places of note in that town are visited and their points of interest explained,

Towns and Villages

and also that time is not wasted by wrong turnings etc.

They may be obtained, at very modest cost, from the appropriate Tourist Information Centre. The only exceptions are the following:
Lydd – from New Romney TIC
Sittingbourne – from Swale Council Office TIC
Tonbridge – from Tunbridge Wells TIC

Broadstairs
The Seven Bays of Broadstairs. Smugglers Walk. A Walk around Historic Broadstairs. A Walk around St Peter's and Reading Street.

Canterbury
City Walls and Gates. Pilgrimage to Cathedral. Cathedral Precinct. Riverside Walks. Streets and Buildings.

Cranbrook
A Look at Cranbrook.

Deal
Deal Town Walk.

Faversham
A Walk around the Town and Port of Faversham

Folkestone
A Walk around Sandgate.

Gravesend
Gordon Memorial Walk. Town Trail.

Herne Bay
A Walk back in Time.

Lydd
A Town Walk around Lydd.

Maidstone
Town Trail. A Walk around Maidstone. Maidstone's Coat of Arms.

Margate
Smugglers Walk. A Walk around Central Margate.

New Romney
A Town Walk around New Romney.

Ramsgate
Smugglers Walk. Ramsgate Royal Harbour Trail.

Rochester
Dickens Trail.

Sevenoaks
Sevenoaks Town Trail.

Sittingbourne
Town Trail

Tenterden
A Walk about Tenterden.

Tonbridge
A Historical Guide to Tonbridge.

Tunbridge Wells
(In preparation)

Unusual Excursions

AEROPLANES

Challock: Kent Gliding Club
Squids Gate, near Challock, Faversham (0233 74307)
Off A252, 2½ miles W of Challock
Pleasure flights (7-15 minutes): no children under 8. Canteen, bar (evening only). Viewing.
Weekdays and Wednesdays when conditions are suitable. Also 3 Open Days at Easter. From 8 a.m. – 'first come, first served'

Headcorn: Headcorn Aerodrome
Headcorn (Weather: 0622 890226; Booking: 0622 890997)
On A274, 1 mile S of town
Private flights, 'Round Kent' or 'Over Kent Castles'; tandem parachute jump with instructor; flying lessons. Any time, weather permitting

BOATS

Canterbury: The Weavers
1-3 King's Bridge, Canterbury (0227 462329)
In main street, near GPO
Splendid group of 15th-century gabled and black-and-white houses, bright with window-boxes (now shops and restaurant) overlooking the River Stour on which self-row boats can be hired for fascinating short trip past some of Canterbury's oldest buildings. Guided trips also available.

Boats only in season, Easter–October. Monday–Saturday tours start at 11; Sundays (June–September) noon

Dover: Jetfoil
P & O European Ferries, Russell Street, Dover (0304 203388)
Corner of Townwall Street and A20
Skim the waves in air-line comfort. Ostend's vast shopping complex is soon alongside.
Throughout the year at times varying according to the season. All departures from Dover *Western* Docks.

Dover: Sealink British Ferries
Eastern Dock, Dover (0304 206090)
At E end of Marine Parade
Sealink, which run 16 sailings a day, offers a wide variety of choices: Same Day Returns, Family Day Out, Take Your Car, ferry/coach excursions, No passport Non-Landing cruises etc. Duty-free and bar and restaurant facilities.
See also Sealink, under Folkestone, below.
Daily: virtually day and night

Folkestone: Sealink British Ferries
Tontine House, Tontine Street, Folkestone (0303 42954)
Departures from the harbour at the end of Tontine Street.
Bar, restaurant, shop.
Crossing takes 1 hour 50 minutes. Passport or British Excursion Document required. Reporting time: 45 minutes before sailing. Reservations are advisable on all sailings and obligatory on 8 a.m., 10 a.m. and 1.15 outward voyages, on return at 2, 5.45 and 8.30.
June to last week in September: 8, 10, 1.15, 3.30, 8, 11. Check by phone.

Grove Ferry: River Trips on 'Reneroy VI'
The Boat House, Grove Ferry Road, Upstreet (0227 86/345)
½ mile off A28, Canterbury–Margate road, at Upstreet
Leisurely 50-minute cruise on River Stour in spanking new 70-seater catamaran with bar (and snacks) and room for 10 wheelchairs. Longer trips (with or without meal) to Richborough Castle or Sandwich by prior arrangement.

Unusual Excursions

Departures from Grove Ferry Inn next to picnic site. D
Daily, May–September: hourly from 1–5

Maidstone: River Medway Hire Cruisers
Undercliffe Boathouse, Bishops Way, Maidstone (0622 53740; evenings 0233 713237)
Promenade in front of the Bishop's Palace beside the Medway
Regular pleasure-boat trips from Maidstone to romantic riverside Allington Castle on *Kentish Lady II*, a new fully covered 100-seater with bar and catering. D
Daily: Easter–October, 1–5 at hourly intervals.

Ramsgate: Sally Viking Line
54 Harbour Parade, Ramsgate (0843 595522)
Opposite the marina
Day trips to France (passport or British Excursion Document from local post office needed). 2½ hours to Dunkirk. Day trips and mini-cruises. On board: children's play area; smorgasbord and carvery, bars, duty-free shop.

Strood: Motor Vessel *Clyde*
Office: Invicta Line Cruises Ltd, 46 New Road, Chatham (0634 41824)
Trips start from Strood Pier; first turn to right after crossing Rochester Bridge in London direction and down Canal Road
Return trips to Southend giving splendid views of Medway and Thames Estuaries. 2-hour voyage each way, with 6-7 hours ashore. Bar, snacks. Commentary, taped music.
Easter holiday: Friday, Sunday, Monday; April: Sunday only; May: Tuesday, Thursday, Sunday; June–September: Tuesday, Wednesday, Thursday, Friday, Sunday; October: Sunday only. All BHs at weekday times. Departure times from Strood: weekdays, 9; Sunday, 10. Arriving back at Strood at 7 p.m. and 9 p.m. respectively.

Strood: Paddle-Steamer *Kingswear Castle*
Historic Dockyard, Chatham (0634 827648)
Cruises leave from Strood Pier. (Down Canal Road, first

turning on right after crossing Rochester Bridge in London direction.) Passengers may join also at Chatham Historic Dockyard and Sun Pier.

Originally built for service on Devon's River Dart; restored and re-fitted with Edwardian panelled saloons, the *Kingswear Castle* re-entered service in 1985. Britain's last coal-fired paddle-steamer. Jazz Jamborees and special events. Bar, snacks, souvenir shops.

Afternoon cruises pass Upnor and Rochester Castles, Hoo Island and Darnet Ness. Mid-May – mid-September: most Sundays; also Wednesdays and Fridays, mid-July – mid-September.

Day cruises (Thursdays and some Saturdays, 11.30–6) have varied destinations down river. Advisable to check.

Fee (non-profit-making)

Tonbridge: Medway Narrowboat Co Ltd
Rilla Mill, Gun Lane, Horsmonden (0892 722874)
1½ hour trips up the Medway from Castle Walk, Tonbridge, in a traditional rose-and-castle decorated narrowboat, *Achilles*. Catering facilities, bar.
Daily Easter–October, except Monday, and subject to availability and weather (approximately noon, 2 and 4)

Tovil: Tovil Bridge Boatyard Services
Tovil, near Maidstone (0622 686341)
Bottom of Wharf Road
Enjoy the Medway to the full. For the lazy landlubber, a powered dinghy; for the energetic 'wet bob', a rowing-boat.
Daily throughout the summer

PONY AND TRAP

Ash: Padbrook Carriage-Driving Centre
Padbrook, Paramour Street, near Ash-with-Sandwich (0304 812574)
In Ash, turn off A257 for Ware; after 2 miles continue ahead into dead-end road
Travel in pony and trap or behind matched 'greys' down

leafy Kentish lanes – with optional pub stops.
All the year, daily. Advance phone-call advisable

RAILWAYS

Hythe: Romney, Hythe & Dymchurch Railway
New Romney (0679 62353)
Starts from Hythe. Off A259, W end of Hythe
Most fully equipped miniature railway in the world. It has a magnificent fleet of 12 steam locomotives and railway stock, one-third full size. The 13½ mile journey across the famous Romney Marsh can be broken at intermediate stations and takes (return) 2½ hours. Workshops and large model exhibition at New Romney HQ. Refreshments, gift shop.
March and October: Saturday and Sunday. Easter–September: daily. See full timetable for varied running times

Sittingbourne: Sittingbourne & Kemsley Light Railway
The Wall, Milton Regis, near Sittingbourne (weekdays: 0634 32320; weekends: 0795 24899)
Off Milton Road, opposite main car-park and Bowater Paper Mill
2 miles of narrow gauge (2 feet 6 inches) track from Sittingbourne to Milton Creek and Kemsley Down. A varied selection of rolling-stock is normally hauled by steam-locomotives. *Premier* and *Leader*, built in 1906, are two of Sittingbourne & Kemsley Light Railway's 10 locomotives. Picnic area, with swings, and refreshments, at Kemsley Down.
Easter–mid-October: Sunday. Mid-July to last week in August: Saturday and Sunday. All BH weekends. See time-tables for varied running times

Stone: Stone Lodge Railway
Cotton Lane, Stone, near Dartford (0634 61879)
Off the Gravesend-Dartford Londron road near Junction 1A on M25
A new, specially-built standard-gauge steam and diesel

railway built and run by a preservation group on a 'green field' site overlooking the Thames. Goods and passenger rolling-stock.
Various weekends and BH, Apr-Jan. But as the scheme is in its infancy, current leaflets should be consulted.

Tenterden: *Kent & East Sussex Railway*
Town Station, Tenterden (0580 65155)
Off High Street
Kent's only full-size steam railway runs through 5 miles of Wealden countryside to Rolvenden and Hexden Bridge. Rolling-stock can be viewed at Rolvenden and Tenterden stations. 'Wine & Dine Specials' on 'Wealden Pullman' on Saturday evenings. Railway shop, picnic areas, buffet at Tenterden. D
New Year, and Easter to end of December: Saturday, Sunday and BH. June–July: also Wednesday and Thursday. August: daily. Phone for latest timings

TOURIST INFORMATION CENTRES

Please note: * = not open in winter months

Ashford
Lower High Street (0233 37311, ext 316)

Broadstairs
Pierremont Hall, 57 High Street (0843 68399)

Canterbury
St Margaret's Street (0227 66567)

*Cranbrook**
Vestry Hall, Stone Street (0580 712538)

Deal
5-11 King Street (0304 361161, ext 263/218)

Dover
Townwall Street (0304 205108)

Faversham
Fleur de Lis Heritage Centre, 13 Preston Street (0795 534542)

Folkestone
Harbour Street (0303 58594)

Folkestone*
Pedestrian Precinct, Sandgate Road (0303 53840/58594)

Gravesend
10 Parrock Street (0474 337600)

Herne Bay
Pierhead (0227 361911)

Hythe
Scanlon's Bridge Road (0303 67799)

Maidstone
The Gatehouse, Old Palace Gardens, Mill Street (0622 673581/602169)

Margate
Marine Terrace (0843 220241)

New Romney
2 Littlebourne Road (0679 64044)

Ramsgate
The Argyle Centre, Queen Street (0843 591086)

Rochester
Eastgate Cottage, High Street (0634 43666)

Sandwich*
St Peter's Church, Market Street (0304 613565)

Sevenoaks
Buckhurst Lane (0732 450305)

Sheerness
Bridge Road car-park (0795 665324)

Tenterden*
Town Hall, High Street (0580 63572)

Tunbridge Wells
Town Hall, Mount Pleasant Road (0892 26121)

Whitstable
Horsebridge (0227 275482)

APPENDIX: ANNUAL EVENTS

The following list of 1988's events gives a useful idea of the wide range of some of Kent's highlight events, lasting just one day or several. It is impossible, however, to guarantee that they will be held *every* year, even though all have been running for two, and some for a number of years. Dates also change occasionally, so it is wise to check with the contact named below – or your local Tourist Information Centre.

January
29–31   King Charles Festival
               Church of King Charles the Martyr, Tunbridge Wells
               Contact: Rev. John Simpson; Tunbridge Wells (0892 25455)

February
8–28   Folkestone Performing and Visual Arts Festival
               Various venues, Folkestone
               Contact: David Allthorpe; Folkestone (0303 54695)

27–17 March   Thanet Music and Drama Festival
               Various venues, Broadstairs
               Contact: Mrs B. Collins; Thanet (0843 68636)

April

1–4	Family Fun Extravaganza Tenterden Town Station, Tenterden Contact: Mark Toynbee, Caxton Advertising, 94 High Street, Tenterden
2–4	Easter Egg Hunt Leeds Castle, Maidstone Contact: Susan Bowen, Maidstone (0622 65400)
2–4	Easter Hockey Festival Cheriton Sports Ground, Folkestone Contact: Mr and Mrs N. Miroy, Staines (0784 52301)
3	Hop Stringing Museum of Kent Rural Life, near Maidstone Contact: Nick Dodd, Maidstone (0622 633936)
4	Motor Racing: British Championship Rallycross Lydden Circuit, near Canterbury Contact: Brenda Harris, Sittingbourne (0795 72926)
9–10	Lucas Truck Superprix Brands Hatch Circuit, near Dartford Contact: Mrs A Hinds; Ash Green (0474 872331)
16-20 (Provisional)	Canterbury Tales Pilgrimage London to Canterbury Contact: Sylvia Denning, London (01 540 1238)
30–1 May	Rochester Chimney Sweeps May Festival Castle Gardens & High Street, Rochester Contact: Dena Oakford, Medway (0634 43666)

Appendix: Annual Events 267

30–2 May	Country Fayre Leeds Castle, Maidstone Contact: Susan Bowen, Maidstone (0622 65400)
30–2 May	Dover Castle Pageant Dover Castle, Dover Contact: Mr M.W. McFarnell, Dover (0304 201711/205368)
30–2 May	Weald of Kent Craft Show Penshurst Place, Penshurst Contact: Mr D.W. Bennett, Highcliffe (04252 72511)
30–21 May	Gillingham Arts Festival Various venues, Gillingham Contact: Mr B Davis, Medway (0634 378898)
May 4–11 June	Kent Opera Tour of Southern England Various venues across South-East Contact: Di Kaufman, Ashford (0233 76406)
13–15	6th Folkestone International Audio-Visual Festival Leas Cliff Hall, Folkestone Contact: Mr D Bridges; Folkestone (0303 57388)
28–30	A Festival of English Wines Leeds Castle, Maidstone Contact: Susan Bowen, Maidstone (0622 65400)
29–30	Sellindge Steam Special Swan Lane, Sellindge, near Ashford Contact: Mrs J.D. Hollingsbee, Sellindge (03 0381 2066)

Leisure Guide to Kent

30	Allington Festival World Pillow Sparring Contest Allington Community Centre, near Maidstone Contact: Linda Payne, Maidstone (0622 65664)
30 (Provisional)	Rural Crafts and Industries Day Museum of Kent Rural Life, Sandling, near Maidstone Contact: Nick Dodd, Maidstone (0622 63936)

June

2–5	Dickens Festival (Rochester) Various venues, Rochester Contact: Mr P. Grimwood, Medway (0634 727777)
10–12	Maidstone Summer Festival Various venues, Maidstone Contact: Mr W.N. Yates, Maidstone (0622 682510)
11	Mammoth Medieval Market Allington Castle, Maidstone Contact: Mrs Molly Kelly, Maidstone (0622 65684/54080)
11–12	International Balloon Fiesta Leeds Castle, Maidstone Contact: Susan Bowen, Maidstone (0622 65400)
11–12	Wrotham Classic Rally Top of Wrotham Hill, Wrotham Contact: Mr W.J. Treadgold, Borough Green (0732 883739)
11–10 September (Provisional)	Kent Repertory Theatre Company Open Air Theatre Season Hever Castle, Edenbridge

Appendix: Annual Events

Contact: Jill Lomax, Edenbridge (0732 866654)

17–26   Stour Music Festival
Boughton Aluph Church, near Wye
Contact: Lady Atkinson, London (01-852 1040)

18–19   Penshurst Game and Country Fair
Penshurst Park, Penshurst
Contact: Dennis Bevan, Westerham (0959 63832)

18–25   Broadstairs Dickens Festival
Various venues, Broadstairs
Contact: Mrs S. Kirkpatrick, 67 High Street, St Peters, Broadstairs

21–1 July   Sevenoaks Summer Festival
Various venues, Sevenoaks
Contact: Mark Pyper, Sevenoaks School, Sevenoaks (0732 455133)

26   Kent Good Food Festival
Museum of Kent Rural Life, Sandling, near Maidstone
Contact: Nick Dodd, Maidstone (0622 63936)

July

July–September   Great Comp Festival
Great Comp, Borough Green
Contact: Mr R. Cameron, Borough Green (0732 882669)

2   Open Air Concert
Leeds Castle, Maidstone
Contact: Susan Bowen, Maidstone (0622 65400)

2   World Custard Pie Championship
Ditton Park Community Centre, Maidstone

Contact: Mr M. Fitzgerald, Maidstone (0622 55808)

2–3 River Festival
Chatham Historic Dockyard & River Medway, Chatham
Contact: Mr P. Grimwood, Rochester Upon Medway City Council, Civic Centre, Strood, Rochester

2–24 Swale Festival 1988
Various venues, Isle of Sheppey, Faversham and Sittingbourne
Contact: Mrs J. West, Sheerness (0795 662395)

9 (Provisional) Elizabethan Festival
Upnor Castle and Village, near Rochester
Contact: Mr P. Grimwood, Medway (0634 727777)

9–10 Custom Bike Show
Near Lydd Airport, Lydd
Contact: Andy Messer, Medway (0634 712381)

14–16 Kent County Show
County Showground, Detling, Maidstone
Contact: The Secretary, Kent County Agricultural Society, Maidstone (0622 30975)

23–29 Sevenoaks Cricket Week
Vine Cricket Ground, Sevenoaks
Contact: Guy Hollamby (Captain), Sevenoaks (0732 451452)

29 Championship Sheep Dog Trial
Chartwell, Westerham
Contact: Kathy Ratcliffe, Lamberhurst (0892 8907651)

Appendix: Annual Events

30	Maidstone River Festival River Medway, Maidstone Contact: Mr I. Gardiner, Maidstone (0622 602189)
30	Open Air Concert: Royal Philharmonic Orchestra – Pop Goes Handel Castle Gardens, Rochester Contact: Mr P. Grimwood, Medway (0634 727777)
30	Sevenoaks Summer Fair High Street, Sevenoaks Contact: Chamber of Commerce, Sevenoaks (0732 455188)
30–5 August	Cricket Week St Lawrence Ground, Canterbury Contact: The Secretary, Kent County Cricket Club, Canterbury (02227 456886)
30–7 August	Whitstable Oyster Festival Various venues, Whitstable Contact: Mr A. Pearce, Chestfield (0227 792164)
30–13 August (Provisional)	Deal Summer Music Festival Various venues in Deal and Walmer Contact: Mrs B. Harwood, 183 Middle Street, Deal, CT14 6LW
August Various	Ramsgate Harbour Heritage Month Various events, Ramsgate Contact: Mr P. Doyle, Thanet (0843 592903)
5–12	Broadstairs Folk Week Various venues, Broadstairs Contact: Pam Porritt, Thanet (0843 603321)
13–20	Folkestone Carnival Week Various venues, Folkestone

Contact: Tourist Information Centre, Folkestone (0303 58594)

17–21 Hythe Music Festival
Parish Church and other venues, Hythe
Contact: Mr F. Martin, Hythe (0303 67138)

20–21 Detling Steam and Transport Rally
Kent County Showground, Detling, Maidstone
Contact: Mr W.J. Treadgold, Borough Green (0732 883739)

20–21 Emmetts Country Fair
Emmetts Garden, Ide Hill, Sevenoaks
Contact: Kathy Ratcliffe, Lamberhurst (0892 890651)

22 (Provisional) Rochester Air Races and Display
Rochester Airport, Chatham
Contact: Mr W. Chesson, Sittingbourne (0795 72926/71978)

22–28 (Provisional) Will Adams Japanese Festival
Hempstead Valley Shopping Centre, Gillingham
Contact: Mr B. Davis, Medway (0634 378898)

28–29 (Provisional) Gillingham Show and Carnival
Gillingham Park, Gillingham
Contact: Mr B. Davis, Medway (0634 378898)

28–29 Maidstone Lions'/Whitbread's Country Fayre
Whitbread Hop Farm, Beltring, Paddock Wood
Contact: Mr J.R. Davies, Maidstone (0622 37266)

28–31 Festival of Flowers
Leeds Castle, Maidstone

Appendix: Annual Events

Contact: Susan Bowen, Maidstone (0622 65400)

29   Motor Racing: British Championship Rallycross Final
Lydden Circuit, near Canterbury
Contact: Brenda Harris, Sittingbourne (0795 72926)

29   7th Great Warbirds Air Display
West Malling Air Station, West Malling
Contact: Mr E. Sallingboe, Copthorne: (0342 716031)

31–3 September   Open Air Shakepeare
Scotney Castle Garden, Lamberhurst
Contact: Caroline Hiller, Lamberhurst (0892 890651)

September
3–25   Finchcocks Festival
Finchcocks, Goudhurst
Contact: Mr and Mrs R. Burnett, Goudhurst (0580 211702)

10   Heavy Horses at Work
Coltfield Farm, Sevenoaks
Contact: Nigel Westacott, Coltfield Farm, Sevenoaks (0732 462458)

10–11 (Provisional)   Hop-Picking and Drying Event
Museum of Kent Rural Life, Sandling, near Maidstone
Contact: Nick Dodd, Maidstone (0622 63936)

17 (Provisional)   The 4th Vintage Motor-Cycle Club International West Kent Run
From Avery Hill College, Eltham, London through West Kent
Contact: Mr Alex Brett, London (01-850 8633)

Leisure Guide to Kent

18	Motor Racing: International Rallycross European Championship Lydden Circuit, near Canterbury Contact: Brenda Harris, Sittingbourne (0795 72926)
18 (Provisional)	6th Vintage Motor-Cycle Club Festival of 1,000 Bikes Brands Hatch Circuit, Fawkham, near Dartford Contact: Mr A. Brett, London (01-850 8633)

October

2–22	Canterbury Festival Various venues, Canterbury Contact: Festival Office, Canterbury (0227 452853)
7–9	Finchcocks Fair Finchcocks, Goudhurst Contact: Mr and Mrs R. Burnett, Goudhurst (0580 211702)
9 (Provisional)	Ploughing Event Museum of Kent Rural Life, Sandling, near Maidstone Contact: Nick Dodd, Maidstone (0622 63936)
17–23	Kent Literature Festival Metropole Arts Centre, Folkestone Contact: Anne Fearey, Folkestone (0303 55070)
25	European and All England Sea Angling Championships Princess Parade, near Hythe Contact: Mr W.L. Brown, Folkestone (0303 76039)
27–29 (in 1988)	Formula Ford Festival and World Cup Brands Hatch Circuit, Fawkham, near

Appendix: Annual Events

	Dartford Contact: Mrs A. Hinds, Ash Green (0474 872331)
28–29 (Provisional)	Hallowe'en Horrors Fort Amherst, Chatham Contact: John Loudwell, Medway (0634 47747)

November

5	Bonfire, Fireworks and Crafts Allington Castle, Maidstone Contact: Mrs Molly Kelly, Maidstone (0622 65684/54080
5	Firework Display Leeds Castle, Maidstone Contact: Susan Bowen, Maidstone (0622 65400)
6	Deal Open Beach Fishing Competition Deal/Walmer Beach Contact: Tourist Information Centre, Deal (0304 369576)
12	Fireworks Display and Torchlight Procession Sevenoaks Contact: John Milest, Sevenoaks (0732 451211)

December

3	Allington Snow Queen Carnival and Olde English Fayre Mid Kent Shopping Centre, Allington, near Maidstone Contact: Mr F. Burton, Maidstone (0622 676196)
3	Motor Racing: Motaquip British Rallycross Grand Prix

Brands Hatch Circuit, Fawkham, near Dartford
Contact: Mrs A. Hinds, Ash Green (0474 872331)

The following popular biennial events are scheduled for 1989:

August

19 Hythe Venetian Fête
    On the Royal Military Canal, Hythe. Generally held on a mid-August Wednesday afternoon and evening
    Contact: Mr S.C. Godden, Hythe (0303 68234)

31 Dymchurch Day of Syn
    'Smugglers' capture Dymchurch beach, streets and recreation ground. Generally held on August Bank Holiday Saturday

FURTHER READING

For those who want to enjoy all aspects of Kent in depth, I would warmly recommend:

Allen and Imrie, *Discovering the North Downs* (Shire, 1988): The backbone of Kent yields untold delights.

Bignell, Alan, *Kent Lore* (Robert Hale): A fascinating collection of myth, legend and anecdote.

Bignell, Alan, *Kent Village Book* (Countryside Books, 1986): Rich in local interest, history and anecdote.

Blaxland, G., *SE Britain, Eternal Battlefront* (Meresborough, 1986): Kent has been in the front-line for 2000 years.

Boorman, R.M., *Kent – Our County* (*Kent Messenger*, 1979, reprint 1988): Mainly pictorial – Kent through the 20th century.

Darby, Ben, *Journey Through The Weald* (Robert Hale, 1986): A detailed journey through the varied Wealden landscapes.

Douch, John, *Smuggling: Flogging Joey's Warriors* (Crabwell Publications, Dover, 1985): Fascinating background to Kent's once most flourishing industry.

Lambert, Roger, and Cann, John, *Heritage Walking Trails 1-3 (Compass Publications, 1985-7):* Intriguingly illustrated and comprehensive; Carnegie Award winners.

MacDonnell, Kevin, *Photographer's Guide Book to Kent* (Wildwood House, 1986): Explains how and shows where to get the best 'snaps'.

Mee, Arthur, *Kent* (Hodder & Stoughton, 1961): Rather dramatic and flowery but never 'misses a trick'. Definitive!

Newman, John, *Kent: Buildings of England Series* (Penguin,

1969): Absolutely invaluable. Succinctly, expertly and with neat turn of phrase, describes Kent's architectural heritage in depth.

Nicolson, Nigel, *Kent*, (Weidenfeld & Nicolson, 1988).

Plascott, R., *Kent Rambles* (Countryside Books, 1987): Speaks for itself – clearly too.

Roper, Anne, *Gift of the Sea* (Birlings, 1984): Romney Marsh – by a lifelong devotee.

Searle, M.V., *Down the Line to Dover* (Midas, 1984): Iron horse and 'Invicta' – a fascinating pair.

Spence, Keith, *Kent and Sussex* (Collins, 1973): Lively, informative and enthusiastic.

Syms, J.A., *Kent Country Churches* (Meresborough, 1984): Admirably but interestingly concise and well illustrated.

Webb, William, *Kent's Historic Buildings* (Robert Hale): Few counties are richer in castle or stately home.

Whitney, C.E., *Discovering the Cinque Ports* (Shire, 1988): Pithy pocket-book for those who want to miss nothing of the 5 historic ports.

Index

Entries are indexed under their nearest town or village so that all attractions in one locality can be seen at a glance.

Addington Green, Angel Inn, 94
Aldington, Walnut Tree, 94
Allington Castle, 134
Appledore
  Appledore's Answer, 116
  Horne's Place Chapel, 126
Ash
  Five Acres Nurseries Garden, 116
  St Nicholas Vineyard, 109
Ashford, 231
  Godinton House and Garden, 134
  Golf Club, 204
  Intelligence Corps Museum, 145
  Lenacre Hall Farm, 108
  Markets, 189
  Railway Research Room, 160
  School of Spinning and Weaving, 185
  Singleton Barn, 98
  Stour Centre, 212
  Stour Centre, Bowls, 202
  Tufton Centre, 181
  Valley Point-to-Point, 226
  WI Markets, 193
Aylesford, 237
  Friary, 121
  Friary Pottery, 185
  Kits Coty and Little Kits Coty, 35

Badlesmere, Deepdene Stables, 219
Barfreston, St Nicholas Church, 126
Barton's Point, 168

Bearsted
  Golf Club, 204
  WI Market, 193
Beckley, Children's Farm, 104
Bekesbourne, Howletts Zoo Park, 34
Beltring
  Whitbread's Hop Farm, 104
  Whitbread's Hop Farm Crafts, 185
Benenden, 237
  Walled Garden, 111
Bethersden, Stevenson Bros Rocking-Horses, 185
Bewl Bridge Reservoir, 217
Biddenden, 238
  Bettenham Manor Baby Carriage Collection, 148
  Claris's Café, 90
  House for Pure Wool, 186
  Vineyard, 109
Birchington, 168
  Powell-Cotton Museum, 148
  Quex House and Garden, 134
Bishopsbourne, 238
Blean Bird Park, 33
Bodiam Castle, 122
Borough Green
  Crowhurst Farm, 108
  Great Comp Garden, 112
  WI Market, 193
Bough Beech Reservoir and Information Centre, 59
Boughton Malherbe, 239
Boughton Monchelsea Place, 135

279

Brands Hatch, 224
Bredgar, The Sun, 94
Brenchley, 239
  Gate House Farm, 104
  Marle Place Garden and Nursery, 112
Brenzett, Aeronautical Museum, 145
Broadstairs, 169
  Bleak House, 149
  Crampton Tower, 161
  Dickens' House Museum, 149
  North Foreland Golf Club, 204
  North Foreland Lighthouse, 177
  Pavilion Theatre, 42
  Pierremont Park, 118
  Victoria Garden, 118
  Westwood Hypermarket, 182
Brook, Wye College Agricultural Museum, 144
Brookland
  Foster House Studio, 186
  Philippine Village Craft Centre, 186
  St Augustine's Church, 126
Broome Park Golf and Country Club, 206
Burham Downs, 59
Burmarsh, Lathe Barn, 90
Bursted Manor Riding Centre, 219
Burwash, Bateman's, 135

Camber, 169
Canterbury, 232
  Bigbury Fort, 35
  Buffs Regimental Museum, 145
  Canterbury Centre, 154
  Cathedral, 125
  Church Wood, Blean, 56
  Coach House Antiques, 179
  Conquest House, 179
  Dane John Gardens, 118
  Eastbridge Hospital, 141
  Golf Club, 205
  Graphics Gallery, 39
  Greyhound Track, 224
  Gulbenkian Theatre, 42
  Heritage Museum, 154
  Markets, 190
  Marlowe Arcade, 182
  Marlowe Theatre, 43
  Motor Museum, 161
  Pilgrim's Way Time-Walk, 154
  Revivals, 180
  Roman Pavement, 36
  Royal Museum and Art Gallery, 154
  Sports Centre, 212
  Swimming-Pool, 226
  St Augustine's Abbey, 121
  St Lawrence Cricket Ground, 221
  St Martin's Church, 126
  Tabor Barns, 155
  Walks, 71, 72
  Waterfields Restaurant, 100
  Weavers, The, 257
  Westgate Gardens, 118
  Westgate Towers Museum, 149
  WI Market, 193
Challock
  Kent Country Nurseries, 116
  Kent Gliding Club, 257
  King's Wood, 51
  Park Wood, 53
Charing, 239
  WI Market, 194
Chartham
  The Master Makers, 186
  Walks, 72
Chartwell, 140
Chatham and Gillingham, 232
  Alpine Ski Centre, 220
  Brook Market, The, 190
  Brook Pumping Station, 152
  Capstone Farm Country Park, 48
  Central Hall Theatre, 43
  Dockyard Museum, 146
  Football Clubs, 222, 223
  Fort Amherst, 132
  Golf Centre, 205
  Historic Dockyard, 146
  Lordswood Leisure Centre, 212
  Medway Heritage Centre, 155
  Medway Indoor Bowls Centre, 202
  Pentagon Centre, 182
  Royal Engineers' Museum, 146
  St Bartholomew's Chapel, 126
  Sir John Hawkins Hospital, 141
Chestfield Golf Club, 205
Chevening, St Botolph's Church, 127
Chiddingstone, 240
  Castle, 135
  Village Tea-shop, 91
Chilham, 240
  Castle Gardens, 112
  Chestnuts, 186

Index

Cliftonville, 169
   Bowl, 203
   Tom Thumb Theatre, 43
Cobham, 240
   Brass Rubbing, Church of St Mary Magdalene, 40
   Hall, 136
   Owletts, 136
   St Mary Magdalene Church, 127
Cooling, St James' Church, 127
Cranbrook, 241
   Hemsted Forest, 50
   Kingsmead Stables, 219
   Museum, 155
   St Dunstan's Church, 127
   Union Mill, 163
   Walks, 74
Crayford Greyhound Track, 224

Darent Valley Path, 88
Dartford, 232
   Blue Water Shopping Precinct, 182
   Central Park, 119
   Downs Sports Centre, 212
   Fairfield Pool, 227
   Golf Club, 205
   Hesketh Park, 216
   Markets, 190
   Museum, 155
   Orchard Theatre, 43
   Stone Lodge Indoor Bowls Club, 203
Deal, 169
   Archaeological Collection, 156
   Astor Theatre, 43
   Castle, 123
   Clarendon Hotel, 94
   Costume and Accessories Museum, 149
   Maritime and Local History Museum, 161
   Markets, 190
   Royal Cinque Ports Golf Club, 206
   Swimming-Pool, 227
   Time-Ball Tower, 161
   Victoriana Museum, 150
   Walks, 82
Doddington Place Gardens, 112
Dover, 170
   Castle, 123
   Connaught Park, 118
   Gaskin Bros, Glass, 187
   Grand Shaft, 133
   Great Farthingloe CP, 50
   Jetfoil, 258
   Kearsney Abbey, 119
   Langdon Cliffs, 52
   Maison Dieu, 156
   Markets, 191
   Museum, 156
   Old Town Gaol, 156
   Painted House, 37
   Pharos, 37
   Port of Dover Tours, 162
   Queen's Regiment Museum, 147
   St Edmund's Chapel, 128
   Sealink British Ferries, 258
   Sports Centre, 212
   Transport Museum, 162
   WI Market, 194
Downe, Darwin Museum, 150
Dungeness, 170
   'A' Power Station, 152
   Bird Reserve, 57
   Lifeboat, 177
   New Lighthouse, 177
   Old Lighthouse, 178
   Pilot Inn, The, 94
Dymchurch, 170
   Martello Tower No. 24, 133
   New Hall, 156
   Phoenix Amusements, 167

East Kent Circular Walks, 70
East Kent Country Tour, Car, 62
East Kent Heritage Walking Trails, 73
East Kent Hunt Point-to-Point, 225
East Peckham WI Market, 194
Eastwell Manor, 100
Edenbridge
   Honours Mill, 101
   Market, 191
Elham, 241
   Elham Valley Vineyards, 109
   Park Gate Down CP 57
Etchingham, Sussex Shire Horses, 105
Eynsford
   Castle, 123
   Malt Shovel, 95

Fairfield, St Thomas à Becket's Church, 128
Farnborough, Viners Farm, 108
Farningham, 242
   Farningham Woods, 58

Index

Pied Bull, 95
Faversham, 233
  Abbey Street, 141
  Chart Gunpowder Mills, 153
  Chimney Boy, 95
  Fleur de Lis Heritage Centre and Museum, 157
  Golf Club, 206
  Market, 191
  McKenade Garden Centre, 116
  Notcutts Garden Centre, 116
  Shepherd Neame Ltd, 187
  St Mary of Charity Church, 128
  WI Market, 194
Flimwell, Pillory Corner, 54
Folkestone, 171
  Antiques Centre, 180
  Earl Grey, 95
  East Cliff, 217
  Football Club, 223
  Kennedy's Garden Centre, 117
  Kingsnorth Gardens, 119
  La Tavernetta, 101
  Leas Bandstand, 41
  Leas Cliff Hall, 43
  Markets, 191
  Metropole Arts Centre, 39
  Museum and Art Gallery, 157
  Racecourse, 225
  Rotunda, 167
  Rowland's Rock (Confectionery) Factory, 187
  St Mary and St Eanswythe's Church, 128
  Sealink British Ferries, 258
  Sene Valley, Folkestone & Hythe Golf Club, 207
  Shepway Indoor Bowls Club, 202
  Ski Slope, 221
  Sports Centre, 213
  Warren, 49
  WI Market, 194
Fordwich, 242
  Fordwich Arms, 95
  George & Dragon, 91
  Town Hall, 141
Frant, Bartley Mill, 164

Gillingham
  Black Lion Sports Centre, 213
  Eastcourt Meadows Country Park, 49
  Football Club, 223

Golf Courses, 207
Hempstead Valley Shopping Centre, 182
Ice Bowl, 221
Kent Windsurfing Centre, 229
Markets, 191
Matthew Riding Centre, 219
Medway Badminton Association, 221
Oast House Theatre, 44
Priestfield Sports Complex, 213
Riverside Country Park and Berengrave Nature Reserve, 58
Star Farm, 105
Strand Leisure Park, 217
United Services Sports Ground, 222
Goodnestone Park Gardens, 113
Goudhurst
  Bedgebury National Pinetum, 113
  Finchcocks, 150
  St Mary's Church, 128
  Star & Eagle, 96
  Weekes of Goudhurst, 91
Gravesend, 233
  Football Club, 223
  Gordon Promenade and Gardens, 119
  Markets, 191
  Mid-Kent Golf Club, 207
  Milton Chantry, 142
  Museum, 157
  New Tavern Fort, 133
  St George's Church, 129
  Thong Lane Sports Centre, 213
  Three Daws, 96
  Woodville Halls, 44
Great Chart, Blue Barn Riding Stables, 219
Great Mongeham, Solley's Farm Tour, 106
Greatstone-on-Sea, 171
  Dunrobin Shire Horse Stud, 106
  Nursery, 117
Greensand Way, 83
Groombridge, 242
  Crown Inn, 96
Grove Ferry
  Picnic Site, 50
  River Trips on 'Reneroy VI', 258

Hadlow, La Crémaillère, 101
Halstow, Three Tuns, 96

Ham Street
  Ham Street Woods, 58
  Romney Marsh Garden Centre, 117
Hawkhurst
  Golf Club, 207
  Springfield Garden Centre, 117
Hawkinge, Battle of Britain Museum, 147
Haxsted Watermill Museum, 164
Headcorn, 243
  Aerodrome, 257
  Lashenden Air Warfare Museum, 147
Heart of Kent Country Tour, 62
Heritage Coast Walks, 74
Herne
  Fox & Hounds, 96
  St Martin's Church, 129
  Windmill, 164
Herne Bay, 171
  Brambles English Wildlife and Rare Breeds, 32
  King's Hall, 44
  Market, 191
  Pier Pavilion Sports Centre, 214
Hernhill, 243
  Crafts Centre, 187
  Mount Ephraim Gardens, 113
  Mount Ephraim Gardens, Farm Walk, 106
Hever
  Castle, 136
  Hever Castle Theatre, 44
High Halstow, Northward Hill Nature Reserve, 58
Higham
  Mockbeggar Farm, 108
  The Knowle, 101
High Weald Country Tour by Car, 64
Hildenborough
  Frank Berry Pottery, 187
  Great Hollenden Farm, 106
  Riding Stables, 220
Hollingbourne, 244
  Eyhorne Manor, 137
Holly Hill Wood, 51
Hoo
  Deangate Ridge Sports Complex, 217
  Deangate Ridge Golf Club, 207
  Swimming-Pool, 227
Horsmonden, Sprivers, 113

Hothfield
  Common, 59
  Picnic Site, 51
Hythe, 172
  Kipps Tea-Rooms, 91
  Local History Room, 157
  Malthouse Arcade, 183
  Royal Military Canal, 119
  St Leonard's Church, 129
  Swimming-Pool, 227

Ide Hill
  Country Park, 51
  Emmetts Garden, 114
  Hanging Bank and Brockhoult Mount CP, 50
  WI Market, 194
Ightham, 244
  George & Dragon, 97
  Ightham Mote, 137
  Oldbury Fort, 35
Isle of Harty, St Thomas's Church, 129

Kearsney Abbey Park, 119
Kemsing, 245
  Walks, 74
Kenardington Park Wood, 53
Kent & East Sussex Railway, 262
Kilndown, Christ Church, 130
Kingsdown, 172
Kingsnorth Museum, 150
Knole, 139
  Knole Park CP, 51
  Knole Park Golf Club, 209

Lamberhurst
  Bayham Abbey, 121
  Chequers, 97
  Mr Heaver's Noted Model Museum and Craft Village, 151
  Owl House Gardens, 114
  Scotney Castle Garden, 114
  Vineyards, 109
Langdon Bay, 172
Larkfield Leisure Centre, 214
Leeds
  Castle, 137
  Leeds Castle Aviaries, 33
  Leeds Castle Golf Course, 208
Lenham, 245
  Dog & Bear, 97
Leysdown, 173

Index

Shell Ness, 59
The Swale, 59
Little Chart, St Mary's Church, 130
Littlestone-on-Sea, 173
  Golf Club, 208
Longfield, WI Market, 194
Loose, 246
Lower Halstow, 246
  St Margaret's Church, 130
Lower Mersham, Swanton Mill, 164
Luddenham, Four Oaks, 108
Lullingstone
  Castle, 136
  Lullingstone Park CP, 52
  Villa, 37
Lydd
  All Saints Church, 130
  Romney Marsh Windsurf Centre, 229
  Town Museum, 158
Lydden Circuit, 224
Lydd-on-Sea, 173
Lyminge, West Wood, 55
Lympne
  Castle, 138
  Port Lympne Mansion and Gardens, 138
  Port Lympne Zoo Park, 34
  Stutfall Castle, 37

Maidstone, 234
  All Saints Church, 130
  British Queen, 97
  Cobtree Manor Golf Course, 208
  Hazlitt Theatre, 45
  London Dinghy Centre Sailsports, 229
  Markets, 191
  Medway Hire Cruisers, 259
  Mote Park, 218
  Mote Park Cricket Ground, 222
  Mote Park Swimming-Pool, 227
  Mr Jones's Pie Shop, 102
  Museum and Art Gallery, 158
  Queen's Own Royal West Kent Regiment Museum, 147
  Rugby Club, 222
  Stoneborough Centre, 183
  Tyrwhitt Museum of Carriages, 151
  Walks in Maidstone and Vicinity, 75-7
  Westborough Sports Centre, 214
  WI Market, 194

Manston, Spitfire Memorial Pavilion, 148
Marden
  Goffs Oak Shire Horses, 106
  Reed Court Farm, 105
Margate, 173
  Bembon Brothers Theme Park, 167
  Caves, 36
  Cliftonville Aquarium, 32
  Dane Park, 119
  Draper's Windmill, 165
  Hartsdown Sport and Leisure Centre, 214
  Lifeboat, 178
  Markets, 192
  Northdown Park, 119
  Old Town Hall Museum, 158
  Salmestone Grange, 122
  Shell Grotto, 36
  Thanet United Football Club, 223
  Tudor House and Museum, 158
  Winter Gardens, 45
Marshside, Gate Inn, 97
Matfield, 247
  Badsell Park Farm, PYO, 108
  Badsell Park Farm, Farm Trail, 107
  Cherry Trees Tea Gallery, 92
Medway Narrowboat Co Ltd, 260
Medway Towpath, 88
Meopham
  Camer CP, 48
  Windmill, 165
Mereworth
  Parrot Park, 33
  St Lawrence's Church, 131
Milstead, 247
Milton Regis, Court Hall Museum, 159
Minster Abbey, Thanet, 122
Minster in Sheppey, 173
  Abbey Church, 122
  Abbey Gatehouse, 159
  The Leas and Cliff-Top, 52
Monkton Nature Reserve, 60

Nettlestead, St Mary's Church, 131
Newington Walks, 75
New Romney, WI Market, 194
Northbourne, Paul Harrison, Silversmith, 188
North Downs Way, 84, 85
Northfleet
  Blue Circle Heritage Centre, 153
  St Botolph's Church, 131

Index

Northiam, Great Dixter House and Garden, 138

Oare Marshes, 57
Offham, 248
Oldbury Hill and Styants Wood, 53
Old Romney, 248
Orlestone, Faggs Wood, 49
Orpington, Hewitts Farm, 108
Ospringe, Maison Dieu, 159
Otford, 249
Otham, 249
   Stoneacre, 142

Padbrook Carriage-Driving Centre, 219, 260
Palm Bay, 173
Pegwell Bay and Cliffsend, 174
Pembury, Pippins Fruit Farm, 108
Penshurst
   Fir Tree House, 92
   Penshurst Place, 139
   Penshurst Vineyards, 110
Pilgrims' Way, 85
Platt, Potters Hole CP, 54
Plaxtol, Old Soar Manor, 142
Pluckley, Lambden Trout Fishery, 199
Port of Dover Tours, 162

Rainham
   Mierscourt Farm Shop, 108
   Walks, 78
Ramsgate, 174
   Golf Club, 208
   Granville Theatre, 45
   Greyhound Stadium, 224
   King George VI Park, 119
   Lavender Farm, 105
   Maritime Museum, 162
   Market, 192
   Model Village, 151
   Motor Museum, 162
   Pegwell Bay Picnic Site, 53
   Pleasure Park, 168
   St Augustine's Church, 131
   Sally Viking Line, 259
   Viking Ship *Hugin*, 162
   Warre Swimming-Pool, 228
   Westcliff Leisure Park and Boating-Pool, 218

Reculver
   Roman Fort, 38
   Towers, 142
Richborough
   Roman Amphitheatre, 38
   Roman Fort, 38
Rochester, 234
   Bluebell Hill Picnic Site, 47
   Castle, 124
   Castle Gallery, 188
   Cathedral, 125
   Cathedral Brass-Rubbing Centre, 40
   Dickens Centre, 151
   Eastgate House, 120
   Esplanade Gardens, 120
   Fagin's Alley, 183
   Guildhall Museum, 159
   Indoor Bowls Club, 202
   Kenneth Bills Motor Cycle Museum, 163
   Markets, 192
   Mr Tope's Gatehouse, 92
   Six Poor Travellers' House, 142
   WI Market, 194
Rolvenden, 249
   C.M. Booth Collection of Historic Vehicles, 163
   Falstaff Antiques, 180
   Great Maytham Hall, 139
   Lake at Pooh Corner, 199
Romney, Hythe & Dymchurch Railway, 261
Romney Marsh Circular Walks, 78
Royal Military Canal Walks, 89
Rye (Sussex), 250

St Margaret's Bay, 174
   Bockell Hill Viewing Point CP, 48
   Bockhill Farm and The Leas CP, 48
   Lighthouse Down CP, 52
   Pines Garden, 114
St Mary's Bay, 174
Saltwood
   Brockhill CP, 48
   Fountain Tea-Rooms, 92
   Hayne Barn Stables, 220
Sandgate, 174
   Antiques Centre, 180
   Peckwater Antiques, 180
   Windsurfing South-East, 229
Sandling, Museum of Kent Rural Life, 144
Sandwich, 234

Index

Guildhall Museum, 160
Market, 192
Precinct Toy Museum, 152
Prince's Golf Club, 208
Royal St George's Golf Club, 209
White Mill and Folk Museum, 165
WI Market, 195
Sandwich Bay, 175
  Nature Reserve, 60
Sarre, Crown Inn (or Cherry Brandy House), 98
Saxon Shore Way, 85-7
Seasalter, 175
  Alberta Riding Centre, 220
  South Swale Nature Reserve, 60
Sellindge Pottery and Crafts, 188
Selling
  Perry Wood and Selling Wood, 54
  White Lion, 98
Sevenoaks, 235
  Barnetts Wood CP, 47
  Buck's Head, Golden Green, 95
  Dryhill Picnic Park, 49
  Knole, 139
  Markets, 192
  Museum, 160
  One Tree Hill, 53
  Riverhill House and Gardens, 140
  Royal Oak, 102
  Swimming-Pool, 228
  Walks Around Sevenoaks, 78-80
  WI Market, 195
  Wildernesse Sports Centre, 215
  Wildfowl Reserve, 60
  Woodlands Manor Golf Club, 209
Sheerness, 175
  Elmley Marshes Nature and Bird Reserve, 60
  Golf Club, 209
  Markets, 192
  Sea-Front, 215
Shell Ness, 175
Shipbourne, Dene Park CP, 49
Shoreham, Andrews Wood, Badger's Mount CP, 47
Shorne
  Inn on the Lake, 102
  Shorne Wood CP, 54
Sissinghurst
  Castle Garden, 115
  Rankins, 102
Sittingbourne, 235
  Dolphin Yard Sailing Barge Museum, 163

Golf Club, 210
Market, 192
Sittingbourne & Kemsley Light Railway, 261
WI Market, 195
Slough Fort Riding Club, 218
Smallhythe Place, 152
Smarden, 250
Smeeth, Evegate Mill, 165
Southborough, Wind-Surfing Tuition, 229
Southfleet, The Ship Inn, 98
Staple Vineyard, 110
Staplehurst
  Brattle Farm Museum, 145
  Iden Croft Herb Garden, 115
  King's Head, 98
  Walks in Staplehurst and Vicinity, 77
Stelling Minnis
  Marberdan Riding Stables, 220
  Windmill, 165
Stodmarsh Nature Reserve, 57
Stone
  Stone Lodge Farm Park, 107
  Stone Lodge Railway, 261
Stourmouth, Theobalds Barn Cider, 188
Stour Walks, 73
Strood
  Crispin and Crispianus Inn, 99
  Market, 192
  Motor Vessel *Clyde*, 259
  Paddle-Steamer *Kingswear Castle*, 259
  Pocock Garden Centre, 117
  Sports Centre, 215
  Temple Manor, 143
Sutton-at-Hone, St John's Jerusalem Garden, 115
Sutton-By-Dover, Sutton Court Farm, 109
Sutton Valence, 251
  Sutton Valence Antiques, 180
Swan Inn, 99
Swale Nature Reserve, 175
Swingfield Butterfly Reserve, 34
Syndale Valley Vineyards, 110

Tankerton, 176
Tenterden, 236
  Boswell's Coffee House, 102
  Golf Club, 210
  Market, 193

Index

Museum, 160
Vineyards, 110
Walks, 70
WI Market, 195
Teston Bridge Picnic Site, 54
Thanet Nature Trails, 80
Tickham Hunt Point-to-Point, 226
Tonbridge, 236
  Angel Centre, 216
  Castle, 124
  Castle Grounds, 120
  Football Club, 223
  Indoor Bowls Club, 203
  Markets, 193
  Medway Hall, 45
  Milne Museum, 153
  Poult Wood Golf Course, 210
  Sportsground, 218
  Swimming-Pool, 228
  Walks, 77
  WI Market, 195
Tonge, Old Mill, 188
Tovil Bridge Boatyard Services, 260
Toys Hill CP, 54
Trosley CP, 55
  Waymarked Walks, 81
Trottiscliffe, Coldrum Long Barrow, 36
Tudeley, All Saints Church, 132
Tunbridge Wells, 236
  Assembly Hall, 46
  Binns Corner House, 92
  Brass-Rubbing Centre, 40
  Calverley Gardens, 120
  David Salomon's House, 153
  Downstairs at Thackeray's, 103
  Dunorlan Park, 120
  High Rocks, 51
  Indoor Bowls Club, 203
  King Charles the Martyr Church, 132
  Markets, 193
  Mission Antiques Centre, 181
  Museum and Art Gallery, 160
  Nevill Golf Club, 210
  Pantiles, 183
  Pantiles Bandstand, 41
  Royal Victoria Hall, 45
  Sawdust and Lace, 181
  Sports & 'Y' Centre, 216
  The Common, 120
  The Common CP, 55
  Trinity Arts Centre, 46
  Walks in Town and Vicinity, 81

WI Market, 195

Ulcombe, The Pepper Box, 99
Upnor Castle, 124

Walmer, 176
  Castle, 124
  Castle Garden, 115
  Golf Course, 206
  Lifeboat, 178
Warden Point, 176
Wateringbury
  Brattles Mill, 166
  Riverside Restaurant, 92
Weald Walks, 82
Wealdway, 87
Westbrook, 176
Westerham, 251
  Dunsdale Lodge Antiques, 181
  Pitt's Cottage, 93
  Quebec House, 148
  Squerryes Court, 140
Westgate-on-Sea, 176
  Golf Course, 211
West Malling, 252
  Golf and Country Club, 211
  Manor Park CP, 52
    Waymarked Walks, 77, 78
  Mill Yard Craft Centre, 189
  St Leonard's Tower, 133
  Woods Meadow CP, 55
West Street Hunt Point-to-Point, 225
Westwell, 252
  Watermill, 166
Whitstable, 177
  Clowes Wood CP, 49
  Golf Club, 211
  Harbour Gallery, 189
  Market, 193
  Oyster Indoor Bowls Centre, 203
  Pearson's Crab and Oyster House, 103
  Playhouse, 46
  Sports Centre, 216
  WI Market, 195
  Whitstable Bowl, 204
  Windsurfing, 230
Wickhambreux, 252
Winchelsea (Sussex), 253
Wingham
  Bird Park, 33
  Red Lion, 99
Wittersham, Stocks Mill, 166

Woodchurch, 253
  Stonebridge Inn, 99
  Windmill, 166
Wrotham, 254
  Wrotham Hill Viewpoint, 55
  Rose & Crown, 100
Wye
  Tickled Trout, 100
  Wye and Crundale Downs, 61

Wye College Agricultural Museum, 144
Wye College Farm, 107

Yalding, 254
  Cobblestones, 103
  Ju Du Crafts, 189
Yockletts Bank Nature Reserve, 56